REALSIMPLE

easy, delicious home cooking

250 RECIPES FOR *every* SEASON AND OCCASION

Edited by Allie Lewis Clapp, Lygeia Grace, and Candy Gianetti

REALSIMPLE  Time HOME ENTERTAINMENT

"home cooking"

What do these words evoke for you? If they make you think of comfort food—well, you're right. If they make you think of seasonal, healthy ingredients prepared in a way that maximizes their flavor and your enjoyment, then you're right about that, too. If they make you think of endless recipes and long hours sweating over a stove—well, there you're wrong.

The last 15 years have brought a revolution to the American kitchen. Gone are the days when talented, creative cooks worked in restaurants and the rest of us relied on convenience foods at home. We have become a nation that appreciates fresh ingredients grown locally, including a wide variety of tastes from cultures around the world.

Real Simple magazine, which debuted in April 2000, has helped change the way we all eat. From its inception, the magazine has promoted delicious dishes that are both healthy and easy to prepare. We have proved that you don't need a long list of ingredients to make a satisfying dish. That cutting down on prep time does not mean sacrificing taste. And that seasonal ingredients usually make the most delicious meals.

It's been 12 years since the launch of the magazine, and our food coverage continues to grow. With 250 recipes, this is our biggest cookbook yet. It's divided into the four seasons, with recipes ranging from starters (like six simple-yet-addictive dips) to desserts (six inventive ways to use leftover Halloween candy, anyone?). Treat it as you would a food calendar, if such a thing existed: Find your time of year; find the fresh, seasonal ingredients at your local market; and find the recipe that appeals to you. That's what "home cooking" means to all of us at *Real Simple*. We trust it means the same thing to you.

KRISTIN VAN OGTROP
Managing Editor

spring

Dishes that bring the pick of the season to your table, like spinach and pea risotto or baked salmon with asparagus. Plus: six crowd-pleasing dips, four family-friendly spaghetti suppers, and the only cake recipes you'll ever need.

summer

Time to crank up the barbecue and take dinner (like skewered chicken and oranges) outdoors. Cool off with gazpacho or a steak and mango salad. Plus: three twists on lemonade, and ice cream cones that will make your kids finally admit how awesome you are.

fall

Back-to-school season = no time to cook, so here you'll find 18 dinners—like steak fajitas with sweet potato—that you can whip up in 30 minutes or less. Plus: all the fixings for Turkey Day, including knockout side dishes and desserts.

winter

'Tis the season for hearty soups and chowders, pastas like ravioli with Brussels sprouts and bacon, and delicious roasts. Plus: creative crostini and sparkling cocktails for holiday parties, comforting slow-cooker meals, and festive cookies that are perfect for sharing.

spring

shrimp with tarragon mayonnaise

hands-on time: 5 minutes / **total time: 5 minutes** / **serves 8**

¾ cup mayonnaise

¼ cup chopped dill pickles

1 tablespoon chopped fresh tarragon

Kosher salt and black pepper

1¼ pounds cooked peeled and deveined large shrimp

1 cup store-bought cocktail sauce

▸ In a small bowl, combine the mayonnaise, pickles, tarragon, and ¼ teaspoon each salt and pepper.

▸ Serve the shrimp with the tarragon mayonnaise and cocktail sauce.

TIP
The tarragon mayonnaise can be made up to 2 days in advance; refrigerate, covered.

6 IDEAS FOR DIP

tomatillo and avocado dip

hands-on time: 15 minutes
total time: 15 minutes
serves 8 (makes 2 cups)

- 4 medium tomatillos, husked and quartered
- 1 avocado, pitted and peeled
- 1 jalapeño pepper, chopped
- 1/2 cup fresh cilantro sprigs
- 1/4 white onion, chopped
- 2 tablespoons fresh lime juice
  Kosher salt and black pepper
  Blue corn tortilla chips, for serving

▶ In a food processor, pulse the tomatillos, avocado, jalapeño, cilantro, onion, lime juice, 1 teaspoon salt, and 1/4 teaspoon black pepper until the mixture is the texture of relish. Serve with tortilla chips.

lemon, pepper, and pecorino dip

hands-on time: 5 minutes
total time: 5 minutes
serves 8 (makes 1 1/4 cups)

- 1 cup sour cream
- 1/2 cup grated pecorino (2 ounces)
- 1 tablespoon finely grated lemon zest
  Kosher salt and black pepper
  Potato chips, for serving

▶ In a medium bowl, mix together the sour cream, pecorino, lemon zest, 1/4 teaspoon salt, and 1/2 to 1 teaspoon pepper. Serve with potato chips.

spinach and white bean dip

hands-on time: 5 minutes
total time: 15 minutes
serves 8 (makes 1 1/2 cups)

- 1/4 cup olive oil
- 1 clove garlic
- 1 15.5-ounce can cannellini beans, rinsed
- 2 1/2 cups spinach (about 2 ounces)
- 1/4 cup fresh dill sprigs
- 1 tablespoon fresh lemon juice
  Kosher salt and black pepper
  Crostini (store-bought or Basic Crostini, page 256), for serving

▶ In a small saucepan, heat the oil with the garlic over medium heat until fragrant, 2 to 3 minutes; let cool.

▶ In a food processor, puree the garlic oil, beans, spinach, dill, lemon juice, 3/4 teaspoon salt, and 1/4 teaspoon pepper until smooth. Serve with crostini.

Feta and sun-dried tomato dip

hands-on time: 5 minutes
total time: 5 minutes
serves 8 (makes 1¹/₂ cups)

4 ounces Feta, crumbled (1 cup)
1 cup plain low-fat Greek yogurt
2 tablespoons olive oil
¹/₂ cup chopped drained oil-packed
   sun-dried tomatoes
   Kosher salt and black pepper
   Pretzel crisps, for serving

▶ In a medium bowl, mash together the Feta, yogurt, and oil until mostly smooth.

▶ Mix in the tomatoes, ¹/₂ teaspoon salt, and ¹/₄ teaspoon pepper. Serve with pretzel crisps.

roasted eggplant and basil dip

hands-on time: 10 minutes
total time: 1 hour
serves 8 (makes 2 cups)

2 medium eggplants, halved
   lengthwise
¹/₂ red onion, finely chopped
¹/₂ cup chopped fresh basil
2 tablespoons olive oil
1 teaspoon red wine vinegar
   Kosher salt and black pepper
   Vegetable chips, for serving

▶ Heat oven to 400° F. Place the eggplants cut-side down on a rimmed baking sheet and roast until very soft, 30 to 40 minutes; let cool.

▶ Scoop out the flesh from the eggplants and roughly chop.

▶ In a medium bowl, mix together the eggplant, onion, basil, oil, vinegar, ³/₄ teaspoon salt, and ¹/₄ teaspoon pepper. Serve with vegetable chips.

curried yogurt and lime dip

hands-on time: 5 minutes
total time: 1 hour, 5 minutes
serves 8 (makes 1¹/₂ cups)

1¹/₂ cups plain low-fat Greek yogurt
1 tablespoon curry powder
1 tablespoon fresh lime juice
   Kosher salt and black pepper
   Sweet potato chips, for serving

▶ In a medium bowl, mix together the yogurt, curry powder, lime juice, ¹/₂ teaspoon salt, and ¹/₄ teaspoon pepper.

▶ Chill the dip for at least 1 hour and up to 1 day. Serve with sweet potato chips.

3 IDEAS FOR ROASTED RED PEPPERS

roasted red pepper canapés

hands-on time: 5 minutes
total time: 25 minutes / serves 4

1/4 cup walnuts
1/4 cup chopped roasted red peppers
2 scallions, sliced
1 tablespoon olive oil
    Kosher salt and black pepper
12 thick-cut potato chips

▶ Heat oven to 350° F. Spread the walnuts on a rimmed baking sheet and toast, tossing occasionally, until fragrant, 8 to 10 minutes. Let cool, then chop.

▶ In a small bowl, mix together the walnuts, red peppers, scallions, oil, 1/4 teaspoon salt, and 1/8 teaspoon black pepper. Spoon onto potato chips.

goat cheese and red pepper quesadillas

hands-on time: 10 minutes
total time: 10 minutes / serves 4

2 8-inch flour tortillas
3/4 cup sliced roasted red peppers
1/2 cup arugula leaves, thick stems removed
4 ounces fresh goat cheese, crumbled (1 cup)
    Kosher salt and black pepper
2 teaspoons olive oil

▶ Top 1 tortilla with the red peppers, arugula, and goat cheese. Season with 1/4 teaspoon each salt and black pepper and top with the remaining tortilla.

▶ Heat 1 teaspoon of the oil in a large skillet over medium heat. Add the quesadilla and cook until golden brown and crisp, 2 to 3 minutes per side, adding the remaining teaspoon of oil to cook the second side. Cut into 8 wedges.

crudités with red pepper aïoli

hands-on time: 5 minutes
total time: 25 minutes / serves 4

1/2 cup coarsely chopped roasted red peppers
1 cup plain low-fat Greek yogurt
1/2 small clove garlic
    Kosher salt and black pepper
    Cut-up vegetables, for serving

▶ In a food processor, puree the red peppers, yogurt, garlic, 1/4 teaspoon salt, and 1/8 teaspoon black pepper until smooth.

▶ Refrigerate the dip until chilled and thickened, at least 20 minutes and up to 2 days. Serve with vegetables.

roasted turkey with Cheddar-stuffed potatoes

hands-on time: 20 minutes / total time: 1 hour / serves 4 (with leftovers)

1 boneless, skinless turkey breast half (about 2¹/₂ pounds)

2 tablespoons olive oil

2 teaspoons chopped fresh thyme

Kosher salt and black pepper

2 russet potatoes (about 1 pound)

¹/₄ cup whole milk

4 tablespoons (¹/₂ stick) unsalted butter, cut into pieces

4 ounces Cheddar, grated (1 cup)

1 pound green beans, trimmed

▸ Heat oven to 450° F. Place the turkey breast on a rimmed baking sheet and rub with 1 tablespoon of the oil; season with the thyme, ¹/₂ teaspoon salt, and 1 teaspoon pepper. Roast until cooked through, 50 to 55 minutes.

▸ Meanwhile, pierce the potatoes all over with a fork and microwave on high until tender, 10 to 12 minutes. Halve them lengthwise and, preserving the skins, scoop the flesh into a large bowl. Mash the flesh with the milk, butter, ¹/₂ teaspoon salt, and ¹/₄ teaspoon pepper. Mix in half the Cheddar.

▸ Spoon the mixture into the potato skins. Place them on a baking sheet and sprinkle with the remaining Cheddar.

▸ After the turkey has been roasting for 30 minutes, place the stuffed potatoes in oven and bake until golden, 20 to 25 minutes. Let the turkey rest for 5 minutes before slicing.

▸ Meanwhile, bring a large pot of salted water to a boil. Add the green beans and cook until tender, 5 to 7 minutes. Drain and toss with the remaining tablespoon of oil. Serve with the turkey and potatoes.

TIP

For lunch the next day, mix the leftover turkey with mayonnaise, halved grapes, chopped celery, and toasted walnuts and tuck into pitas or serve over greens.

chicken with white beans and tomatoes

hands-on time: 10 minutes / total time: 55 minutes / serves 4

2 15.5-ounce cans cannellini
   beans, rinsed
1 pint grape tomatoes
4 sprigs fresh thyme
4 sprigs fresh oregano, plus
   leaves for garnish
2 cloves garlic, smashed
1/4 teaspoon crushed red pepper
2 tablespoons olive oil
   Kosher salt and black pepper
8 bone-in, skin-on chicken
   thighs (about 3 pounds total)

▸ Heat oven to 425° F. In a 9-by-13-inch (or some other large, shallow) baking dish, toss the beans and tomatoes with the thyme and oregano sprigs, garlic, red pepper, 1 tablespoon of the oil, 1/2 teaspoon salt, and 1/4 teaspoon black pepper.

▸ Pat the chicken dry and place on top of the bean mixture, skin-side up. Rub with the remaining tablespoon of oil. Season with 1/2 teaspoon salt and 1/4 teaspoon black pepper.

▸ Roast until the chicken is golden and cooked through, 35 to 45 minutes. Sprinkle with the oregano leaves.

TIP
Patting chicken dry before cooking helps ensure a crispy crust and seals in juices. This also works with steaks and chops.

oven-"fried" chicken with crunchy broccoli slaw

hands-on time: 30 minutes / total time: 1 hour, 10 minutes / serves 4

Canola oil, for the rack

$^1/_2$ teaspoon paprika

$1^1/_4$ cups buttermilk

Kosher salt and black pepper

$2^3/_4$ pounds bone-in chicken parts (thighs, legs, or breasts), skin removed

1 cup crushed buttery round crackers (such as Ritz; about 4 ounces)

$^1/_4$ cup reduced-fat mayonnaise

1 tablespoon cider vinegar

$^3/_4$ pound broccoli, chopped (about 4 cups), or 12 ounces broccoli slaw

1 large carrot, coarsely grated

$^1/_2$ small shallot, chopped

▸ Heat oven to 375° F. Set a wire rack inside a rimmed baking sheet and lightly coat the rack with oil.

▸ In a shallow baking dish, combine the paprika, 1 cup of the buttermilk, and $^1/_2$ teaspoon each salt and pepper. Add the chicken and turn to coat.

▸ Place the crackers in a shallow bowl. Remove the chicken from the buttermilk mixture and coat with the crackers, pressing gently to help them adhere.

▸ Place the chicken on the rack and bake, turning halfway through, until crispy and an instant-read thermometer inserted in the center of the thickest piece of chicken registers 160° F for white meat or 165° F for dark meat, 40 to 45 minutes.

▸ Meanwhile, in a large bowl, whisk together the mayonnaise, vinegar, the remaining $^1/_4$ cup of buttermilk, $^1/_2$ teaspoon salt, and $^1/_4$ teaspoon pepper. Add the broccoli, carrot, and shallot and toss to combine. Serve with the chicken.

TIP
This dish is also delicious served cold. Let the chicken cool on a wire rack so the air can circulate around it. This will keep the crust from becoming soggy.

red curry chicken skewers
hands-on time: 35 minutes / total time: 1 hour, 15 minutes (includes marinating) / serves 4

¾ cup coconut milk
1 to 2 tablespoons Thai red curry paste
Kosher salt and black pepper
4 6-ounce boneless, skinless chicken breasts, cut into 1-inch pieces
1 cup long-grain white rice
1 tablespoon canola oil
½ pound snap peas, trimmed
4 scallions, sliced
Lime wedges, for serving

▶ In a medium bowl, whisk together the coconut milk, curry paste, and ¾ teaspoon salt. Add the chicken and turn to coat; refrigerate, covered, for 1 hour.

▶ Meanwhile, soak 8 wooden skewers in water for at least 10 minutes. Heat grill to medium. Cook the rice according to the package directions.

▶ Thread the chicken onto the skewers and grill, turning occasionally, until cooked through, 4 to 5 minutes.

▶ Meanwhile, heat the oil in a large skillet over medium-high heat. Add the snap peas, scallions, ½ teaspoon salt, and ¼ teaspoon pepper and cook, tossing, until the vegetables are tender, 3 to 5 minutes. Serve with the chicken, rice, and lime wedges.

TIP
Although you'll find several types of Thai curry paste in the supermarket, the red variety—typically made from red chili peppers, lemongrass, ginger, and kaffir limes—is the most common. A spoonful instantly adds depth of flavor to marinades, soups, curries, and stir-fries.

sweet and spicy chicken with soba salad

hands-on time: 25 minutes / total time: 25 minutes / serves 4

6 ounces soba noodles

4 heads baby bok choy, cut into strips

1 small red bell pepper, thinly sliced

2 tablespoons canola oil

2 tablespoons rice vinegar

1/2 to 1 teaspoon Sriracha or some other hot pepper sauce (such as Tabasco)

Kosher salt

1/2 cup red currant jelly

2 tablespoons ketchup

1 tablespoon grated fresh ginger

4 6-ounce boneless, skinless chicken breasts

▶ Cook the noodles according to the package directions, adding the bok choy during the last minute of cooking. Drain the noodles and bok choy and run under cold water to cool; transfer to a large bowl. Add the bell pepper, oil, vinegar, Sriracha, and 1/4 teaspoon salt and toss to combine.

▶ Meanwhile, heat broiler. In a small bowl, combine the jelly, ketchup, and ginger.

▶ Place the chicken on a foil-lined broilerproof baking sheet and season with 1/4 teaspoon salt. Broil the chicken until it is cooked through, 4 to 5 minutes per side, brushing with the jelly mixture twice during the last 3 minutes of cooking. Serve with the noodles.

TIP
Japanese soba noodles are made from buckwheat and wheat flours. If you don't find them, substitute thicker udon (another Japanese noodle, made from wheat or corn flour) or spaghetti.

turkey burgers with creamy romaine slaw
hands-on time: 20 minutes / **total time: 20 minutes** / **serves 4**

1 pound ground dark-meat turkey (93 percent lean or less)

2 scallions, sliced

1 tablespoon Dijon mustard

1 tablespoon fresh thyme leaves

Kosher salt and black pepper

1 tablespoon olive oil

2 tablespoons mayonnaise

1 tablespoon white wine vinegar

2 leaves romaine lettuce, thinly sliced crosswise (about 2 cups)

1 medium carrot, coarsely grated

4 soft rolls, split and toasted

Potato chips and pickles, for serving

▸ In a medium bowl, gently combine the turkey, scallions, mustard, and thyme. Form the mixture into four $^3/_4$-inch-thick patties; season with $^1/_2$ teaspoon salt and $^1/_4$ teaspoon pepper.

▸ Heat the oil in a large nonstick skillet over medium heat. Cook the patties until cooked through, 6 to 8 minutes per side.

▸ Meanwhile, in a medium bowl, whisk together the mayonnaise, vinegar, and $^1/_4$ teaspoon each salt and pepper. Add the lettuce and carrot and toss to coat.

▸ Place the burgers on the rolls and top with the slaw. Serve with chips and pickles.

TIP
As the patties cook, resist the urge to press down on them or you will squeeze out (and lose) the flavorful juices.

beef quesadillas with watercress and corn salad

hands-on time: 15 minutes / total time: 20 minutes / serves 4

2 tablespoons plus 4 teaspoons canola oil

1 red onion, half chopped and half thinly sliced

³/₄ pound ground beef

Pinch cayenne pepper

Kosher salt and black pepper

4 8-inch flour tortillas

6 ounces Monterey Jack, grated (1¹/₂ cups)

1 bunch watercress, trimmed (about 4 cups)

1 cup frozen corn, thawed

1 tablespoon fresh lime juice

▸ Heat 1 tablespoon of the oil in a large skillet over medium heat. Add the chopped onion and cook, stirring occasionally, until beginning to soften, 2 to 3 minutes. Add the beef, cayenne, ¹/₂ teaspoon salt, and ¹/₄ teaspoon black pepper and cook, breaking up the beef with a spoon, until no longer pink, 3 to 5 minutes more.

▸ Heat broiler. Brush one side of each tortilla with 1 teaspoon of the remaining oil. Place 2 tortillas, oiled-side down, on a foil-lined baking sheet. Dividing evenly, top with the beef mixture, Monterey Jack, and the remaining tortillas (oiled-side up). Broil until the tortillas are crisp and the cheese has melted, 1 to 2 minutes per side.

▸ Meanwhile, in a large bowl, toss the watercress, corn, and sliced onion with the lime juice, the remaining tablespoon of oil, and ¹/₄ teaspoon each salt and black pepper. Cut the quesadillas into wedges and serve with the salad.

TIP
You can prepare the beef mixture and assemble the quesadillas up to 1 day ahead. (Let the beef mixture cool before placing it on the tortillas.) Refrigerate, covered, until ready to cook.

steak salad with bacon, potatoes, and blue cheese dressing
hands-on time: 30 minutes / total time: 30 minutes / serves 4

8 slices bacon (about
$^1/_4$ pound), cut into 1-inch
pieces

$^1/_2$ pound Yukon gold or
fingerling potatoes, cut into
$^1/_2$-inch pieces

Kosher salt and black pepper

2 teaspoons canola oil

$1^1/_2$ pounds sirloin steak
(1 inch thick)

3 ounces blue cheese (such
as Stilton or Roquefort),
crumbled ($^3/_4$ cup)

$^1/_4$ cup sour cream

$^1/_4$ cup buttermilk

1 teaspoon red wine vinegar

1 scallion, chopped

1 head romaine lettuce,
torn into bite-size pieces
(about 8 cups)

▶ In a large skillet, cook the bacon over medium heat, stirring occasionally, until crisp, 5 to 7 minutes. Using a slotted spoon, transfer to a paper towel–lined plate.

▶ Add the potatoes to the bacon drippings in the skillet and season with $^1/_4$ teaspoon each salt and pepper. Increase heat to medium-high and cook, tossing occasionally, until browned and tender, 12 to 15 minutes. Transfer to the paper towel–lined plate.

▶ Meanwhile, heat the oil in a second large skillet over medium-high heat. Season the steak with $^1/_4$ teaspoon each salt and pepper; cook to the desired doneness, 5 to 7 minutes per side for medium-rare. Let rest for at least 5 minutes before slicing.

▶ In a small bowl, mix together the blue cheese, sour cream, buttermilk, vinegar, scallion, and $^1/_4$ teaspoon each salt and pepper. Divide the lettuce among plates. Top with the steak, bacon, and potatoes and drizzle with the dressing.

TIP
If you don't have buttermilk, you can substitute 3 tablespoons plain yogurt thinned with 1 tablespoon milk.

lamb kebabs with lima bean salad

hands-on time: 25 minutes / **total time: 40 minutes** / **serves 4**

3 tablespoons olive oil

2 tablespoons red wine vinegar

2 cloves garlic, chopped

1 tablespoon chopped fresh oregano

Kosher salt and black pepper

3/4 pound boneless lamb top round steak or shoulder chop, cut into 16 pieces

1 lemon, cut into 8 pieces

1 medium red onion, cut into 8 wedges (stem end left intact)

1 pound frozen baby lima beans

1 ounce Feta, crumbled (1/4 cup)

1/4 cup pitted kalamata olives, coarsely chopped

1/4 cup torn fresh mint leaves

▸ Soak 8 wooden skewers in water for at least 10 minutes. Bring a large saucepan of water to a boil.

▸ Meanwhile, in a medium bowl, whisk together the oil, vinegar, garlic, oregano, and 1/4 teaspoon each salt and pepper. Transfer half the vinaigrette to a second medium bowl, add the lamb, and toss to coat.

▸ Heat broiler. Thread the lamb, lemon, and onion onto the skewers and place on a broilerproof baking sheet. Broil 3 to 4 minutes per side for medium-rare.

▸ Add the beans and 1 tablespoon salt to the boiling water and cook until the beans are tender, 2 to 3 minutes. Run under cold water to cool, drain well, and add to the bowl with the remaining vinaigrette. Add the Feta, olives, and mint and toss to combine. Serve with the kebabs.

TIP
You can assemble the skewers and make the lima bean salad up to 1 day in advance; refrigerate separately, covered.

slow-cooker chipotle beef tacos with cabbage-radish slaw

hands-on time: 30 minutes / total time: 4 to 8 1/2 hours / serves 6

3 pounds beef chuck, trimmed and cut into 2-inch pieces

1 large onion, thinly sliced

4 cloves garlic, chopped

1 to 3 tablespoons chopped chipotle chilies in adobo sauce

2 bay leaves

1 teaspoon dried oregano

Kosher salt

4 cups thinly sliced cabbage (about 1/3 medium head)

4 radishes, halved and sliced

1/4 cup chopped fresh cilantro

2 tablespoons fresh lime juice, plus lime wedges for serving

12 6-inch corn tortillas

Sour cream, pickled jalapeño peppers, and hot sauce, for serving

▸ In a 4- to 6-quart slow cooker, toss together the beef, onion, garlic, chipotles, bay leaves, oregano, and 1 teaspoon salt. Cover and cook until the beef is very tender, on low for 7 to 8 hours or on high for 3 1/2 to 4 hours.

▸ Twenty minutes before serving, heat oven to 350° F. In a large bowl, toss the cabbage, radishes, and cilantro with the lime juice and 1/4 teaspoon salt. Wrap the tortillas in foil and bake until warm, 5 to 10 minutes.

▸ Transfer the beef to a medium bowl (reserve the cooking liquid) and shred, using 2 forks. Strain the cooking liquid through a fine-mesh sieve into the bowl and toss with the beef to coat.

▸ Fill the warm tortillas with the beef and slaw. Serve with sour cream, pickled jalapeños, hot sauce, and lime wedges.

TIP
For an authentic, tasty char, toast the tortillas (one at a time) directly over a low gas flame, using tongs to move and turn them. Keep them warm in foil or in a clean kitchen towel until you're ready to serve.

spicy hoisin skirt steak with cucumber salad
hands-on time: 10 minutes / total time: 35 minutes / serves 4

1 cup quick-cooking brown rice

Canola oil, for the grill

2 tablespoons hoisin sauce

1 teaspoon Sriracha or some other hot pepper sauce (such as Tabasco)

1½ pounds skirt steak, cut into 4 pieces

1 English cucumber, halved lengthwise and thinly sliced

2 scallions, thinly sliced, white and green parts separated

1 tablespoon rice vinegar

½ teaspoon sugar

Kosher salt and black pepper

¼ cup salted roasted peanuts, chopped

▸ Heat grill to medium-high. Cook the rice according to the package directions.

▸ Meanwhile, oil grill. In a small bowl, stir together the hoisin and Sriracha. Brush the mixture on the steak and grill, 2 to 3 minutes per side. Let rest for 5 minutes before slicing.

▸ In a medium bowl, toss the cucumber and scallion whites with the vinegar, sugar, and ¼ teaspoon each salt and pepper. Serve with the steak and rice and sprinkle with the peanuts and scallion greens.

TIP
Turn the leftovers from this sweet-and-spicy dish into a sandwich. Serve the steak on whole-wheat bread with the cucumber salad and sliced avocado.

chipotle pork loin with black bean salad
hands-on time: 10 minutes / total time: 1 hour, 5 minutes / serves 4

1 teaspoon ground chipotle chili pepper or chili powder

1 teaspoon paprika

$^1/_2$ teaspoon ground cumin

$^1/_4$ teaspoon ground coriander

4 tablespoons olive oil

Kosher salt

$1^1/_2$ pounds boneless pork loin

2 15.5-ounce cans black beans, rinsed

1 avocado, cut into bite-size pieces

$^1/_2$ cup fresh cilantro leaves

2 scallions, thinly sliced

1 red chili pepper (such as jalapeño or serrano), chopped

2 tablespoons fresh lime juice, plus lime wedges for serving

▸ Heat oven to 375° F. In a small bowl, combine the chipotle pepper, paprika, cumin, coriander, 1 tablespoon of the oil, and 1 teaspoon salt.

▸ Place the pork on a rimmed baking sheet and coat with the spice mixture. Roast until the internal temperature of the pork registers 145° F, 40 to 50 minutes. Let rest for at least 5 minutes before slicing.

▸ Meanwhile, in a medium bowl, toss the beans, avocado, cilantro, scallions, and chili with the lime juice, the remaining 3 tablespoons of oil, and $^1/_2$ teaspoon salt. Let stand while the pork roasts.

▸ Serve the pork with the bean salad and lime wedges.

TIP
Turn the leftovers into an easy burrito for the next day's lunch: Roll the sliced pork and the bean salad (and cooked rice, if you have any) in a warm tortilla. Serve with salsa and sour cream.

oven-"fried" pork cutlets with fennel-chickpea slaw
hands-on time: 15 minutes / total time: 30 minutes / serves 4

- 4 slices whole-wheat sandwich bread
- 3 tablespoons olive oil
  Kosher salt and black pepper
- 1/4 cup all-purpose flour
- 2 large egg whites
- 4 pork cutlets (1 pound total), pounded 1/4 inch thick
- 1 15.5-ounce can chickpeas, rinsed
- 1 bulb fennel, very thinly sliced
- 2 celery stalks, thinly sliced, plus 1/4 cup celery leaves
- 1/4 small red onion, thinly sliced
- 2 tablespoons fresh lemon juice, plus lemon wedges for serving

▸ Heat oven to 425° F. In a food processor, pulse the bread until fine crumbs form (you should have about 2½ cups). Add 1 tablespoon of the oil, ½ teaspoon salt, and ¼ teaspoon pepper and pulse once or twice to moisten the crumbs. Spread them on a rimmed baking sheet and bake, tossing once, until golden brown, 4 to 6 minutes. Let cool, then transfer to a shallow bowl.

▸ Place the flour in a second shallow bowl. In a third, beat the egg whites with 1 tablespoon water.

▸ Season the pork with ½ teaspoon salt and ¼ teaspoon pepper. Coat with the flour (tapping off any excess), dip in the egg whites (shaking off any excess), then coat with the bread crumbs, pressing gently to help them adhere. Place the pork on a wire rack set on a rimmed baking sheet and bake until cooked through, 8 to 10 minutes.

▸ Meanwhile, in a medium bowl, toss the chickpeas, fennel, celery slices and leaves, and onion with the lemon juice, the remaining 2 tablespoons of oil, ½ teaspoon salt, and ¼ teaspoon pepper. Serve the pork with the slaw and lemon wedges.

TIP
To pound the pork, place each cutlet between 2 sheets of wax paper or inside a large plastic freezer bag. Pound with a meat mallet or the bottom of a heavy skillet until the cutlet reaches the desired thickness.

deep-dish pepperoni pizza with arugula salad
hands-on time: 15 minutes / total time: 50 minutes / serves 4

3 tablespoons olive oil

¾ pound pizza dough, at room temperature

½ pound mozzarella, grated (2 cups)

1 14.5-ounce can diced tomatoes, drained

½ teaspoon dried oregano

¼ small red onion, thinly sliced

¼ cup pitted kalamata olives, halved

4 mushrooms, thinly sliced

1 ounce sliced pepperoni

2 bunches arugula, thick stems removed (about 8 cups)

1 tablespoon red wine vinegar

Kosher salt and black pepper

▸ Heat oven to 400° F. Coat a 9-inch ovenproof skillet or cake pan with 1½ tablespoons of the oil. Press the dough into the pan, covering the bottom and sides. Top with half the mozzarella, then the tomatoes, oregano, and the remaining mozzarella.

▸ In a small bowl, toss the onion, olives, mushrooms, and pepperoni with ½ tablespoon of the remaining oil; scatter over the pizza. Bake until the crust is golden brown, 30 to 35 minutes.

▸ Meanwhile, in a large bowl, toss the arugula with the vinegar, the remaining tablespoon of oil, ½ teaspoon salt, and ¼ teaspoon pepper. Serve with the pizza.

TIP
Make Parmesan bread sticks with the extra pizza dough: Roll it into 12-inch strips, brush with olive oil, and sprinkle with grated Parmesan. Bake at 400° F until golden brown, 15 to 20 minutes.

pork chops with tangy rhubarb chutney
hands-on time: 30 minutes / total time: 30 minutes / serves 4

3 tablespoons olive oil

1 small red onion, chopped
   Kosher salt and black pepper

1/2 pound rhubarb, sliced
   1/2 inch thick

3 tablespoons sugar

1 tablespoon plus 1 teaspoon
   red wine vinegar

4 bone-in pork chops (about
   1 inch thick; 2 pounds total)

1 1/2 teaspoons ground coriander

1 small head Boston or
   Bibb lettuce, leaves torn
   (about 5 cups)

2 tablespoons coarsely
   chopped fresh chives

▸ Heat 1 tablespoon of the oil in a medium sauce-pan over medium heat. Add the onion, 1/2 teaspoon salt, and 1/4 teaspoon pepper and cook, stirring occasionally, until tender and beginning to brown, 5 to 7 minutes.

▸ Add the rhubarb, sugar, and 1/4 cup water to the saucepan and cook, stirring occasionally, until the rhubarb is just tender, 4 to 6 minutes. Stir in 1 teaspoon of the vinegar and remove from heat.

▸ Meanwhile, heat 1 tablespoon of the remaining oil in a large skillet over medium heat. Season the pork with the coriander and 1/2 teaspoon each salt and pepper and cook until browned and cooked through, 7 to 9 minutes per side.

▸ In a large bowl, toss the lettuce with the chives, the remaining tablespoon of oil and tablespoon of vinegar, and 1/4 teaspoon each salt and pepper. Serve with the pork and chutney.

TIP
A little tart and a little sweet, this chutney is also a great accompaniment to Brie or blue cheese on a cheese board.

seared salmon with potato and watercress salad

hands-on time: 20 minutes / **total time: 30 minutes** / **serves 4**

1 pound new potatoes
(about 10)

Kosher salt and black pepper

4 tablespoons olive oil

1½ pounds skinless salmon
fillet, cut into 4 pieces

2 tablespoons prepared
horseradish

1 tablespoon white wine
vinegar

2 scallions, sliced

½ small bunch watercress,
thick stems removed
(about 2 cups)

▸ Place the potatoes in a medium saucepan and add enough cold water to cover. Add 1 teaspoon salt and bring to a boil. Reduce heat and simmer until tender, 15 to 18 minutes. Drain and run under cold water to cool. Cut into quarters.

▸ Meanwhile, heat 1 tablespoon of the oil in a large nonstick skillet over medium-high heat. Season the salmon with ½ teaspoon salt and ¼ teaspoon pepper and cook until opaque throughout, 4 to 5 minutes per side.

▸ In a large bowl, mix together the horseradish, vinegar, scallions, the remaining 3 tablespoons of oil, ½ teaspoon salt, and ¼ teaspoon pepper. Add the potatoes and watercress and toss to combine. Serve with the salmon.

TIP
This dish is also delicious served at room temperature— a perfect spring lunch for company.

curry shrimp and snow peas
hands-on time: 20 minutes / total time: 20 minutes / serves 4

1 cup long-grain white rice

1 14-ounce can coconut milk

1 to 2 tablespoons Thai red curry paste

Kosher salt and black pepper

1½ pounds peeled and deveined large shrimp

3 tablespoons fresh lime juice, plus lime wedges for serving

¾ cup snow peas, sliced lengthwise

½ cup bean sprouts

¼ cup torn fresh basil leaves

1 tablespoon canola oil

▶ Cook the rice according to the package directions.

▶ In a large saucepan, whisk together the coconut milk, curry paste, and ¼ teaspoon each salt and pepper; bring to a boil. Add the shrimp, reduce heat, and simmer, stirring occasionally, until the shrimp are opaque throughout, 2 to 4 minutes. Stir in 2 tablespoons of the lime juice.

▶ Meanwhile, in a medium bowl, toss the snow peas and sprouts with the basil, oil, the remaining tablespoon of lime juice, and ¼ teaspoon each salt and pepper.

▶ Top the rice with the shrimp and sauce and the snow pea mixture. Serve with lime wedges.

TIP
Tail-on shrimp make for a pretty presentation. If you prefer not to deal with tails at the table, slide them off before cooking.

roasted tilapia, potatoes, and lemons
hands-on time: 10 minutes / **total time: 45 minutes** / **serves 4**

1 pound baby potatoes
  (about 16), halved

1 lemon, thinly sliced

8 sprigs fresh thyme

2 tablespoons plus 1 teaspoon
  olive oil

  Kosher salt and black pepper

½ cup pitted kalamata olives

4 6-ounce skinless tilapia fillets

½ teaspoon paprika

▸ Heat oven to 400° F. On a large rimmed baking sheet, toss the potatoes and lemon with the thyme, 2 tablespoons of the oil, and ¼ teaspoon each salt and pepper; arrange in a single layer. Roast, tossing once, until the potatoes begin to soften, about 20 minutes.

▸ Add the olives to the potato mixture, toss to combine, and place the tilapia on top. Drizzle the tilapia with the remaining teaspoon of oil and season with the paprika and ¼ teaspoon each salt and pepper. Continue to roast until the tilapia is opaque throughout and the potatoes are golden brown and crisp, 12 to 15 minutes more.

TIP
To pit an olive, place it on a cutting board and firmly press on it with the side of a chef's knife (with the blade facing away from you). When the olive splits, pull out the pit.

lemony baked salmon with asparagus and bulgur

hands-on time: 10 minutes / total time: 40 minutes / serves 4

1 cup bulgur

1¹/₂ cups low-sodium vegetable or chicken broth

Kosher salt and black pepper

1 pound asparagus, trimmed

1¹/₄ pounds skinless salmon fillet, cut into 4 pieces

1 lemon, very thinly sliced

2 tablespoons chopped fresh dill

Olive oil, for serving

▸ Heat oven to 375° F. In a large, shallow baking dish, stir together the bulgur, broth, and ¹/₄ teaspoon each salt and pepper. Arrange the asparagus in a single layer over the bulgur, then place the salmon on top of the asparagus. Season the salmon with ¹/₂ teaspoon salt and ¹/₄ teaspoon pepper and top with the lemon.

▸ Tightly cover the baking dish with foil and bake until the bulgur and asparagus are tender and the salmon is cooked through, 25 to 30 minutes.

▸ Serve the salmon with the bulgur and asparagus. Sprinkle the salmon with the dill and drizzle with oil.

TIP
Prefer a milder fish? Substitute striped bass for the salmon.

shrimp, leek, and spinach pasta
hands-on time: 10 minutes / total time: 20 minutes / serves 4

3/4 pound gemelli, fusilli, or some other short pasta

2 tablespoons unsalted butter

2 leeks (white and light green parts only), halved lengthwise and sliced crosswise

Kosher salt and black pepper

1 pound peeled and deveined medium shrimp

Zest of 1 lemon, finely grated

3/4 cup heavy cream

12 cups baby spinach (about 10 ounces)

▸ Cook the pasta according to the package directions. Drain and return it to the pot.

▸ Meanwhile, heat the butter in a large skillet over medium heat. Add the leeks, 1/2 teaspoon salt, and 1/4 teaspoon pepper and cook, stirring occasionally, until softened, 3 to 5 minutes.

▸ Add the shrimp and lemon zest to the skillet and cook, tossing frequently, until the shrimp are opaque throughout, 4 to 5 minutes more.

▸ Add the cream and 1/2 teaspoon salt to the pasta and cook over medium heat, stirring, until slightly thickened, 1 to 2 minutes. Add the shrimp mixture and the spinach and toss to combine.

TIP
Give this dish an even richer, more complex flavor by adding 1/2 cup dry white wine to the leeks after they have softened. Cook until the wine has almost evaporated, then add the shrimp and lemon zest.

pesto orecchiette with chicken sausage
hands-on time: 20 minutes / total time: 20 minutes / serves 4

3/4 pound orecchiette

1/2 pound green beans, trimmed and cut into 1-inch pieces

1 cup frozen peas

1 tablespoon olive oil

1/2 pound fully cooked Italian-style chicken sausage links, thinly sliced

1/3 cup pesto

1/2 cup grated Parmesan (2 ounces)

▸ Cook the pasta according to the package directions, adding the green beans and peas during the last 3 minutes of cooking. Reserve 1 cup of the cooking water; drain the pasta and vegetables and return them to the pot.

▸ Meanwhile, heat the oil in a large skillet over medium-high heat. Add the sausage and cook, turning occasionally, until browned, 6 to 8 minutes.

▸ Add the sausage, pesto, Parmesan, and 1/2 cup of the reserved cooking water to the pasta and vegetables and toss to combine. (Add more cooking water if the pasta seems dry.)

TIP
This recipe is also delicious with pork sausage. Brown and slice it before adding it to the pasta and vegetables.

spaghetti primavera with basil

hands-on time: 20 minutes / total time: 20 minutes
serves 4

- ³/₄ pound spaghetti
- ¹/₄ cup olive oil
- 3 cups small broccoli florets
- 1 bell pepper, sliced
- 1 zucchini, sliced
- 4 cloves garlic, sliced
- Kosher salt and black pepper
- ¹/₂ cup chopped fresh basil

▸ Cook the pasta according to the package directions. Reserve ¹/₂ cup of the cooking water; drain the pasta and return it to the pot.

▸ Meanwhile, heat the oil in a large skillet over medium heat. Add the broccoli, bell pepper, zucchini, garlic, ¹/₂ teaspoon salt, and ¹/₄ teaspoon black pepper and cook, tossing occasionally, until tender, 8 to 10 minutes.

▸ Add the vegetables, basil, and reserved cooking water to the pasta and toss to combine.

peanut noodles with snap peas and cabbage

hands-on time: 20 minutes / total time: 20 minutes
serves 4

- ¹/₂ pound spaghetti
- ¹/₂ cup creamy peanut butter
- ¹/₄ cup soy sauce
- 2 tablespoons rice vinegar
- 2 tablespoons light brown sugar
- 1 teaspoon grated fresh ginger
- 1 clove garlic
- 3 cups thinly sliced red cabbage (about ¹/₄ medium head)
- 1 cup thinly sliced snap peas
- ¹/₄ cup chopped salted roasted peanuts

▸ Cook the pasta according to the package directions. Drain and return it to the pot.

▸ Meanwhile, in a blender, blend the peanut butter, soy sauce, vinegar, sugar, ginger, garlic, and ¹/₂ cup water until smooth.

▸ Add the peanut sauce, cabbage, and snap peas to the pasta and toss to combine. Sprinkle with the peanuts.

spaghetti with ricotta and roasted tomatoes

**hands-on time: 20 minutes / total time: 20 minutes
serves 4**

- 2 pints grape tomatoes
- 4 cloves garlic, smashed
- 2 teaspoons olive oil
- ³/₄ pound spaghetti
- 1 cup ricotta
- ¹/₄ cup chopped parsley
  Kosher salt and black pepper

▸ Heat oven to 450° F. On a rimmed baking sheet, toss the tomatoes with the garlic and oil. Roast until the tomatoes burst, 8 to 10 minutes.

▸ Meanwhile, cook the pasta according to the package directions. Reserve ³/₄ cup of the cooking water; drain the pasta and return it to the pot.

▸ Add the tomatoes, ricotta, parsley, reserved cooking water, ³/₄ teaspoon salt, and ¹/₄ teaspoon pepper to the pasta and toss to combine.

spaghetti with pesto and shrimp

**hands-on time: 5 minutes / total time: 20 minutes
serves 4**

- ³/₄ pound spaghetti
- 4 cups baby spinach (about 4 ounces)
- ¹/₃ cup grated Parmesan (about 1¹/₂ ounces)
- ¹/₃ cup olive oil
- 2 tablespoons pine nuts
  Kosher salt and black pepper
- 1 pound cooked peeled and deveined large shrimp

▸ Cook the pasta according to the package directions. Reserve ¹/₄ cup of the cooking water; drain the pasta and return it to the pot.

▸ Meanwhile, in a food processor, puree 2¹/₂ cups of the spinach with the Parmesan, oil, pine nuts, ³/₄ teaspoon salt, and ¹/₄ teaspoon pepper.

▸ Add the pesto, shrimp, reserved cooking water, and the remaining 1¹/₂ cups of spinach to the pasta and toss to combine.

pappardelle with Swiss chard, onions, and goat cheese
hands-on time: 20 minutes / total time: 20 minutes / serves 4

³/₄ pound pappardelle or
     fettuccine

2 tablespoons olive oil

1 small red onion, thinly sliced

4 cloves garlic, sliced

2 bunches Swiss chard, stems
   discarded and leaves cut into
   1-inch strips

   Kosher salt and black pepper

4 ounces fresh goat cheese,
   crumbled (1 cup)

▸ Cook the pasta according to the package directions. Reserve 1 cup of the cooking water; drain the pasta and return it to the pot.

▸ Meanwhile, heat the oil in a large skillet over medium-high heat. Add the onion and garlic and cook, stirring occasionally, until the onion is soft, 3 to 5 minutes.

▸ Add the chard and ¹/₄ teaspoon each salt and pepper to the skillet and cook, tossing often, until tender, 3 to 5 minutes more.

▸ Add the chard mixture, 3 ounces of the goat cheese, ³/₄ cup of the reserved cooking water, and ¹/₂ teaspoon salt to the pasta and toss until the cheese melts and coats the pasta. (If the pasta seems dry, add more cooking water.) Serve sprinkled with the remaining ounce of goat cheese.

TIP
If you can't find Swiss chard or aren't a fan of its earthy taste, spinach will work well in this recipe—and deliver a similarly healthy dose of antioxidants and vitamins.

quinoa and vegetable salad with tahini dressing

hands-on time: 30 minutes / total time: 30 minutes / serves 4

1 cup quinoa

1 cup frozen shelled edamame

1/3 cup tahini (sesame seed paste)

2 tablespoons fresh lemon juice

2 teaspoons grated fresh ginger

1 teaspoon honey

Kosher salt and black pepper

1 bunch watercress, thick stems removed (about 4 cups)

1 pound raw beets (about 2 medium), peeled and coarsely grated

8 radishes, thinly sliced

▸ Cook the quinoa according to the package directions. Spread it out on a plate or rimmed baking sheet and refrigerate until cool. Cook the edamame according to the package directions.

▸ Meanwhile, in a small bowl, whisk together the tahini, lemon juice, ginger, honey, 1/2 cup water, 1/2 teaspoon salt, and 1/4 teaspoon pepper.

▸ Divide the watercress, beets, radishes, quinoa, and edamame among plates and drizzle with the dressing.

TIP

To prevent staining your hands or work surface with beet juice, cover a cutting board with plastic wrap or wax paper and hold each beet in a paper towel as you grate it.

asparagus and ricotta pizzas

hands-on time: 15 minutes / total time: 45 minutes / serves 4

1 pound pizza dough, at room temperature

Cornmeal, for the baking sheets

1 pound asparagus, halved lengthwise and crosswise

5 ounces cremini or button mushrooms, thinly sliced

2 cloves garlic, thinly sliced

1¹/₂ cups ricotta

¹/₂ cup grated Parmesan (2 ounces)

3 tablespoons olive oil

Kosher salt and black pepper

2 cups baby arugula (about 1¹/₂ ounces)

2 teaspoons fresh lemon juice

▸ Heat oven to 400° F. Shape the dough into 4 rounds and place on 2 cornmeal-dusted baking sheets.

▸ Dividing evenly, top the dough with the asparagus, mushrooms, and garlic, then the ricotta, Parmesan, 2 tablespoons of the oil, ³/₄ teaspoon salt, and ¹/₄ teaspoon pepper. Bake, switching the pans halfway through, until the crust is golden brown and crisp, 25 to 30 minutes.

▸ Meanwhile, in a medium bowl, toss the arugula with the lemon juice, the remaining tablespoon of oil, and ¹/₄ teaspoon each salt and pepper. Top the pizzas with the arugula salad just before serving.

TIP
Dusting the pan with cornmeal is an easy way to keep the dough from sticking and adds a tasty bit of crunch.

baked spinach and pea risotto

hands-on time: 10 minutes / total time: 35 minutes / serves 4

2 tablespoons unsalted butter

1 shallot, chopped

Kosher salt and black pepper

$1/2$ cup dry white wine

3 cups low-sodium vegetable or chicken broth

1 cup Arborio rice

1 cup frozen peas

2 cups roughly chopped flat-leaf spinach (about $1/4$ pound)

$1/4$ cup grated Parmesan (1 ounce), plus more for serving

▶ Heat oven to 425° F. Heat the butter in a Dutch oven or large ovenproof pot over medium-high heat. Add the shallot, $1/2$ teaspoon salt, and $1/4$ teaspoon pepper and cook, stirring often, until soft, 3 to 5 minutes.

▶ Add the wine to the pot and cook, stirring, until almost evaporated, 2 to 3 minutes. Add the broth and rice and bring to a boil.

▶ Cover the pot and transfer to oven. Cook until the rice is tender and creamy, 20 to 25 minutes.

▶ Add the peas, spinach, Parmesan, $1/2$ teaspoon salt, and $1/4$ teaspoon pepper to the pot and stir to combine. If the risotto is too thick, stir in up to $1/4$ cup hot water. Sprinkle with additional Parmesan before serving.

TIP

Looking for a dry white wine for cooking? Try Sauvignon Blanc, Pinot Grigio, or Chablis. Avoid "cooking wines" sold in the condiment aisle of the supermarket. They lack flavor and often contain salt. (As a general rule, don't cook with anything that you wouldn't drink.)

Thai curry vegetable and tofu soup

hands-on time: 30 minutes / total time: 30 minutes / serves 4

2 cups low-sodium vegetable broth

1 14-ounce can coconut milk

1 tablespoon Thai red curry paste

1 teaspoon grated fresh ginger

Kosher salt

1/2 pound shiitake mushrooms, stems removed and caps thinly sliced

1/4 pound green beans, trimmed and halved

2 carrots, halved lengthwise and sliced crosswise

14 ounces extra-firm tofu, drained and cut into cubes

1/4 pound snow peas

2 tablespoons fresh lime juice

1/4 cup torn fresh basil leaves

Asian chili-garlic sauce, for serving

▶ In a large saucepan, whisk together the broth, coconut milk, curry paste, ginger, and 1 teaspoon salt; bring to a boil.

▶ Add the mushrooms, green beans, and carrots to the saucepan and simmer until just tender, 3 to 5 minutes. Add the tofu and snow peas; simmer until the snow peas are bright green, about 1 minute more.

▶ Stir in the lime juice. Sprinkle with the basil and serve with chili-garlic sauce.

TIP
Made by cooking down, then straining, fresh coconut meat and water, coconut milk adds a rich, creamy sweetness to foods and balances out spicy dishes like Thai curries. It's high in saturated fat, but there's also a low-fat version. Look for both kinds in the international aisle of the supermarket.

baked stuffed artichokes with pecorino
hands-on time: 15 minutes / total time: 1 hour, 20 minutes / serves 4

$1/4$ pound baguette or country bread, torn into large pieces

$1/2$ cup grated pecorino (2 ounces)

2 tablespoons olive oil, plus more for brushing the artichokes

2 tablespoons chopped fresh chives, plus more for serving

Kosher salt and black pepper

2 large artichokes (about $1^3/4$ pounds total)

Vinaigrette (optional)

▸ Heat oven to 400° F. In a food processor, pulse the bread until pea-size crumbs form (you should have about $1^1/2$ cups). Transfer the crumbs to a medium bowl and toss with the pecorino, oil, chives, and $1/4$ teaspoon pepper.

▸ Using a vegetable peeler, peel the stems of the artichokes. Using a serrated knife, slice off the top third of each artichoke (discard), then halve each artichoke lengthwise through the choke (the fuzzy fibers at the center) and stem. Using a spoon, scoop out the choke and thorny inner petals and discard them.

▸ Place the artichoke halves cut-side up in a large baking dish, brush the edges of the leaves with oil, and season with $1/2$ teaspoon salt. Dividing evenly, fill the halves with the bread crumb mixture, mounding slightly. Fill the baking dish with $3/4$ inch of water and tightly cover with foil.

▸ Bake until the artichokes are tender, 45 to 60 minutes. Uncover the baking dish and bake until the crumbs are golden, 5 to 7 minutes more. Sprinkle with chives. Serve with vinaigrette for dipping, if desired.

TIP
Look for deep green artichokes, heavy for their size, with a thorn at the tip of each leaf; they have a nuttier flavor and a firmer texture than the thornless variety. The leaves should be tightly packed and squeak when rubbed together; splayed leaves and a blackened stem are signs that an artichoke is old. The roundest artichokes have the largest hearts.

pea, Feta, and crispy prosciutto salad

hands-on time: 10 minutes / total time: 15 minutes
serves 4

- 2 thin slices prosciutto (2 ounces)
  Kosher salt and black pepper
- 1¹/₂ pounds fresh peas in the pod, shelled (about 2 cups), or 2 cups frozen peas
- 2 scallions, thinly sliced
- 2 ounces Feta, crumbled (¹/₂ cup)
- 2 tablespoons olive oil

▶ Heat oven to 450° F. Place the prosciutto in a single layer on a rimmed baking sheet and bake until it begins to darken, 10 to 12 minutes. Let cool (it will crisp as it cools), then crumble.

▶ Meanwhile, bring a large saucepan of salted water to a boil. Add the peas and cook until tender, 5 to 7 minutes (1 to 2 minutes if frozen). Drain and rinse under cold water to cool.

▶ In a large bowl, toss the peas, prosciutto, scallions, and Feta with the oil and ¹/₄ teaspoon each salt and pepper.

roasted potatoes and lemon with dill

hands-on time: 5 minutes / total time: 40 minutes
serves 4

- 2 pounds new potatoes (about 20), halved
- 1 lemon, thinly sliced
- 2 tablespoons olive oil
  Kosher salt and black pepper
- 2 tablespoons chopped fresh dill

▶ Heat oven to 450° F. On a rimmed baking sheet, toss the potatoes and lemon with the oil, ³/₄ teaspoon salt, and ¹/₄ teaspoon pepper.

▶ Roast, tossing once, until tender, 25 to 35 minutes. Toss with the dill before serving.

roasted asparagus with olive vinaigrette

hands-on time: 5 minutes / total time: 15 minutes
serves 4

- 2 pounds asparagus, trimmed
- 3 tablespoons olive oil
  Kosher salt and black pepper
- 1/2 cup chopped pitted kalamata olives
- 2 tablespoons chopped fresh flat-leaf parsley
- 1 tablespoon sherry vinegar or red wine vinegar

▸ Heat oven to 450° F. On a rimmed baking sheet, toss the asparagus with 1 tablespoon of the oil, 1/2 teaspoon salt, and 1/4 teaspoon pepper. Roast, tossing once, until tender, 8 to 12 minutes.

▸ Meanwhile, in a small bowl, mix together the olives, parsley, vinegar, the remaining 2 tablespoons of oil, and 1/4 teaspoon each salt and pepper. Spoon over the asparagus.

gingery sautéed watercress and shiitakes

hands-on time: 10 minutes / total time: 10 minutes
serves 4

- 2 tablespoons canola oil
- 1/2 pound shiitake mushrooms, stems removed and caps thinly sliced
- 4 cloves garlic, sliced
- 1 tablespoon chopped fresh ginger
- 2 bunches watercress, thick stems removed (about 6 cups)
  Kosher salt
- 1/2 teaspoon toasted sesame oil

▸ Heat the canola oil in a large skillet over medium-high heat. Add the mushrooms and cook, tossing occasionally, until soft, 3 to 4 minutes.

▸ Add the garlic and ginger to the skillet and cook until fragrant, about 1 minute.

▸ Add the watercress and 1/2 teaspoon salt and cook, tossing, until tender, 2 to 3 minutes more. Remove from heat, add the sesame oil, and toss to combine.

3 IDEAS FOR RICE

tomato and Parmesan rice

hands-on time: 5 minutes
total time: 25 minutes / serves 6

- 1 cup long-grain white rice
  Kosher salt
- 1 14.5-ounce can diced tomatoes, drained
- $1/2$ cup grated Parmesan (2 ounces)
- $1/4$ cup chopped fresh basil

▸ In a medium saucepan, combine the rice, $1^1/_2$ cups water, and $1/2$ teaspoon salt and bring to a boil. Stir once, reduce heat to low, cover, and simmer until the water is absorbed and the rice is tender, 18 minutes.

▸ Sprinkle the rice with the tomatoes and Parmesan. Remove from heat, cover, and let stand for 5 minutes. Fold in the basil before serving.

apricot and almond rice

hands-on time: 10 minutes
total time: 25 minutes / serves 6

- $1/2$ cup sliced almonds
- 1 cup long-grain white rice
  Kosher salt
- $1/2$ cup sliced dried apricots
- 2 teaspoons grated lemon zest

▸ Heat oven to 350° F. Spread the almonds on a rimmed baking sheet and toast, tossing occasionally, until golden, 4 to 6 minutes.

▸ Meanwhile, in a medium saucepan, combine the rice, $1^1/_2$ cups water, and $1/2$ teaspoon salt and bring to a boil. Stir once, reduce heat to low, cover, and simmer until the water is absorbed and the rice is tender, 18 minutes.

▸ Sprinkle the rice with the apricots and lemon zest. Remove from heat, cover, and let stand for 5 minutes. Fold in the almonds before serving.

broccoli and sesame rice

hands-on time: 10 minutes
total time: 25 minutes / serves 6

- 1 cup long-grain white rice
  Kosher salt
- 2 cups finely chopped broccoli florets
- 2 thinly sliced scallions
- 2 tablespoons toasted sesame seeds
- 1 teaspoon toasted sesame oil

▸ In a medium saucepan, combine the rice, $1^1/_2$ cups water, and $1/2$ teaspoon salt and bring to a boil. Stir once, reduce heat to low, cover, and simmer for 12 minutes. Sprinkle the rice with the broccoli, cover, and cook for 6 minutes more.

▸ Remove from heat and let stand, covered, for 5 minutes. Fold in the scallions, sesame seeds, and oil before serving.

A MIX-AND-MATCH GUIDE TO CAKES

On the following pages, you'll find all the recipes, how-tos, and inspiration that you need to make party-perfect desserts like these.

1. Yellow cake with pastry cream filling, chocolate ganache frosting, and shaved chocolate.

2. Yellow cake with lemon curd filling, lemon frosting, chopped pistachios, and candied lemons.

3. Chocolate cake with caramel frosting and gumdrop roses.

4. Yellow cake with vanilla frosting and white chocolate chips.

5. Yellow cupcake with vanilla frosting and chocolate nonpareils.

6. Chocolate cupcake with chocolate sour cream frosting and M&M's Minis.

7. Chocolate cupcake with vanilla frosting and colored sprinkles.

8. Chocolate cupcake with chocolate ganache frosting and mini marshmallows.

9. Yellow cupcake with chocolate sour cream frosting and toasted sliced almonds.

10. Chocolate cake with coffee frosting and crushed cookies.

11. Yellow cake with fresh strawberry filling, chocolate sour cream frosting, and a strawberry fan.

CAKES

These two essential recipes make enough for various pan sizes (see Pan Options and Baking Times, to the right of each recipe). For baking and frosting tips, see Tricks of the Trade (page 85).

yellow cake

hands-on time: 15 minutes / total time: 1 hour, 45 minutes (includes cooling) / serves 12 (or makes 24 cupcakes)

1 cup (2 sticks) unsalted butter, at room temperature, plus more for the pan(s)

2½ cups all-purpose flour, spooned and leveled, plus more for the pan(s)

1½ teaspoons baking powder

¼ teaspoon baking soda

½ teaspoon kosher salt

1½ cups sugar

2 teaspoons pure vanilla extract

3 large eggs, at room temperature

1 cup whole milk

▸ Heat oven to 350° F. Butter the pan or pans, line the bottom(s) with parchment, butter again, and dust with flour, tapping out the excess. (For cupcakes, there is no need for parchment or rebuttering.)

▸ In a medium bowl, whisk together the flour, baking powder, baking soda, and salt; set aside.

▸ Using an electric mixer, beat the butter and sugar on medium-high until fluffy, 2 to 3 minutes. Beat in the vanilla, then beat the eggs in one at a time, scraping down the sides of the bowl as necessary.

▸ Reduce mixer speed to low. Add the flour mixture in 3 additions and the milk in 2 additions, beginning and ending with the flour mixture. Mix just until combined (do not overmix).

▸ Transfer the batter to the prepared pan(s) and bake until a toothpick inserted in the center comes out clean (see Pan Options and Baking Times, right). Cool the cake(s) in the pan(s) for 15 minutes, then turn out onto rack(s) to cool completely.

PAN OPTIONS AND BAKING TIMES

For two 8-inch rounds: 25 to 30 minutes.

For two 9-inch rounds: 22 to 25 minutes.

For one 9-by-13-inch rectangle: 25 to 30 minutes.

For 24 cupcakes: 15 to 20 minutes.

chocolate cake

hands-on time: 15 minutes / total time: 1 hour, 45 minutes (includes cooling) / serves 12 (or makes 24 cupcakes)

1 cup (2 sticks) unsalted butter, at room temperature, plus more for the pan(s)

³/₄ cup unsweetened cocoa powder, plus more for the pan(s)

2 cups all-purpose flour, spooned and leveled

1 teaspoon baking powder

1 teaspoon baking soda

1 teaspoon kosher salt

1¹/₂ cups sugar

2 teaspoons pure vanilla extract

3 large eggs, at room temperature

1¹/₂ cups whole milk

▸ Heat oven to 350° F. Butter the pan or pans, line the bottom(s) with parchment, butter again, and dust with cocoa, tapping out the excess. (For cupcakes, there is no need for parchment or rebuttering.)

▸ In a medium bowl, whisk together the flour, cocoa, baking powder, baking soda, and salt; set aside.

▸ Using an electric mixer, beat the butter and sugar on medium-high until fluffy, 2 to 3 minutes. Beat in the vanilla, then beat the eggs in one at a time, scraping down the sides of the bowl as necessary.

▸ Reduce mixer speed to low. Add the flour mixture in 3 additions and the milk in 2 additions, beginning and ending with the flour mixture. Mix just until combined (do not overmix).

▸ Transfer the batter to the prepared pan(s) and bake until a toothpick inserted in the center comes out clean (see Pan Options and Baking Times, right). Cool the cake(s) in the pan(s) for 15 minutes, then turn out onto rack(s) to cool completely.

PAN OPTIONS AND BAKING TIMES

For two 8-inch rounds: 30 to 35 minutes.

For two 9-inch rounds: 25 to 30 minutes.

For one 9-by-13-inch rectangle: 35 to 40 minutes.

For 24 cupcakes: 20 to 25 minutes.

FILLINGS

Using a filling between layers instead of frosting lets you add another flavor and texture to your cake. Here, choose from sweet-tart lemon curd, fresh berries, and a light, luscious cream.

lemon curd

hands-on time: 25 minutes
total time: 2 hours, 25 minutes
(includes cooling) / makes 1³/₄ cups

4 large eggs

1 cup sugar

1 tablespoon finely grated lemon zest, plus ¹/₂ cup fresh lemon juice (from about 4 medium lemons)

Pinch kosher salt

8 tablespoons (1 stick) unsalted butter, cut into pieces

▶ In a heatproof bowl, whisk together the eggs, sugar, lemon zest and juice, and salt. Add the butter. Set the bowl over (but not in) a saucepan of simmering water and cook, whisking constantly, until the mixture has thickened to the consistency of mayonnaise, 12 to 15 minutes.

▶ Pour the egg mixture through a fine-mesh sieve into a medium bowl. Place a piece of parchment or wax paper directly on the surface of the lemon curd (to prevent a skin from forming) and refrigerate until completely cool, at least 2 hours and up to 2 days.

fresh strawberry

hands-on time: 10 minutes
total time: 10 minutes
makes 1²/₃ cups

1 pound strawberries, hulled and halved (about 2³/₄ cups)

¹/₄ cup seedless raspberry jam

Pinch kosher salt

▶ In a food processor, pulse the strawberries, jam, and salt 10 to 12 times, just until the strawberries are coarsely chopped (about the consistency of relish).

▶ Refrigerate the filling until ready to use, up to 6 hours.

pastry cream

hands-on time: 10 minutes
total time: 2 hours, 10 minutes
(includes cooling) / makes 2 cups

4 large egg yolks

¹/₂ cup sugar

¹/₄ cup cornstarch

¹/₄ teaspoon kosher salt

1¹/₂ cups whole milk

1 teaspoon pure vanilla extract

4 tablespoons (¹/₂ stick) unsalted butter, cut into small pieces

▶ In a medium saucepan, whisk together the egg yolks, sugar, cornstarch, and salt. Whisk in the milk. Cook over medium-high heat, whisking constantly, until the mixture has thickened to the consistency of creamy salad dressing, 2 to 4 minutes.

▶ Remove the mixture from heat and whisk in the vanilla, then the butter, a few pieces at a time, until melted and smooth.

▶ Pour the mixture into a medium bowl. Place a piece of parchment or wax paper directly on the surface of the pastry cream (to prevent a skin from forming) and refrigerate until completely cool, at least 2 hours and up to 2 days.

CARAMEL   CHOCOLATE   LEMON   COFFEE   VANILLA   CHOCOLATE
SOUR CREAM   GANACHE

FROSTINGS

They're (literally) the icing on the cake—the delicious finish. Each recipe makes enough to frost an 8- or 9-inch double-layer cake, a 9-by-13-inch sheet cake, or 24 cupcakes.

vanilla

hands-on time: 5 minutes
total time: 10 minutes
makes 4½ cups

2 cups (4 sticks) unsalted butter, at room temperature
1 pound confectioners' sugar (about 3¾ cups), sifted
1 teaspoon pure vanilla extract
Pinch kosher salt

▸ Using an electric mixer, beat the butter on high until light and fluffy, 3 to 5 minutes. Reduce mixer speed to low. Gradually add the sugar, then the vanilla and salt, and beat until smooth, scraping down the sides of the bowl as necessary.

3 VARIATIONS
Follow the recipe above, with these modifications.
Lemon: Beat in 2 tablespoons finely grated lemon zest with the butter. Omit the vanilla.
Coffee: In a small bowl, stir together 1 tablespoon instant espresso powder and 1 table-spoon hot water until the powder has dissolved. Add to the frosting along with the vanilla and salt.
Caramel: Add ½ cup prepared dulce de leche to the frosting along with the vanilla and salt.

chocolate sour cream

hands-on time: 10 minutes
total time: 30 minutes
makes 5 cups

¾ pound semisweet chocolate, chopped
1½ cups (3 sticks) unsalted butter, at room temperature
3 cups confectioners' sugar
¾ cup sour cream
Pinch kosher salt

▸ Heat the chocolate in a double boiler or medium heatproof bowl set over (but not in) a saucepan of simmering water, stirring often, until melted and smooth. Remove from heat and let cool, 10 to 15 minutes.

▸ Using an electric mixer, beat the butter on high until light and fluffy, 3 to 5 minutes. Reduce mixer speed to low. Gradually add the sugar and beat until smooth, scraping down the sides of the bowl as necessary. Add the chocolate, sour cream, and salt and beat to combine.

chocolate ganache

hands-on time: 5 minutes
total time: 5 hours, 10 minutes
(includes cooling) / makes 4½ cups

1 pound semisweet chocolate, chopped
2 cups heavy cream
Pinch kosher salt

▸ Place the chocolate in a large heatproof bowl.

▸ In a medium saucepan, bring the cream to a bare simmer. Pour over the chocolate, add the salt, and let stand for 2 minutes.

▸ Whisk until the chocolate is melted and the mixture is smooth. Let the frosting cool, stirring occasionally, until thick and spreadable, 4 to 5 hours. (Note: Don't try to speed the cooling process by putting the frosting in the refrigerator; it will become lumpy.)

TOPPINGS

Feeling fancy? Try one of these impressive—and surprisingly easy—decorations that add a little razzle-dazzle to your masterpiece. (Or cover up a less-than-pristine frosting job!)

meringues

Arrange store-bought meringue cookies around the edge of the cake as a crunchy alternative to piped-frosting rosettes.

cookie balloons

Spread several vanilla wafer cookies with frosting, sprinkle with colored sprinkles, and cluster on the cake. Form the balloon strings with shoestring licorice. (Knot the strings for an added effect.)

chocolate nonpareils

Arrange the candies in geometric patterns. Try alternating large disks with clusters of little ones.

strawberry fan

Thinly slice 1 quart hulled fresh strawberries. Starting from the outside perimeter, place a ring of overlapping strawberries around the cake, points facing out. Continue layering concentric rings around the cake until you reach the center. Carefully brush the berries with $1/4$ cup warmed seedless raspberry jam.

gumdrop rose

Lightly dust a work surface with granulated sugar. With a rolling pin, roll 3 gumdrops to a thickness of $1/8$ inch, then cut the rounds in half. Roll 1 piece into a tight bud and pinch it at one end to form the center of the flower. Place the remaining pieces around the center, overlapping them slightly and pressing them together at the base. Trim the bottom to form a flat base before setting the rose on the cake.

candied lemons

In a small saucepan, bring $3/4$ cup water and $3/4$ cup sugar to a boil, stirring until the sugar dissolves. Add 1 thinly sliced lemon, reduce heat, and simmer until tender and translucent, 5 to 7 minutes. Drain and let cool completely on a rack before placing on the cake.

more ideas

Have fun with your toppings. Sprinkle the top of a cake or coat the sides with any of the following:

▸ toasted coconut
▸ chopped dried fruit
▸ colored sprinkles
▸ caramel corn
▸ shaved chocolate
▸ chocolate chips
▸ mini marshmallows
▸ M&M's Minis
▸ crushed cookies
▸ chopped pistachios
▸ toasted sliced almonds

TRICKS OF THE TRADE

Experienced bakers learn how to create light, moist cakes through trial and error. Here's a crib sheet with the Real Simple food department's time-tested advice.

tips for better baking

▸ **AVOID USING COLD EGGS.** Sure, you know to bring the butter to room temperature, but it's just as important for eggs—otherwise the mixture won't emulsify properly. If you're short on time, microwave cut-up butter on low in 5-second intervals, checking in between, and place eggs in a bowl of warm water for 10 to 15 minutes.

▸ **MEASURE THE FLOUR PROPERLY.** Spoon it into a dry measuring cup, then sweep off the excess with a knife. Don't scoop it directly from the bag with a measuring cup; the flour will be compacted, and you'll get more than you need for the recipe.

▸ **USE A PASTRY BRUSH TO BUTTER THE PANS.** You'll get better coverage than with a piece of butter in paper. Plus, it makes buttering parchment a breeze. Simply swipe the brush over a tablespoon of very soft butter, then onto the pan or paper.

▸ **CENTER THE PANS IN THE OVEN.** If your oven isn't wide enough to position pans side by side without their touching each other or the walls, place them on different racks (as close to the center of the oven as possible) and slightly offset, to allow for air circulation.

▸ **ROTATE THE PANS DURING BAKING.** This will ensure even cooking. But wait until the cake is set (about two-thirds of the way through the baking time) to prevent collapse. If you're using more than one rack, this is also the time to swap the pans.

▸ **COOL CAKES UPSIDE DOWN.** This will flatten out the tops, creating easy-to-stack disks for layer cakes. If the top of a cake is still too rounded, slice it off with a serrated knife.

frosting a layer cake

▸ **STEP 1.** Elevate the cake—frosting is easier when the cake is closer to eye level. No cake stand? Turn a large, wide-bottom mixing bowl upside down and place a plate on top of it.

▸ **STEP 2.** Dab a couple of tablespoons of frosting on the plate before putting down the first layer. This will prevent the cake from sliding.

▸ **STEP 3.** Tuck pieces of wax paper under the cake's edge to protect the plate from frosting drips.

▸ **STEP 4.** Put a big dollop of frosting or filling (1 to 1$^1/_2$ cups) on top of the first layer. Using an offset spatula, start in the middle and spread the frosting or filling evenly over the top.

▸ **STEP 5.** Place the second cake layer on top and press gently. Step back and check to make sure that it is level and centered. If you're using a filling (rather than a frosting) between layers, chill the cake for 30 minutes to firm up the filling a bit, making the cake more stable for frosting.

▸ **STEP 6.** Frost the top of the cake and then the sides. It's best to start with a lot and remove excess if necessary. Aim for coverage first, then go back to beautify.

▸ **STEP 7.** Add toppings if desired (for ideas, see page 83), then remove the wax paper.

summer

flaky tomato and mozzarella tart

hands-on time: 10 minutes / total time: 1 hour (includes chilling) / serves 4

All-purpose flour, for the work surface

½ sheet frozen puff pastry (one-quarter of a 17.3-ounce package), thawed

1 cup grape or cherry tomatoes, halved if large

¼ pound mozzarella, grated (1 cup)

1 tablespoon olive oil

Kosher salt and black pepper

▸ Heat oven to 425° F. Line a baking sheet with parchment. On a lightly floured surface, roll the pastry into a 9-by-6-inch rectangle. Place on the prepared baking sheet and refrigerate until firm, at least 30 minutes.

▸ Prick the pastry all over with a fork, then top with the tomatoes and mozzarella. Drizzle with the oil; season with ½ teaspoon salt and ¼ teaspoon pepper.

▸ Bake the tart until golden brown and cooked through, 20 to 25 minutes. Cut into pieces before serving.

TIP
Be sure to use commercially packaged mozzarella in this recipe. Fresh mozzarella loses its water during baking and will leave the pastry soggy.

hummus and cucumber crostini

hands-on time: 5 minutes / total time: 5 minutes
serves 4

12 large bagel chips (preferably "everything" flavor)
½ cup hummus
¼ English cucumber, thinly sliced
1 tablespoon olive oil
Kosher salt and black pepper

▸ Dividing evenly, top the bagel chips with the hummus and cucumber, drizzle with the oil, and season with ¼ teaspoon each salt and pepper.

Mexican grilled corn with cilantro

hands-on time: 10 minutes / total time: 25 minutes
serves 4

2 ears corn, shucked and cut into 6 pieces each
1 tablespoon olive oil
Kosher salt and black pepper
¼ cup chopped fresh cilantro
1 teaspoon fresh lime juice, plus lime wedges for serving

▸ Heat grill to medium. In a medium bowl, toss the corn with the oil and ¼ teaspoon each salt and pepper.

▸ Reserving the bowl, grill the corn, uncovered, turning occasionally, until tender, 10 to 12 minutes.

▸ Transfer the cooked corn to the reserved bowl and toss with the cilantro and lime juice. Serve with lime wedges.

roast beef and horseradish canapés

hands-on time: 10 minutes / total time: 25 minutes
serves 4

12 frozen waffle fries

3 ounces thinly sliced roast beef, torn into pieces

2 tablespoons horseradish sauce

Kosher salt and black pepper

▸ Cook the waffle fries according to the package directions.

▸ Dividing evenly, top the fries with the roast beef, horseradish sauce, and ⅛ teaspoon each salt and pepper.

grilled spiced chicken wings

hands-on time: 20 minutes / total time: 30 minutes
serves 4

8 chicken wings (about 1½ pounds), halved through the joint

1 teaspoon olive oil

2 teaspoons seafood seasoning (such as Old Bay)

3 tablespoons unsalted butter, melted

Ranch dressing, for serving

▸ Heat grill to medium. In a large bowl, toss the wings with the oil and 1 teaspoon of the seafood seasoning. Grill, uncovered, until cooked through, 8 to 10 minutes per side.

▸ Meanwhile, in a second large bowl, combine the butter and the remaining teaspoon of seafood seasoning. Add the cooked wings and toss to coat. Serve with ranch dressing for dipping.

grilled Feta with thyme

hands-on time: 5 minutes / **total time: 30 minutes** / **serves 8**

1 12-ounce piece Feta,
  at room temperature

6 sprigs fresh thyme

2 tablespoons olive oil
  Black pepper
  Grilled pitas, for serving

▸ Heat grill to medium-low. Place the Feta in the center of a large piece of heavy-duty foil. Top with the thyme, drizzle with the oil, and season with $1/4$ teaspoon pepper. Seal the foil to form a packet.

▸ Grill the packet, covered, until the Feta is soft in the center when pressed, 15 to 17 minutes.

▸ Transfer the Feta, herbs, and oil to a shallow bowl and serve with pitas.

TIP
You can assemble the foil packet up to 1 day in advance; refrigerate. Bring to room temperature before grilling.

chicken and orange skewers with zucchini rice

hands-on time: 30 minutes / **total time: 45 minutes** / **serves 4**

1 cup long-grain white rice

1 medium zucchini, coarsely grated

1¼ pounds boneless, skinless chicken thighs (6 or 7), cut into 1½-inch pieces

1 small red onion, cut into 1½-inch pieces

1 navel orange, cut into 16 pieces

1 tablespoon olive oil, plus more for the grill

½ teaspoon ground cumin

¼ teaspoon cayenne pepper

Kosher salt and black pepper

▶ Soak 8 small wooden skewers in water for at least 10 minutes.

▶ Cook the rice according to the package directions. Remove from heat. Sprinkle the zucchini over the rice, cover, and let stand for 5 minutes. Fluff the rice with a fork and fold in the zucchini.

▶ Meanwhile, heat grill to medium. In a large bowl, toss the chicken, onion, and orange with the oil, cumin, cayenne, ¾ teaspoon salt, and ¼ teaspoon black pepper; thread onto the skewers.

▶ Lightly oil grill and grill the skewers, uncovered, turning occasionally, until the chicken is cooked through and the onion is just tender, 15 to 18 minutes. Serve with the rice.

TIP
Play up the citrus flavor of the kebabs by adding a teaspoon of finely grated orange zest to the rice along with the zucchini.

grilled chicken and corn salad with avocado and Parmesan
hands-on time: 30 minutes / total time: 30 minutes / serves 4

¼ cup fresh lemon juice

2 tablespoons chopped fresh rosemary

4 cloves garlic, finely chopped

4 tablespoons olive oil

Kosher salt and black pepper

2 6-ounce boneless, skinless chicken breasts

3 ears corn, shucked

5 ounces baby spinach (about 5 cups)

1 avocado, cut into bite-size pieces

2 ounces Parmesan, shaved

▶ Heat grill to medium-high. In a medium bowl, whisk together the lemon juice, rosemary, garlic, 3 tablespoons of the oil, ½ teaspoon salt, and ¼ teaspoon pepper. Transfer half the dressing to a small bowl; set aside. Add the chicken to the remaining dressing and turn to coat.

▶ Rub the corn with the remaining tablespoon of oil and season with ¼ teaspoon each salt and pepper. Grill the corn and chicken, covered, turning occasionally, until the corn is tender and lightly charred, 4 to 6 minutes, and the chicken is cooked through, 8 to 10 minutes. Cut the kernels off the cobs and slice the chicken.

▶ Toss the spinach, chicken, corn, and avocado with the reserved dressing and sprinkle with the Parmesan.

TIP
If you prefer a less garlicky salad, add garlic only to the half of the dressing used to marinate the chicken.

lemon and olive chicken with arugula and white bean salad

hands-on time: 25 minutes / total time: 40 minutes / serves 4

2½ to 3 pounds bone-in, skin-on chicken pieces
     Kosher salt and black pepper
2   teaspoons olive oil
4   cups arugula
1   15.5-ounce can cannellini beans, rinsed
⅓   cup pesto
1   lemon, thinly sliced
½   cup pitted kalamata olives

▸ Heat oven to 400° F. Season the chicken with ½ teaspoon salt and ¼ teaspoon pepper.

▸ Heat the oil in a large skillet over medium-high heat. Working in batches if necessary, cook the chicken until golden brown, 5 to 6 minutes per side.

▸ Reserving the skillet, transfer the chicken to a rimmed baking sheet and bake until cooked through, 15 to 20 minutes.

▸ Meanwhile, in a medium bowl, toss the arugula and beans with the pesto and ¼ teaspoon each salt and pepper.

▸ Add the lemon to the drippings in the reserved skillet and cook until golden, 1 to 2 minutes per side. Mix in the olives. Top the chicken with the olives and lemon and serve with the salad.

TIP
Any white bean will work in this salad. If you don't have cannellini, try great Northern or navy beans.

chicken pitas with tzatziki

hands-on time: 25 minutes / total time: 25 minutes / serves 4

2 tablespoons olive oil

1½ pounds boneless, skinless chicken thighs (about 8)

¼ teaspoon cayenne pepper
Kosher salt and black pepper

1 cup plain low-fat Greek yogurt

1 cucumber, seeded and grated (about 1¼ cups)

¼ cup chopped fresh mint

½ small clove garlic, finely chopped

4 pocketless pitas or flat breads, warmed

1 small romaine heart, leaves torn

8 cherry tomatoes, quartered

▸ Heat the oil in a large skillet over medium-high heat. Season the chicken with the cayenne, ½ teaspoon salt, and ¼ teaspoon black pepper. Cook until cooked through, 6 to 7 minutes per side. Cut into bite-size pieces.

▸ Meanwhile, in a medium bowl, mix together the yogurt, cucumber, mint, garlic, ½ teaspoon salt, and ¼ teaspoon black pepper.

▸ Top the pitas with the romaine, chicken, tomatoes, and tzatziki sauce.

TIP
The tzatziki can be made up to 1 day ahead; refrigerate, covered. For a change of pace, substitute dill or basil for the mint.

grilled hoisin chicken and scallions with sweet potatoes

hands-on time: 30 minutes / total time: 30 minutes / serves 4

4 6-ounce boneless, skinless chicken breasts

1½ pounds medium sweet potatoes (about 3), peeled and cut into ½-inch wedges

2 tablespoons canola oil

Kosher salt and black pepper

2 bunches scallions, trimmed

¼ cup hoisin sauce

1 teaspoon toasted sesame oil

2 teaspoons toasted sesame seeds

▸ Heat grill to medium. In a large bowl, toss the chicken and potatoes with 1½ tablespoons of the canola oil and ½ teaspoon each salt and pepper.

▸ In a medium bowl, toss the scallions with the remaining ½ tablespoon of canola oil and ¼ teaspoon each salt and pepper.

▸ Grill the chicken and potatoes, covered, until the chicken is cooked through, 5 to 7 minutes per side. After 5 minutes, add the scallions and cook, turning occasionally, until tender, 2 to 4 minutes. During the last 3 minutes of cooking, brush the chicken with the hoisin sauce and turn occasionally.

▸ Drizzle the potatoes with the sesame oil. Serve with the chicken and scallions and sprinkle with the sesame seeds.

TIP
Turn leftovers into a spicy-sweet Asian sandwich: Thinly slice the chicken and serve it on white bread with the scallions, shredded lettuce, mayonnaise, and Sriracha or Asian chili sauce.

chicken niçoise salad

hands-on time: 25 minutes / total time: 30 minutes / serves 4

½ pound green beans, trimmed

½ pound baby potatoes (about 8), halved

4 large eggs

6 cups mixed greens

1½ cups shredded rotisserie chicken

½ small red onion, sliced

½ cup cured black olives

3 tablespoons red wine vinaigrette

▶ Fill a large pot with 1 inch of water and fit with a steamer basket; bring the water to a boil. Place the beans in the basket, cover, and steam until tender, 4 to 5 minutes; run under cold water to cool.

▶ Steam the potatoes until tender, 10 to 12 minutes.

▶ Meanwhile, place the eggs in a large saucepan and add enough cold water to cover by 1 inch; bring to a boil. Remove the saucepan from heat, cover, and let stand for 12 minutes. Drain the eggs and run under cold water to cool. Peel and halve the eggs.

▶ Divide the greens among plates and top with the beans, potatoes, eggs, chicken, onion, and olives. Drizzle with the vinaigrette.

TIP
For an authentic French touch, add 2 oil-packed anchovy fillets to each plate.

GRILLED STEAK DINNER

grilled steak with caper sauce

hands-on time: 20 minutes
total time: 30 minutes
serves 8

2 cups chopped fresh flat-leaf parsley
$^1/_2$ cup olive oil
$^1/_4$ cup capers, chopped
2 tablespoons red wine vinegar
1 clove garlic, chopped
  Kosher salt and black pepper
3 T-bone steaks (about 1$^1/_4$ inches thick; 4$^1/_2$ pounds total) or 3 pounds strip or flank steak

▸ Heat grill to medium-high. In a medium bowl, mix together the parsley, oil, capers, vinegar, garlic, 1 teaspoon salt, and $^1/_4$ teaspoon pepper.

▸ Season the steaks with 2 teaspoons salt and $^1/_2$ teaspoon pepper and grill to the desired doneness, 5 to 7 minutes per side for medium-rare. Let rest for at least 5 minutes before slicing. Serve with the caper sauce.

grilled asparagus with manchego

hands-on time: 15 minutes
total time: 15 minutes
serves 8

2 bunches asparagus, trimmed
1 tablespoon olive oil
  Kosher salt and black pepper
2 ounces manchego, shaved
$^1/_2$ teaspoon paprika (preferably smoked; also called pimentón)

▸ Heat grill to medium-high. In a large bowl, toss the asparagus with the oil, $^1/_2$ teaspoon salt, and $^1/_4$ teaspoon pepper.

▸ Grill the asparagus, turning occasionally, until just tender, 4 to 6 minutes. Transfer to a platter and sprinkle with the manchego and paprika.

tomato salad with pickled onion

hands-on time: 10 minutes
total time: 1 hour, 10 minutes
(includes marinating) / serves 8

1 medium red onion, halved and thinly sliced
  Zest of 1 lime, finely grated, plus 3 tablespoons fresh lime juice
3 tablespoons olive oil
  Kosher salt
4 large tomatoes (about 2$^1/_2$ pounds), sliced

▸ In a medium bowl, toss the onion with the lime juice, oil, and $^1/_2$ teaspoon salt. Let stand, tossing occasionally, until the onion has softened, at least 1 hour and up to 3 hours.

▸ Arrange the tomatoes on a platter and season with $^1/_2$ teaspoon salt. Top with the onion and sprinkle with the lime zest.

lamb chops with orzo and cucumber salad
hands-on time: 30 minutes / total time: 1 hour (includes marinating) / serves 4

4 cloves garlic, chopped

1 tablespoon grated lemon zest, plus 2 tablespoons fresh lemon juice

4 tablespoons olive oil

Kosher salt and black pepper

8 small lamb chops (rib or loin; 3/4 inch thick; about 2 pounds total)

1 cup orzo (6 ounces)

1/2 English cucumber, chopped

3 scallions, thinly sliced

1/2 cup pitted black olives, halved

1/4 cup chopped fresh mint

▶ In a shallow baking dish, combine the garlic, lemon zest, 2 tablespoons of the oil, and 1/2 teaspoon each salt and pepper. Add the lamb chops and turn to coat. Refrigerate, covered, for 30 minutes.

▶ Meanwhile, cook the orzo according to the package directions. Drain, run under cold water to cool, and shake well to remove excess water. In a medium bowl, toss with the cucumber, scallions, olives, mint, lemon juice, the remaining 2 tablespoons of oil, 1/2 teaspoon salt, and 1/4 teaspoon pepper.

▶ Heat a large skillet over medium-high heat. Remove the lamb from the marinade and, working in batches, cook until medium-rare, 2 to 4 minutes per side. Serve with the orzo salad.

TIP
The salad can be prepared and the lamb marinated up to 1 day in advance; refrigerate, covered.

5 IDEAS FOR BURGERS

MASTER RECIPE

hands-on time: 15 minutes
total time: 15 minutes / serves 4

1¼ pounds ground beef chuck
Kosher salt and black pepper
Canola oil, for the grill

▸ Heat grill to medium-high. Form the beef into four ³/₄-inch-thick patties. Use your fingers to make a shallow well in the top of each. (This will prevent overplumping during cooking.) Dividing evenly, season the patties with ½ teaspoon each salt and pepper.

▸ Oil grill and cook the patties with the wells facing up until the burgers release easily, 4 to 5 minutes. Flip and cook until an instant-read thermometer inserted in the center registers 160° F for medium, 4 to 5 minutes more.

Cheddar, avocado, and sprouts burgers

hands-on time: 15 minutes
total time: 15 minutes / serves 4

Ingredients for Master Recipe (left)
4 ounces Cheddar, sliced
8 slices multigrain bread
½ cup mayonnaise
4 leaves red leaf lettuce
1 avocado, sliced
½ cup alfalfa or radish sprouts

▸ Cook the burgers following the Master Recipe. During the last 3 minutes of cooking, top them with the Cheddar.

▸ Spread the bread with the mayonnaise and form sandwiches with the lettuce, burgers, avocado, and sprouts.

ricotta salata and pickled zucchini burgers

hands-on time: 25 minutes
total time: 35 minutes / serves 4

Ingredients for Master Recipe (left)
2 zucchini
¼ cup distilled white vinegar
2 tablespoons sugar
½ teaspoon crushed red pepper
Kosher salt
4 brioche buns, split
¼ head radicchio
4 ounces ricotta salata or Feta, thinly sliced

▸ With a vegetable peeler, cut the zucchini into ribbons. In a medium bowl, toss with the vinegar, sugar, red pepper, and 1 teaspoon salt; let stand for 10 minutes.

▸ Meanwhile, cook the burgers following the Master Recipe.

▸ Form sandwiches with the buns, radicchio, burgers, ricotta salata, and pickled zucchini.

celery, olive, and blue cheese burgers

hands-on time: 20 minutes
total time: 20 minutes / serves 4

Ingredients for Master Recipe (left)
2 small celery stalks, thinly sliced
¹/₂ cup sliced green olives
¹/₄ small red onion, thinly sliced
1 tablespoon olive oil
1 tablespoon fresh lemon juice
4 sandwich-size English muffins, split
¹/₂ cup chunky blue cheese dressing

▸ In a medium bowl, toss the celery, olives, and onion with the oil and lemon juice.

▸ Cook the burgers following the Master Recipe. Grill the muffins until toasted, 1 to 2 minutes.

▸ Spread the muffins with the blue cheese dressing and form sandwiches with the burgers and celery mixture.

onion dip and potato chip burgers

hands-on time: 15 minutes
total time: 15 minutes / serves 4

Ingredients for Master Recipe (left)
4 soft onion rolls, split
¹/₂ cup onion dip
4 leaves Bibb lettuce
16 bread-and-butter pickle chips
1 cup ridged potato chips

▸ Cook the burgers following the Master Recipe. Grill the rolls until toasted, 1 to 2 minutes.

▸ Spread the rolls with the dip and form sandwiches with the burgers, lettuce, pickles, and potato chips.

chipotle mayo and grilled onion burgers

hands-on time: 25 minutes
total time: 25 minutes / serves 4

Ingredients for Master Recipe (left)
¹/₂ cup mayonnaise
1 to 2 tablespoons chopped chipotle chilies in adobo sauce
2 teaspoons fresh lime juice
1 medium red onion, cut into ¹/₂-inch-thick slices
8 thick slices white bread
¹/₂ cup fresh cilantro leaves

▸ In a small bowl, mix together the mayonnaise, chipotles, and lime juice.

▸ Cook the burgers following the Master Recipe. At the same time, grill the onion until tender, 4 to 5 minutes per side. Grill the bread until toasted, 1 to 2 minutes per side.

▸ Spread the bread with the chipotle mayonnaise and form sandwiches with the burgers, onion, and cilantro.

Asian steak salad with mango
hands-on time: 30 minutes / total time: 30 minutes / serves 4

³/₄ pound sirloin steak
(1 inch thick)

Kosher salt and black pepper

1 teaspoon grated lime zest,
plus 3 tablespoons fresh
lime juice

3 tablespoons canola oil

1 tablespoon honey

1 tablespoon chopped pickled
ginger (found in the
international aisle)

2 teaspoons low-sodium
soy sauce

1 large head romaine lettuce,
thinly sliced (about 7 cups)

1 mango, cut into bite-size
pieces

1 red bell pepper, thinly sliced

¹/₂ cup fresh basil leaves, sliced

2 scallions, thinly sliced

1 teaspoon toasted sesame
seeds

▸ Heat a large skillet over high heat. Season the steak with ¹/₄ teaspoon each salt and black pepper and cook to the desired doneness, 4 to 5 minutes per side for medium-rare. Let rest for at least 5 minutes before slicing.

▸ Meanwhile, in a large bowl, whisk together the lime zest and juice, oil, honey, ginger, soy sauce, and ¹/₄ teaspoon salt. Add the lettuce, mango, bell pepper, basil, and scallions and toss to combine. Gently fold in the steak and sprinkle with the sesame seeds.

TIP
For a hearty next-day lunch, tuck the leftovers into a toasted baguette spread with wasabi mayonnaise.

steak with skillet tomatoes and spicy green beans

hands-on time: 30 minutes / **total time: 30 minutes** / **serves 4**

Kosher salt and black pepper

3 tablespoons plus 3 teaspoons olive oil

2 strip steaks (1 inch thick; about 1½ pounds total)

2 pints grape tomatoes

¼ cup fresh oregano leaves

1 pound green beans, trimmed

2 cloves garlic, thinly sliced

¼ to ½ teaspoon crushed red pepper

▶ Bring a large pot of salted water to a boil. Heat 2 teaspoons of the oil in a large skillet over medium-high heat. Season the steaks with ½ teaspoon salt and ¼ teaspoon black pepper and cook to the desired doneness, 4 to 6 minutes per side for medium-rare. Let rest for at least 5 minutes before slicing.

▶ Wipe out the skillet and heat 1 teaspoon of the remaining oil over medium-high heat. Add the tomatoes and ¼ teaspoon each salt and black pepper. Cook, tossing occasionally, until beginning to soften, 4 to 6 minutes. Mix in the oregano.

▶ Meanwhile, cook the green beans in the boiling water until tender, 3 to 4 minutes; drain. Wipe out the pot and heat the garlic in the remaining 3 tablespoons of oil over medium heat, stirring frequently, until fragrant, 1 to 2 minutes. Add the green beans, ½ teaspoon salt, and ¼ teaspoon black pepper and toss to combine. Sprinkle with the red pepper and serve with the steak and tomatoes.

TIP
Slowly heating the garlic in the oil (rather than adding it to hot oil) infuses the oil with flavor and keeps the garlic from burning.

Thai pork salad with chilies and mint

hands-on time: 25 minutes / total time: 25 minutes / serves 4

2 teaspoons canola oil

1 pound ground pork

5 tablespoons Asian fish sauce

3 teaspoons sugar

1/2 cup fresh lime juice (from about 4 limes)

1 to 2 jalapeño or serrano chili peppers, seeded (if desired) and thinly sliced

2 small heads Boston lettuce, torn into bite-size pieces (about 8 cups)

1 small shallot, thinly sliced

2 medium carrots, coarsely grated

1 cup fresh mint leaves

1/4 cup salted roasted peanuts, chopped

▸ Heat the oil in a large skillet over medium-high heat. Add the pork and cook, breaking it up with a spoon, until no longer pink, 2 to 3 minutes. Add 1/4 cup water, 1 tablespoon of the fish sauce, and 1 teaspoon of the sugar and cook, stirring, until the liquid is almost evaporated, 2 to 4 minutes more.

▸ In a small bowl, stir together the lime juice, jalapeños, and the remaining 4 tablespoons of fish sauce and 2 teaspoons of sugar.

▸ Divide the lettuce among bowls. Top with the pork mixture, shallot, carrots, mint, and peanuts. Drizzle with the lime dressing.

TIP

In spite of its name, fish sauce does not add a fishy taste to food. Rather, it enriches dressings, dips, marinades, and soups with a deep, savory flavor that chefs call "umami." The condiment—made from fermented anchovies, salt, and water—is found in the international aisle of the supermarket, often labeled "nuoc mam" (Vietnamese) or "nam pla" (Thai).

pork and pineapple kebabs

hands-on time: 10 minutes / total time: 25 minutes / serves 4

1 cup long-grain white rice

2 tablespoons chopped fresh cilantro

1 1¼-pound pork tenderloin, cut into 1-inch chunks

½ medium pineapple, cut into 1-inch chunks

1 red onion, cut into 1-inch chunks

1 cup grape tomatoes

Kosher salt and black pepper

¼ cup honey

▸ Soak 8 wooden skewers in water for at least 10 minutes.

▸ Cook the rice according to the package directions. Just before serving, fold in the cilantro.

▸ Meanwhile, heat broiler. Thread the pork, pineapple, onion, and tomatoes onto the skewers. Season with ½ teaspoon salt and ¼ teaspoon pepper.

▸ Place the skewers on a foil-lined baking sheet and broil, turning once and brushing occasionally with the honey, until browned, 8 to 10 minutes. Serve with the rice.

TIP
Soaking the wooden skewers keeps them from scorching under the broiler. Alternatively, you can thread the meat and vegetables onto the skewers, then wrap the tips with foil.

chorizo and potato tacos with black bean salsa
hands-on time: 25 minutes / total time: 25 minutes / serves 4

1 pound fresh chorizo or Italian sausage, casings removed

1 russet potato (about 1/2 pound), cut into 1/4-inch pieces

1 15-ounce can black beans, rinsed

4 radishes, cut into small pieces

1/2 cup chopped fresh cilantro

2 tablespoons fresh lime juice

1 tablespoon olive oil

1/2 teaspoon ground cumin

Kosher salt and black pepper

8 hard taco shells, warmed

1 avocado, sliced

1/4 cup sour cream

▸ In a large nonstick skillet, cook the chorizo and potato over medium-high heat, breaking up the chorizo with a spoon, until it has browned and the potato is tender, 12 to 15 minutes.

▸ Meanwhile, in a medium bowl, combine the beans, radishes, cilantro, lime juice, oil, cumin, 1/2 teaspoon salt, and 1/4 teaspoon pepper.

▸ Fill the taco shells with the chorizo mixture, black bean salsa, avocado, and sour cream.

TIP
To remove sausage casings easily, cut down the side of the sausage with a paring knife or scissors, then scrape or squeeze out the meat.

apricot-glazed pork chops with brown rice–pecan pilaf
hands-on time: 20 minutes / total time: 1 hour / serves 4

1 cup brown rice

$^1/_2$ cup pecans

2 teaspoons olive oil

4 bone-in pork chops (1 inch thick; about 2$^1/_2$ pounds total)

Kosher salt and black pepper

$^1/_2$ cup apricot preserves

1 tablespoon balsamic vinegar

3 tablespoons chopped fresh dill

2 tablespoons unsalted butter, cut into small pieces

▸ Heat oven to 350° F. Cook the rice according to the package directions. Spread the pecans on a rimmed baking sheet and toast, tossing occasionally, until fragrant, 8 to 10 minutes. Let cool, then coarsely chop.

▸ After the rice has been cooking for 35 minutes, heat the oil in a large skillet over medium-high heat. Season the pork chops with $^1/_2$ teaspoon each salt and pepper and cook until browned and cooked through, 6 to 8 minutes per side.

▸ Add the apricot preserves and vinegar to the skillet and cook the pork, turning once, until coated, 1 to 2 minutes more.

▸ Fold the pecans, dill, butter, $^1/_2$ teaspoon salt, and $^1/_4$ teaspoon pepper into the rice and serve with the pork chops.

TIP
This easy apricot glaze is also a great finish for chicken breasts or cutlets.

pork loin with mustard sauce and sautéed squash
hands-on time: 20 minutes / total time: 1 hour / serves 4

2 tablespoons olive oil
1½ pounds boneless pork loin
   Kosher salt and black pepper
¼ cup red wine vinegar
¼ cup Dijon mustard
¼ cup coarsely chopped fresh
   flat-leaf parsley
1 small onion, cut into 1-inch
   pieces
3 zucchini and/or yellow squash,
   cut into 1-inch pieces

▸ Heat oven to 400° F. Heat 1 tablespoon of the oil in a large ovenproof skillet over medium-high heat. Season the pork with ¼ teaspoon each salt and pepper and cook, turning occasionally, until browned, 6 to 8 minutes.

▸ Transfer the skillet to oven and roast the pork, turning once, until the internal temperature registers 145° F, 40 to 45 minutes. Remove the pork from the skillet and let rest for 5 minutes before slicing.

▸ Carefully add the vinegar, mustard, and parsley to the hot skillet and stir to combine; set aside.

▸ Meanwhile, in a second large skillet, heat the remaining tablespoon of oil over medium-high heat. Add the onion, squash, and ¼ teaspoon each salt and pepper and cook, tossing occasionally, until tender, 8 to 10 minutes. Serve with the pork and mustard sauce.

TIP
Don't have two large skillets? After browning the pork, transfer it to a rimmed baking sheet for roasting and use the skillet for the mustard sauce and then the vegetables.

red curry salmon with bok choy and pineapple slaw
hands-on time: 20 minutes / total time: 30 minutes / serves 4

1 pound baby bok choy, thinly sliced (4 cups)

$1/2$ medium pineapple, cut into bite-size pieces

1 cup fresh cilantro leaves

4 tablespoons canola oil

Kosher salt and black pepper

1 tablespoon Thai red curry paste

1 teaspoon light brown sugar

$1^1/4$ pounds skinless salmon fillet, cut into 4 pieces

▸ In a medium bowl, toss the bok choy and pineapple with the cilantro, 3 tablespoons of the oil, $1/2$ teaspoon salt, and $1/4$ teaspoon pepper. Let sit for 15 minutes before serving.

▸ Meanwhile, heat broiler. In a small bowl, mix together the curry paste, sugar, the remaining tablespoon of oil, $1/2$ teaspoon salt, and $1/4$ teaspoon pepper.

▸ Place the salmon on a foil-lined broilerproof baking sheet and, dividing evenly, brush with the curry paste mixture. Broil until the salmon is opaque throughout, 5 to 7 minutes. Serve with the slaw.

TIP
This refreshing slaw also works well with mint or basil in place of the cilantro.

grilled halibut with salt-and-vinegar potatoes
hands-on time: 40 minutes / **total time: 40 minutes** / **serves 4**

2 russet potatoes (about
   1 pound), peeled and sliced
   into ¹/₂-inch-thick rounds

2 tablespoons cider vinegar

2 tablespoons olive oil, plus
   more for the grill

   Kosher salt and black pepper

1¹/₂ pounds halibut, cod, or
   striped bass fillet, cut into
   4 pieces

1 large red onion, sliced into
   ¹/₂-inch-thick rings

2 cups baby arugula

2 tablespoons fresh lemon
   juice, plus lemon wedges
   for serving

▸ Heat grill to medium-high. Dividing evenly, place the potatoes on 2 large pieces of heavy-duty foil and toss with the vinegar, 1 tablespoon of the oil, and ¹/₂ teaspoon each salt and pepper. Fold the foil over the potatoes and seal the edges to form 2 packets. Place the packets on grill and cook, turning once, until the potatoes are tender, 20 to 25 minutes.

▸ Meanwhile, rub the halibut and onion with the remaining tablespoon of oil and season with ¹/₄ teaspoon each salt and pepper. After the potatoes have cooked for 15 minutes, oil grill. Add the halibut and onion and cook until the halibut is opaque throughout, 3 to 5 minutes per side, and the onion is tender, 4 to 5 minutes per side.

▸ In a small bowl, toss the arugula with the lemon juice. Top the halibut with the arugula and serve with the potatoes, onion, and lemon wedges.

TIP
This foil-packet method works well with other cut-up vegetables, such as mushrooms, carrots, tomatoes, and broccoli.

grilled shrimp panzanella with basil

hands-on time: 15 minutes / total time: 25 minutes / serves 4

1½ pounds peeled and deveined large shrimp

1 teaspoon finely grated lemon zest, plus 2 tablespoons fresh lemon juice

4 tablespoons olive oil
Kosher salt and black pepper

1 small baguette (about 8 ounces), split lengthwise

2½ pounds heirloom or beefsteak tomatoes, cut into wedges

2 cups fresh basil leaves

▶ Heat grill to medium-high. In a large bowl, toss the shrimp with the lemon zest, 1 tablespoon of the oil, and ¼ teaspoon each salt and pepper. Brush the baguette with 1 tablespoon of the remaining oil.

▶ Grill the baguette and shrimp, uncovered, until the baguette is golden and crisp, about 1 minute per side, and the shrimp are opaque throughout, 2 to 3 minutes per side. Cut the baguette into bite-size pieces.

▶ In a second large bowl, toss the shrimp, bread, and tomatoes with the basil, lemon juice, the remaining 2 tablespoons of oil, ½ teaspoon salt, and ¼ teaspoon pepper.

TIP
For a vegetarian take on this refreshing salad, omit the shrimp and toss in halved bocconcini (small balls of fresh mozzarella) and thinly sliced red onion.

GRILLED SALMON DINNER

plank-grilled salmon with lemon and fennel

hands-on time: 10 minutes
total time: 1 hour, 10 minutes / serves 8

1 large or 2 small cedar planks
1 bulb fennel, very thinly sliced, plus 1/2 cup fennel fronds
1 lemon, very thinly sliced
1 tablespoon olive oil
1 2³/4- to 3-pound piece salmon fillet (skin on)
   Kosher salt and black pepper

▶ Soak the cedar plank(s) in water for at least 30 minutes. Heat grill to medium.

▶ In a medium bowl, toss the fennel and lemon slices with the oil. Place the salmon on the plank(s), season with 1 1/2 teaspoons salt and 1/2 teaspoon pepper, and top with the lemon-fennel mixture.

▶ Place the plank(s) on grill, cover, and cook until the salmon is cooked through, 35 to 40 minutes. Sprinkle with the fennel fronds before serving.

wild rice and pine nut salad

hands-on time: 15 minutes
total time: 1 hour, 10 minutes / serves 8

2 cups wild and long-grain rice blend (discarding the spice packet, if included)
1/2 cup pine nuts
1 cup chopped fresh flat-leaf parsley
1/4 cup chopped fresh tarragon
1/4 cup olive oil
2 tablespoons fresh lemon juice
   Kosher salt and black pepper

▶ Cook the rice according to the package directions. Spread it on a rimmed baking sheet or large plate and refrigerate until cool.

▶ Meanwhile, heat oven to 350° F. Spread the pine nuts on a rimmed baking sheet and toast, tossing occasionally, until golden, 6 to 8 minutes; let cool.

▶ Transfer the cooled rice to a large bowl and fold in the pine nuts, parsley, tarragon, oil, lemon juice, 1 teaspoon salt, and 1/2 teaspoon pepper.

greens with radishes and snap peas

hands-on time: 15 minutes
total time: 15 minutes / serves 8

3 tablespoons olive oil
2 tablespoons red wine vinegar
1 tablespoon whole-grain mustard
1/2 teaspoon sugar
   Kosher salt and black pepper
1 large head Boston lettuce, leaves torn (about 10 cups)
1 medium head radicchio, leaves torn (about 4 cups)
1 bunch radishes, cut into thin wedges
1/2 pound snap peas, trimmed and cut into 1/2-inch pieces

▶ In a large bowl, whisk together the oil, vinegar, mustard, sugar, 1 teaspoon salt, and 1/2 teaspoon pepper.

▶ Add the lettuce, radicchio, radishes, and snap peas to the dressing and toss to combine.

basil spaghetti with cheesy broiled tomatoes
hands-on time: 15 minutes / total time: 30 minutes / serves 4

$^3/_4$ pound spaghetti

3 large beefsteak tomatoes (about 1$^1/_2$ pounds), cut into $^1/_2$-inch-thick slices

3 tablespoons olive oil, plus more for the baking sheet

Kosher salt and black pepper

8 ounces fresh mozzarella, grated (2 cups)

$^1/_4$ cup grated Parmesan (1 ounce), plus more (shaved) for serving

2 cloves garlic, chopped

$^1/_4$ to $^1/_2$ teaspoon crushed red pepper

$^1/_4$ cup torn fresh basil leaves, plus more for serving

▶ Heat broiler. Cook the pasta according to the package directions. Drain and return it to the pot.

▶ Meanwhile, arrange the tomato slices in a single layer on a lightly oiled rimmed baking sheet. Season with $^1/_4$ teaspoon each salt and black pepper. Dividing evenly, sprinkle the slices with the mozzarella and Parmesan. Broil until the cheese is bubbly and golden, 3 to 5 minutes.

▶ In a small saucepan, heat the oil with the garlic and red pepper over medium heat until fragrant, 1 to 2 minutes.

▶ Add the garlic oil, basil, $^1/_2$ teaspoon salt, and $^1/_4$ teaspoon black pepper to the pasta and toss to combine. Serve topped with the tomatoes, additional basil, and shaved Parmesan.

TIP
These deliciously cheesy tomatoes make a quick and easy side dish for steak or chicken.

campanelle with roasted red peppers and almonds

hands-on time: 20 minutes / total time: 20 minutes / serves 4

3/4 pound campanelle, penne, or some other short pasta

4 red or orange bell peppers, seeded and cut into quarters

3/4 cup pitted kalamata olives

1/2 cup coarsely chopped roasted almonds

1/4 cup olive oil

1 tablespoon fresh thyme leaves

Kosher salt and black pepper

▸ Cook the pasta according to the package directions. Reserve 1/4 cup of the cooking water; drain the pasta and return it to the pot.

▸ Meanwhile, heat broiler. Place the bell peppers skin-side up on a baking sheet and broil until blackened, 8 to 10 minutes. When the bell peppers are cool enough to handle, scrape away the blackened skins with a knife and discard. Cut the flesh into 1-inch pieces.

▸ Add the bell peppers, olives, almonds, oil, thyme, 2 tablespoons of the reserved cooking water, 1/2 teaspoon salt, and 1/4 teaspoon black pepper to the pasta and toss to combine. (Add more cooking water if the pasta seems dry.)

TIP
If you have a gas stove, you can char the bell peppers (whole) directly over a high flame, turning them frequently with tongs.

bucatini with turkey sausage and zucchini

hands-on time: 15 minutes / total time: 35 minutes / serves 4

- ³/₄ pound bucatini or spaghetti
- 1 tablespoon plus 1 teaspoon olive oil
- 1 pound Italian-style turkey sausage links, casings removed
- 1 pound zucchini and/or summer squash (about 4 small), thinly sliced
- 1 large onion, chopped
- 4 cloves garlic, chopped
  Kosher salt and black pepper
- ¹/₂ cup grated Parmesan (2 ounces), plus more for serving
- ¹/₄ cup fresh oregano leaves

▸ Cook the pasta according to the package directions. Reserve ¹/₂ cup of the cooking water; drain the pasta and return it to the pot.

▸ Meanwhile, in a large skillet, heat 1 teaspoon of the oil over medium-high heat. Add the sausage and cook, breaking it up with a spoon, until browned and cooked through, 10 to 12 minutes. Transfer to a plate.

▸ Reduce heat to medium and add the remaining tablespoon of oil to the skillet. Add the squash, onion, garlic, ¹/₂ teaspoon salt, and ¹/₄ teaspoon pepper and cook, tossing occasionally, until the vegetables are golden and very tender, 15 to 18 minutes. (Reduce heat if the pan begins to darken.)

▸ Add the sausage, vegetables, Parmesan, oregano, and ¹/₄ cup of the reserved cooking water to the pasta and toss to combine. (Add more cooking water if the pasta seems dry.) Serve with additional Parmesan.

TIP
Italian-style turkey sausage has a flavor similar to that of its pork counterpart but with about 40 percent fewer calories and 60 percent less fat. Use it in stews and stuffings or on pizzas.

pasta with goat cheese and basil oil

hands-on time: 15 minutes / total time: 20 minutes / serves 4

³/₄ pound gemelli or some other short pasta

3 cups fresh basil leaves

¹/₂ cup olive oil

4 ounces fresh goat cheese, crumbled (1 cup)

Kosher salt and black pepper

▸ Cook the pasta according to the package directions. Drain and return it to the pot.

▸ Meanwhile, in a blender, puree 2 cups of the basil leaves with the oil until smooth. Pour through a fine-mesh sieve and discard the solids.

▸ Toss the pasta with the basil oil, goat cheese, the remaining cup of basil leaves, ¹/₂ teaspoon salt, and ¹/₄ teaspoon pepper.

TIP
This fragrant basil oil is also delicious in salad dressings. Or drizzle it on sandwich bread in place of mayonnaise.

chopped Greek salad with pita chips
hands-on time: 15 minutes / total time: 15 minutes / serves 4

2 pitas, split

4 tablespoons olive oil

2 tablespoons red wine vinegar

$^{1}/_{2}$ teaspoon dried oregano
   Kosher salt and black pepper

1 small head iceberg lettuce, chopped (about 8 cups)

1 pint grape tomatoes, halved

1 green bell pepper, cut into bite-size pieces

$^{1}/_{2}$ English cucumber, sliced

$^{1}/_{2}$ red onion, chopped

1 15.5-ounce can chickpeas, rinsed and coarsely chopped

4 ounces Feta, crumbled (1 cup)

8 pepperoncini (optional)

$^{1}/_{4}$ cup pitted kalamata olives (optional)

▶ Heat oven to 350° F. Place the pita halves cut-side up on a baking sheet, brush with 1 tablespoon of the oil, and bake until golden and crisp, 4 to 6 minutes. Let cool, then break into pieces.

▶ In a large bowl, whisk together the vinegar, oregano, the remaining 3 tablespoons of oil, $^{1}/_{2}$ teaspoon salt, and $^{1}/_{4}$ teaspoon black pepper. Add the lettuce, tomatoes, bell pepper, cucumber, onion, chickpeas, Feta, pita chips, and pepperoncini and olives, if desired, and toss to combine.

TIP
To keep Feta moist and fresh, always buy it in block form and store it in the brine that it came in. Top off with water if the level drops.

lentil fritter pitas with red cabbage slaw
hands-on time: 30 minutes / **total time: 30 minutes** / **serves 4**

2 15-ounce cans lentils, rinsed

1/2 cup fresh cilantro leaves, plus more for serving

1/2 cup fresh flat-leaf parsley leaves

1 clove garlic, smashed

1/2 teaspoon ground cumin

1/2 cup bread crumbs

Kosher salt and black pepper

1/4 head red cabbage, shredded (about 1 1/2 cups)

2 tablespoons fresh lemon juice

3 tablespoons olive oil

1/2 cup plain low-fat Greek yogurt

1/4 teaspoon crushed red pepper, plus more for serving

4 pocketless pitas or flat breads, warmed

▶ In a food processor, puree 1 can of the lentils with the cilantro, parsley, garlic, and cumin until nearly smooth. Transfer to a large bowl and mix in the bread crumbs, the remaining can of lentils, 1/2 teaspoon salt, and 1/4 teaspoon black pepper. Form into sixteen 1/2-inch-thick patties.

▶ In a large bowl, using a wooden spoon, lightly mash the cabbage with the lemon juice, 1 tablespoon of the oil, and 1/4 teaspoon each salt and black pepper; set aside. In a small bowl, stir together the yogurt, red pepper, and 1/4 cup water.

▶ Heat 1 tablespoon of the remaining oil in a large nonstick skillet over medium-high heat. In 2 batches, cook the patties until browned, 3 to 4 minutes per side, adding the remaining tablespoon of oil to the skillet for the second batch.

▶ Dividing evenly, top each pita with the patties, cabbage mixture, yogurt sauce, and additional cilantro and red pepper.

TIP
Love veggie burgers? Form the lentil mixture into 4 large patties, cook in oil until browned, and serve on buns with whatever toppings you like.

cool gazpacho

hands-on time: 15 minutes / total time: 45 minutes (includes chilling) / serves 4

- 2 pounds ripe tomatoes, coarsely chopped
- 1 red bell pepper, coarsely chopped
- 1/2 small red onion, coarsely chopped
- 1 clove garlic
- 1 English cucumber, half coarsely chopped and half finely chopped
- 1/4 cup olive oil, plus more for drizzling
- 2 teaspoons red wine vinegar or sherry vinegar

  Kosher salt and black pepper
- 2 tablespoons chopped fresh flat-leaf parsley

▶ In a blender, working in batches, puree the tomatoes, bell pepper, onion, garlic, and coarsely chopped cucumber. Transfer to a bowl and stir in the oil, vinegar, 1 1/2 teaspoons salt, and 1/2 teaspoon black pepper. Refrigerate for at least 30 minutes and up to 1 day.

▶ Top the gazpacho with the parsley and finely chopped cucumber and drizzle with additional oil.

TIP
Making gazpacho is a great way to use up bruised and less-than-perfect tomatoes. Just cut out any bad spots.

VEGETARIAN DINNER

grilled Mediterranean vegetables

hands-on time: 25 minutes
total time: 25 minutes / serves 8

2 cups couscous

6 zucchini and/or yellow squash (about 2$\frac{1}{2}$ pounds total), sliced $\frac{1}{4}$ inch thick

1 large eggplant (about 1 pound), sliced $\frac{1}{4}$ inch thick

2 pints cherry tomatoes

2 bunches scallions, trimmed

$\frac{1}{2}$ cup olive oil

Kosher salt and black pepper

Spiced Chili Oil (right) or store-bought harissa (North African chili sauce), for drizzling

▸ Prepare the couscous according to the package directions.

▸ Meanwhile, heat grill to medium. In a large bowl, toss the squash, eggplant, tomatoes, and scallions with the olive oil, 1 teaspoon salt, and $\frac{1}{2}$ teaspoon pepper.

▸ Working in batches if necessary, grill the vegetables, covered, turning occasionally, until tender, 4 to 6 minutes for the squash and eggplant and 1 to 2 minutes for the tomatoes and scallions. Serve with the couscous and drizzle with the Spiced Chili Oil.

spiced chili oil

hands-on time: 15 minutes
total time: 20 minutes / makes 1$\frac{1}{4}$ cups

1 cup olive oil

4 cloves garlic, chopped

2 teaspoons crushed red pepper

2 teaspoons paprika

$\frac{3}{4}$ teaspoon ground cumin

2 tablespoons tomato paste

2 teaspoons finely grated orange zest, plus $\frac{1}{4}$ cup fresh orange juice

Kosher salt and black pepper

▸ In a small saucepan, heat 2 table-spoons of the oil over medium heat. Add the garlic, red pepper, paprika, and cumin. Cook, stirring, until fragrant, about 30 seconds.

▸ Add the tomato paste and orange zest to the saucepan and cook, stirring, until slightly darkened, about 30 seconds.

▸ Add the orange juice, the remaining oil, 1 teaspoon salt, and $\frac{1}{4}$ teaspoon black pepper and stir to combine; remove from heat and let cool. Serve immediately or refrigerate for up to 5 days.

chickpea and raisin salad

hands-on time: 10 minutes
total time: 15 minutes / serves 8

1 cup raisins

$\frac{1}{4}$ cup red wine vinegar

2 teaspoons sugar

3 15.5-ounce cans chickpeas, rinsed

1 cup fresh cilantro or flat-leaf parsley leaves

4 scallions, thinly sliced

$\frac{1}{3}$ cup olive oil

$\frac{1}{2}$ teaspoon ground cumin

Kosher salt and black pepper

▸ In a small saucepan, combine the raisins, vinegar, and sugar and bring just to a simmer. Remove from heat and let cool.

▸ In a large bowl, toss the chickpeas, cilantro, scallions, and raisin mixture with the oil, cumin, $\frac{1}{2}$ teaspoon salt, and $\frac{1}{4}$ teaspoon pepper.

corn salad with Feta and walnuts

hands-on time: 10 minutes / total time: 15 minutes / serves 6

1 cup walnuts

4 cups fresh corn kernels
(from 4 ears), raw or cooked

2 jalapeño peppers, seeded and
thinly sliced

2 tablespoons fresh lime juice

2 tablespoons olive oil

Kosher salt and black pepper

2 ounces Feta, crumbled
(1/2 cup)

▶ Heat oven to 400° F. Spread the walnuts on a rimmed baking sheet and toast, tossing occasionally, until fragrant, 6 to 8 minutes. Let cool and roughly chop.

▶ In a large bowl, combine the corn, jalapeños, lime juice, oil, walnuts, 1/2 teaspoon salt, and 1/4 teaspoon black pepper. Sprinkle with the Feta before serving.

TIP
When cutting corn off the cob, place your cutting board in a rimmed baking sheet to catch flying kernels and juices.

grilled zucchini salad with lemon and scallions

hands-on time: 10 minutes / total time: 20 minutes / serves 6

2 pounds medium zucchini (about 6), halved lengthwise

1 tablespoon plus 1 teaspoon olive oil

6 scallions, sliced

2 tablespoons fresh lemon juice

1/4 teaspoon crushed red pepper

Kosher salt

▸ Heat grill to medium-high. Brush the zucchini with 1 teaspoon of the oil and grill until tender, 5 to 7 minutes per side.

▸ Cut the zucchini into 1-inch pieces and toss in a large bowl with the scallions, lemon juice, red pepper, the remaining tablespoon of oil, and 3/4 teaspoon salt. Serve at room temperature.

TIP
This simple salad is a great accompaniment to anything you're throwing on the grill—chicken, steak, or fish. It also makes a delicious pasta topping: Toss with 3/4 pound cooked penne or rigatoni and a little more olive oil and serve hot or at room temperature.

potato salad with bacon and parsley

hands-on time: 10 minutes / **total time: 25 minutes** / **serves 6**

1½ pounds new potatoes
(about 15)

Kosher salt and black pepper

4 slices bacon (about
2 ounces)

3 tablespoons olive oil

2 tablespoons red wine vinegar

2 teaspoons Dijon mustard

1 cup fresh flat-leaf parsley,
roughly chopped

▸ Place the potatoes in a pot with 1 teaspoon salt and enough water to cover and simmer until tender, 15 to 18 minutes. Drain and run under cold water to cool. Cut into quarters.

▸ Meanwhile, cook the bacon in a medium skillet over medium heat, stirring occasionally, until crisp, 6 to 8 minutes. Transfer to a paper towel–lined plate. Let cool, then crumble.

▸ In a large bowl, whisk together the oil, vinegar, mustard, ¾ teaspoon salt, and ¼ teaspoon pepper. Add the potatoes, bacon, and parsley and toss to combine.

TIP
The potatoes can be cooked and tossed with the dressing and parsley up to 1 day in advance; refrigerate, covered. Bring to room temperature and add the bacon just before serving.

baked beans

hands-on time: 20 minutes / total time: 4 hours (plus overnight soaking of the beans) / serves 8

8 slices bacon (about ¼ pound), cut into ½-inch pieces

1 medium onion, chopped
Kosher salt and black pepper

1 pound dried navy beans, soaked in water overnight and drained

½ cup molasses

½ cup ketchup

1 tablespoon dry mustard

2 tablespoons cider vinegar

▶ Heat oven to 300° F. Cook the bacon in a Dutch oven over medium heat, stirring occasionally, until nearly crisp, 4 to 6 minutes. Add the onion, 1 teaspoon salt, and ½ teaspoon pepper and cook, stirring occasionally, until the onion is soft, 4 to 6 minutes more.

▶ Add the beans, molasses, ketchup, mustard, and 5 cups water to the pot and stir to combine; bring to a boil. Cover and transfer to oven. Bake until the liquid is reduced by half, about 2½ hours.

▶ Uncover the pot and bake, stirring once, until the liquid has thickened, 1 to 1¼ hours more. Stir in the vinegar and serve.

TIP
Don't have all night to wait for dried beans to soak? Try this: After discarding any that are discolored or shriveled, rinse the beans with cold water in a colander, then place them in a large saucepan with enough water to cover. Bring to a boil, reduce heat, and simmer for 2 to 3 minutes. Remove from heat; let stand, covered, for 1 hour, then drain and proceed with the recipe.

3 IDEAS FOR LEMONADE

spicy cayenne shandy

hands-on time: 5 minutes
total time: 5 minutes / **serves 4**

$^1/_2$ teaspoon cayenne pepper
Kosher salt

1 lemon wedge

2 12-ounce bottles lager beer

1 cup lemonade

▸ On a small plate, combine the cayenne and 2 tablespoons salt.

▸ With the lemon wedge, moisten the rims of 4 glasses, then dip each rim in the salt mixture to coat.

▸ In a pitcher, combine the beer and lemonade. Serve over ice in the prepared glasses.

thyme and lime lemonade

hands-on time: 10 minutes
total time: 1 hour, 10 minutes
(includes chilling) / **serves 4**

10 fresh thyme sprigs, plus more for serving

$^1/_4$ cup fresh lime juice

3 cups lemonade

$^3/_4$ cup vodka (optional)

▸ In a pitcher, using a wooden spoon, mash the thyme with the lime juice.

▸ Add the lemonade and refrigerate for at least 1 hour and up to 1 day.

▸ Add the vodka, if desired. Serve over ice, garnished with thyme sprigs.

hibiscus and mint lemonade

hands-on time: 10 minutes
total time: 40 minutes
(includes cooling) / **serves 4**

4 bags hibiscus tea (such as Celestial Seasonings Red Zinger)

2 cups fresh mint leaves, plus sprigs for serving

$2^1/_2$ cups lemonade

▸ Steep the tea and mint in 2 cups boiling water, using a wooden spoon to gently mash the mint; let cool. Discard the tea bags and mint.

▸ In a pitcher, combine the tea and lemonade. Serve over ice, garnished with mint sprigs.

nectarine galette

hands-on time: 10 minutes / total time: 50 minutes / serves 4

1 refrigerated rolled piecrust

3 nectarines or peaches, thinly sliced

2 tablespoons unsalted butter, cut up

3 tablespoons turbinado sugar

▸ Heat oven to 375° F with the rack in the lowest position. Line a baking sheet with parchment.

▸ Place the piecrust on the prepared baking sheet. Top the piecrust with the fruit, leaving a 2-inch border. Dot with the butter and sprinkle with 2 tablespoons of the sugar.

▸ Fold the edges of the dough toward the center, overlapping slightly and partially covering the fruit. Brush the dough with 2 teaspoons water and sprinkle with the remaining tablespoon of sugar.

▸ Bake until the juices are bubbling and the crust is golden (tent with foil if it browns too quickly), 35 to 40 minutes.

TIP
The galette can be baked up to 8 hours in advance; keep at room temperature, loosely covered.

strawberry sorbet with balsamic syrup

hands-on time: 5 minutes / total time: 25 minutes
serves 4

- ½ cup balsamic vinegar
- 1 pint strawberry sorbet
- 1 quart strawberries, hulled and chopped

▸ In a small skillet, boil the vinegar until reduced by half, 3 to 4 minutes; let cool.

▸ Divide the sorbet among bowls. Top with the strawberries and balsamic syrup.

chocolate pound cake with ricotta

hands-on time: 5 minutes / total time: 5 minutes
serves 4

- 4 slices chocolate pound cake
- ¾ cup ricotta, at room temperature
- ¼ cup honey

▸ Dividing evenly, top the pound cake with the ricotta and drizzle with the honey.

cantaloupe parfait with salted pistachios

hands-on time: 5 minutes / total time: 5 minutes
serves 4

$^{1}/_{2}$ cantaloupe, cut into bite-size pieces

1 pint vanilla ice cream

$^{1}/_{2}$ cup coarsely chopped salted roasted pistachios

▸ Divide the cantaloupe and ice cream among bowls. Sprinkle with the pistachios.

blackberry and granola crisp

hands-on time: 5 minutes / total time: 35 minutes
serves 4

5 cups blackberries (about 1$^{1}/_{2}$ pounds)

$^{1}/_{4}$ cup packed light brown sugar

$^{1}/_{4}$ teaspoon kosher salt

2 cups granola

4 tablespoons ($^{1}/_{2}$ stick) unsalted butter, at room temperature

▸ Heat oven to 350° F. In a medium bowl, toss the blackberries with the sugar and salt. Transfer to a shallow 2-quart baking dish.

▸ In a second medium bowl, using your hands, knead the granola with the butter until large clumps form. Scatter over the blackberries and bake until they are bubbling, 20 to 30 minutes.

dulce de leche mousse

hands-on time: 5 minutes / total time: 55 minutes (includes chilling) / serves 4

¼ cup sweetened shredded
   coconut
1 cup heavy cream
   Pinch kosher salt
¼ cup dulce de leche

▶ Heat oven to 350° F. Spread the coconut on a rimmed baking sheet and toast, tossing occasionally, until golden, 6 to 8 minutes; let cool.

▶ Meanwhile, with an electric mixer, beat the cream with the salt until soft peaks form. Gently fold in the dulce de leche.

▶ Divide the mousse between bowls and chill for at least 45 minutes and up to 8 hours. Sprinkle with the coconut before serving.

TIP
Dulce de leche, a Latin American favorite, is a sweet, caramel-like sauce made from milk and sugar. To get the swirled effect shown here, fold the dulce de leche into the whipped cream very gently, being careful not to overmix.

3 IDEAS FOR ICE CREAM CONES

ballpark cone

hands-on time: 5 minutes
total time: 5 minutes / serves 1

 2 tablespoons chopped
   caramel corn
 1 tablespoon miniature
   chocolate chips
 ¹/₂ cup chocolate ice cream
 1 ice cream cone

▸ In a small bowl, combine the
caramel corn and chocolate chips.

▸ Scoop the ice cream onto the
cone, then roll in the caramel
corn mixture, pressing gently to
help it adhere.

tropical cone

hands-on time: 5 minutes
total time: 15 minutes / serves 1

 1 tablespoon sweetened
   shredded coconut
 1 tablespoon chopped
   banana chips
 1 tablespoon crumbled dried
   papaya or mango
 ¹/₂ cup vanilla ice cream
 1 ice cream cone

▸ Heat oven to 350° F. Spread the
coconut on a rimmed baking
sheet and toast, tossing occasionally, until golden, 6 to 8 minutes;
let cool.

▸ In a small bowl, combine the
coconut, banana chips, and
papaya.

▸ Scoop the ice cream onto the
cone, then roll in the fruit
mixture, pressing gently to help
it adhere.

nutty crunch cone

hands-on time: 5 minutes
total time: 5 minutes / serves 1

 2 crushed gingersnaps
 1 tablespoon chopped salted
   roasted pistachios
 ¹/₂ cup strawberry ice cream
 1 ice cream cone

▸ In a small bowl, combine the
gingersnaps and pistachios.

▸ Scoop the ice cream onto the
cone, then roll in the gingersnap mixture, pressing gently to
help it adhere.

fall

stuffed mushrooms with spinach

hands-on time: 20 minutes / total time: 40 minutes / serves 8

24 medium button mushrooms
(about 1¹/₂ pounds)

2 tablespoons olive oil, plus
more for the baking sheet

2 cloves garlic, finely chopped

1 5-ounce package baby
spinach, chopped

Kosher salt and black pepper

³/₄ cup panko bread crumbs

2 ounces Gruyère, grated
(¹/₂ cup)

▸ Heat oven to 375° F. Remove the stems from the mushrooms; finely chop the stems and reserve.

▸ Coat a baking sheet with oil. Bake the mushroom caps, stem-side down, until just tender, 10 to 12 minutes.

▸ Meanwhile, heat the oil in a medium skillet over medium heat. Add the garlic and chopped mushroom stems and cook, stirring often, until tender, 3 to 5 minutes.

▸ Add the spinach, ¹/₄ teaspoon salt, and ¹/₈ teaspoon pepper to the skillet and cook, tossing, until wilted, 2 to 3 minutes more.

▸ Transfer the spinach mixture to a medium bowl and combine the panko and Gruyère. Turn the mushroom caps stem-side up, fill with the stuffing, and bake until golden brown, 12 to 15 minutes.

TIP
The mushroom caps can be baked and then stuffed (but not baked for the second time with the stuffing) up to 2 days in advance; refrigerate, covered. Bake again just before serving.

goat cheese with pistachios and cranberries

hands-on time: 5 minutes / total time: 5 minutes serves 8

2 tablespoons roasted pistachios, chopped
2 tablespoons dried cranberries, chopped
1 8- to 10-ounce log fresh goat cheese
  Crackers or bread, for serving

▸ On a large plate, combine the pistachios and cranberries.

▸ Roll the goat cheese in the fruit-and-nut mixture to coat. Serve with crackers. (The cheese can be coated up to 2 days in advance; refrigerate, covered.)

spiced pickled carrots with mint

hands-on time: 5 minutes / total time: 2^1/$_2$ hours (includes chilling) / serves 8

1 pound carrots (about 10 medium), peeled and cut into thin sticks
^{1}/$_2$ cup apple cider vinegar
^{1}/$_4$ cup sugar
1 teaspoon coriander seeds
1 teaspoon mustard seeds
  Kosher salt
^{1}/$_4$ cup fresh mint leaves, torn

▸ Bring a large saucepan of water to a boil. Add the carrots and cook for 2 minutes; drain and run under cold water to cool. Transfer to a large bowl.

▸ Meanwhile, in a small saucepan, combine the vinegar, sugar, coriander and mustard seeds, 1^1/$_2$ cups water, and ^{1}/$_2$ teaspoon salt and bring to a boil. Pour over the carrots and let cool to room temperature. Add the mint and refrigerate, covered, for at least 2 hours or up to 3 days.

Parmesan-scallion pastry pinwheels

hands-on time: 10 minutes / total time: 40 minutes
serves 8

1 sheet frozen puff pastry
   (half a 17.3-ounce box), thawed

1 large egg, beaten

3 scallions, thinly sliced

¼ cup plus 2 tablespoons grated Parmesan
   (1½ ounces)

   Kosher salt and black pepper

▶ Heat oven to 400° F. Unfold the pastry and brush with the egg. Sprinkle with the scallions, ¼ cup of the Parmesan, ¼ teaspoon salt, and ⅛ teaspoon pepper. Roll tightly into a log. Freeze until firm but still sliceable, about 20 minutes.

▶ Slice the log into ¼-inch-thick rounds and place them on a parchment-lined baking sheet. Sprinkle with the remaining 2 tablespoons of Parmesan and bake until golden brown, 12 to 15 minutes. (The pinwheels can be baked up to 6 hours in advance; store, covered, at room temperature. The unbaked log can be frozen, tightly wrapped, for up to 1 week; thaw slightly before slicing and baking.)

caramelized onion dip

hands-on time: 40 minutes / total time: 1 hour
serves 8 (makes 2¼ cups)

2 tablespoons unsalted butter

2 medium onions, thinly sliced
   Kosher salt and black pepper

1 8-ounce bar cream cheese, at room
   temperature

1 cup sour cream

2 tablespoons chopped fresh chives
   Thick-cut potato or vegetable chips,
   for serving

▶ Melt the butter in a large skillet over medium-low heat. Add the onions and ½ teaspoon salt and cook, stirring occasionally, until deep golden brown, 30 to 35 minutes. Remove from heat and let cool.

▶ In a medium bowl, mix together the cooled onions, cream cheese, sour cream, chives, ¼ teaspoon salt, and ⅛ teaspoon pepper. Serve with chips. (The dip can be made up to 2 days in advance; refrigerate, covered.)

3 IDEAS FOR MIXED NUTS

chocolate-drizzled nuts with sea salt
hands-on time: 15 minutes
total time: 35 minutes
serves 10 (makes 3¹/₃ cups)

¹/₄ pound semisweet chocolate, chopped

2 cups lightly salted roasted mixed nuts (one 11.5-ounce can)

¹/₂ teaspoon flaky sea salt

▸ Line a rimmed baking sheet with parchment. In a microwave-safe bowl, microwave the chocolate in 30-second intervals, stirring between each, until smooth.

▸ Spread the nuts on the prepared baking sheet. Drizzle with the chocolate and sprinkle with the salt.

▸ Refrigerate the nuts until set, 15 to 20 minutes. Break apart before serving. (Store at room temperature, between sheets of wax paper in an airtight container, for up to 5 days.)

buttered nuts with rosemary and orange
hands-on time: 5 minutes
total time: 5 minutes
serves 10 (makes 2¹/₂ cups)

1 tablespoon unsalted butter

2 cups lightly salted roasted mixed nuts (one 11.5-ounce can)

2 tablespoons sugar

1 tablespoon fresh rosemary leaves

1 tablespoon thinly sliced orange zest

▸ Melt the butter in a large skillet over medium-high heat.

▸ Add the nuts, sugar, rosemary, and zest to the skillet and cook, tossing, until the sugar is melted and the mixture is fragrant, 2 to 3 minutes. Serve warm or at room temperature.

sweet and spicy candied nuts
hands-on time: 10 minutes
total time: 25 minutes
serves 10 (makes 2¹/₂ cups)

1 large egg white

¹/₄ cup packed brown sugar

2 teaspoons paprika

¹/₄ teaspoon cayenne pepper

2 cups lightly salted roasted mixed nuts (one 11.5-ounce can)

▸ Heat oven to 350° F. Line a rimmed baking sheet with parchment. In a medium bowl, whisk together the egg white, sugar, paprika, and cayenne. Add the nuts and toss to coat.

▸ Spread the nut mixture on the prepared baking sheet and bake until the coating is set, 12 to 15 minutes. Let cool on the baking sheet. (Store in an airtight container at room temperature for up to 5 days.)

6 IDEAS FOR SANDWICHES

chipotle turkey club

hands-on time: 5 minutes
total time: 5 minutes / serves 1

1 tablespoon mayonnaise
1 pinch chipotle chili powder
2 slices multigrain bread
2 ounces thinly sliced roasted turkey
2 slices cooked bacon
$1/4$ cup sprouts
1 ounce Cheddar, sliced

▸ In a small bowl, stir together the mayonnaise and chili powder.

▸ Spread the mixture on the bread and form a sandwich with the turkey, bacon, sprouts, and Cheddar.

ham banh mi sandwich

hands-on time: 10 minutes
total time: 10 minutes / serves 1

$1/2$ Kirby cucumber, cut into thin strips
$1/4$ carrot, cut into thin strips
$1/2$ jalapeño pepper, seeded and sliced
$1/4$ cup fresh cilantro leaves
1 tablespoon fresh lime juice
1 tablespoon olive oil
  Kosher salt and black pepper
1 Portuguese sandwich roll, split
2 ounces thinly sliced ham

▸ In a small bowl, toss the cucumber, carrot, and jalapeño with the cilantro, lime juice, oil, and a pinch each salt and pepper.

▸ Form a sandwich with the roll, ham, and cucumber mixture.

roast beef, Gouda, and apple sandwich

hands-on time: 5 minutes
total time: 5 minutes / serves 1

1 tablespoon Dijon mustard
2 slices challah bread
2 ounces thinly sliced roast beef
1 ounce Gouda, sliced
$1/4$ apple, sliced
$1/2$ cup watercress, thick stems removed

▸ Spread the mustard on the bread and form a sandwich with the roast beef, Gouda, apple, and watercress.

double-onion turkey sandwich

hands-on time: 5 minutes
total time: 5 minutes / serves 1

- 1 tablespoon whole-grain mustard
- 1 soft onion roll, split
- 2 ounces thinly sliced roasted turkey
- 2 slices tomato
- 1/2 dill pickle, thinly sliced
- 1/4 cup store-bought French-fried onions

▸ Spread the mustard on the roll and form a sandwich with the turkey, tomato, pickle, and French-fried onions.

peanut butter, celery, and raisin sandwich

hands-on time: 5 minutes
total time: 5 minutes / serves 1

- 2 tablespoons peanut butter
- 2 slices white bread
- 1/2 stalk celery, sliced
- 2 tablespoons raisins

▸ Spread the peanut butter on the bread and form a sandwich with the celery and raisins.

ham and pineapple sandwich

hands-on time: 5 minutes
total time: 5 minutes / serves 1

- 2 slices pumpernickel bread
- 2 ounces thinly sliced ham
- 2 slices pineapple
- 3 ounces fresh mozzarella, sliced
- 1/4 cup fresh basil leaves
- 2 teaspoons olive oil

▸ Top 1 slice of the bread with the ham, pineapple, mozzarella, and basil.

▸ Drizzle with the oil and top with the remaining slice of bread.

red currant–glazed chicken with spinach

hands-on time: 25 minutes / total time: 40 minutes / serves 4

- 1/2 cup red currant jelly
- 1/4 to 1/2 teaspoon crushed red pepper
- 2 1/2 pounds bone-in, skin-on chicken pieces
- 2 tablespoons olive oil
   Kosher salt and black pepper
- 2 cloves garlic, thinly sliced
- 1/4 cup golden raisins
- 1 10-ounce package fresh spinach, thick stems removed

▸ Heat oven to 425° F. In a small bowl, whisk together the jelly and red pepper.

▸ Place the chicken on a rimmed baking sheet, rub with 1 tablespoon of the oil, and season with 1/2 teaspoon salt and 1/4 teaspoon black pepper. Roast until cooked through, 25 to 30 minutes, basting with the jelly mixture twice during the last 10 minutes of cooking.

▸ Meanwhile, heat the remaining tablespoon of oil in a large skillet over medium heat. Add the garlic and raisins and cook, stirring often, until the garlic is golden, 2 to 3 minutes.

▸ Add the spinach and 1/4 teaspoon each salt and black pepper to the skillet and cook, tossing, until beginning to wilt, 1 to 2 minutes more. Serve with the chicken.

TIP
Though boneless chicken cooks faster, bone-in chicken has more flavor and retains more moisture during cooking. It also tends to cost less.

chicken enchiladas verdes

hands-on time: 20 minutes / **total time: 50 minutes** / **serves 4**

2 pounds bone-in chicken breasts (2 to 3)

1 16-ounce jar mild salsa verde

2 cups fresh cilantro sprigs, plus more for serving

1 cup sour cream, plus more for serving

1½ cups frozen corn, thawed

½ pound Muenster or Monterey Jack cheese, grated (about 2 cups)

Kosher salt and black pepper

8 6-inch flour tortillas

1 cup long-grain white rice

▸ Heat oven to 400° F. Place the chicken in a medium saucepan, add enough water to cover, and bring to a boil. Reduce heat and simmer until cooked through, 15 to 20 minutes; transfer to a plate and let cool. When cool enough to handle, shred the chicken, discarding the skin and bones. Place the meat in a large bowl.

▸ Meanwhile, in a blender, puree the salsa, cilantro, and ½ cup of the sour cream until smooth. Transfer to a small saucepan and simmer until slightly thickened, 10 to 12 minutes. Stir in the remaining ½ cup of sour cream.

▸ Add the corn, 1 cup of the Muenster, ½ cup of the sauce, and ½ teaspoon each salt and pepper to the chicken and toss to combine.

▸ Spread 1 cup of the remaining sauce in a 9-by-13-inch baking dish. Roll up the chicken in the tortillas (about ½ cup each) and place seam-side down in the dish. Top with the remaining sauce and Muenster. Bake until bubbling and beginning to brown, 15 to 20 minutes.

▸ Meanwhile, cook the rice according to the package directions. Serve with the enchiladas, sour cream, and cilantro.

TIP
The unbaked enchiladas can be frozen in the baking dish, tightly wrapped, for up to 3 months. Thaw and bake as directed, adding 10 minutes to the cooking time.

Colombian chicken and potato soup
hands-on time: 20 minutes / total time: 45 minutes / serves 4

4 cups low-sodium chicken broth

1 pound boneless, skinless chicken thighs (about 4)

4 frozen corn-on-the-cob pieces (sometimes called "cobbettes") or 2 ears shucked fresh corn

1 tablespoon olive oil

1 small onion, thinly sliced

1 celery stalk, thinly sliced

4 cloves garlic, thinly sliced

2 medium russet potatoes (about 1 pound), peeled and cut into 1-inch pieces

2 tablespoons fresh lime juice, plus lime wedges for serving

1/4 teaspoon dried oregano

Kosher salt and black pepper

Cut-up avocado, fresh cilantro sprigs, and capers, for serving

▶ In a large saucepan or Dutch oven, combine the broth and 1 cup water and bring to a boil. Add the chicken and corn, reduce heat, and simmer until the chicken is cooked through, 10 to 12 minutes.

▶ Transfer the chicken and corn to a plate. Strain the cooking liquid into a large bowl or measuring cup and reserve.

▶ Wipe out the saucepan and heat the oil over medium heat. Add the onion, celery, and garlic and cook, stirring occasionally, until beginning to soften, 2 to 3 minutes. Add the potatoes and the reserved cooking liquid and bring to a boil. Reduce heat and simmer until the potatoes are cooked through, 15 to 20 minutes.

▶ Meanwhile, shred the chicken and cut the corn pieces into 1-inch-thick rounds. Return the chicken and corn to the soup. Add the lime juice, oregano, 1/2 teaspoon salt, and 1/4 teaspoon pepper and cook until heated through, about 1 minute.

▶ Serve the soup with avocado, cilantro, capers, and lime wedges.

TIP
To ripen an avocado, place it in a paper bag at room temperature for up to 4 days (add an apple to the bag to quicken the process). When ripe, they can be refrigerated for several days.

chicken paprikash

hands-on time: 15 minutes / total time: 45 minutes / serves 4

1 tablespoon olive oil

2½ pounds bone-in, skin-on chicken thighs and drumsticks

Kosher salt and black pepper

1 medium onion, sliced

1 bell pepper, sliced

2 cloves garlic, chopped

1 28-ounce can whole peeled tomatoes

1 tablespoon paprika

6 ounces wide egg noodles

¼ cup sour cream

2 tablespoons chopped fresh dill

▸ Heat the oil in a large Dutch oven over medium-high heat. Season the chicken with ¼ teaspoon each salt and black pepper and cook until browned, 4 to 5 minutes per side; transfer to a plate.

▸ Discard all but 2 tablespoons of the drippings from the pot. Add the onion, bell pepper, and garlic and cook, stirring often, until tender, 4 to 5 minutes.

▸ Add the tomatoes (crushing them with your hands as you add them), paprika, ½ teaspoon salt, and ¼ teaspoon black pepper to the pot and bring to a boil. Nestle the chicken in the mixture, reduce heat, and simmer, partially covered, until cooked through, 15 to 20 minutes.

▸ Meanwhile, cook the noodles according to the package directions. Serve topped with the chicken, sour cream, and dill.

TIP
When browning chicken, patience is key. It's ready to be turned when the meat releases easily from the pan (don't tug).

chicken skewers with bean salad and parsley pesto

hands-on time: 30 minutes / total time: 30 minutes / serves 4

- ¼ cup plain low-fat yogurt
- 2 tablespoons pine nuts
- 1 small clove garlic
- 2¼ cups fresh flat-leaf parsley leaves
- ¼ cup plus 2 tablespoons olive oil
- Kosher salt and black pepper
- 1 15-ounce can cannellini beans, rinsed
- ½ small head radicchio, thinly sliced (about 1 cup)
- 1 tablespoon white wine vinegar
- 1½ pounds boneless, skinless chicken breasts, cut into 2-inch pieces

▸ Soak 8 wooden skewers in water for at least 10 minutes. Meanwhile, in a food processor, puree the yogurt, pine nuts, garlic, 2 cups of the parsley, ¼ cup of the oil, and ¼ teaspoon each salt and pepper; set aside.

▸ By hand, chop the remaining ¼ cup of parsley. In a medium bowl, toss the parsley, beans, and radicchio with the vinegar, 1 tablespoon of the remaining oil, and ¼ teaspoon each salt and pepper; set aside.

▸ Heat grill to medium-high. Thread the chicken onto the skewers, coat with the remaining tablespoon of oil, and season with ¼ teaspoon each salt and pepper. Grill the chicken, turning occasionally, until cooked through, 7 to 10 minutes. Serve with the bean salad and the pesto.

TIP
The pesto and the uncooked skewered chicken can be refrigerated separately, covered, for up to 1 day. Oil and season the chicken just before grilling. Bring the pesto to room temperature before serving.

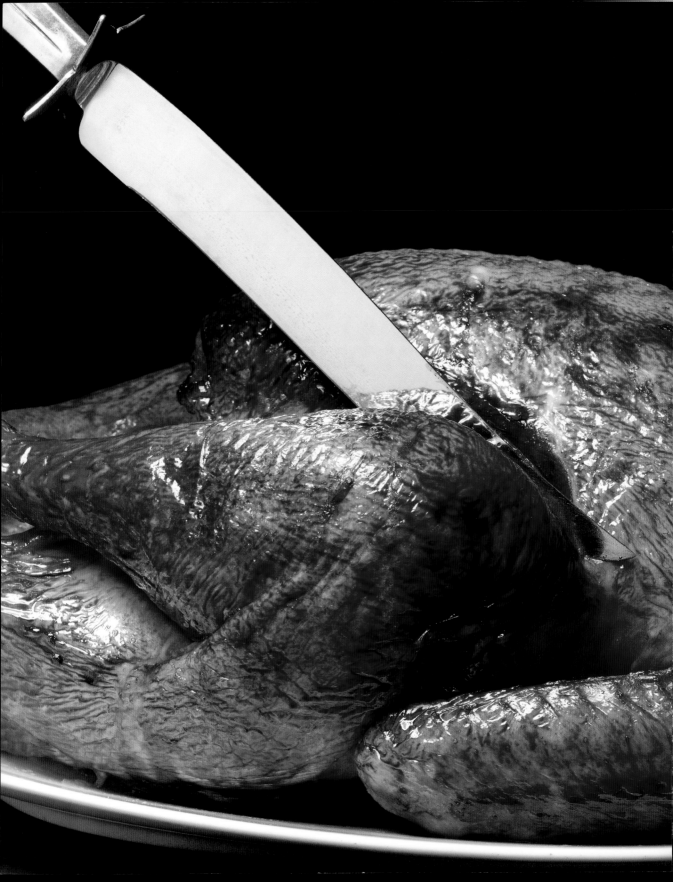

easy Thanksgiving turkey

**hands-on time: 20 minutes / total time: 3 hours, 45 minutes
serves 8 (with leftovers)**

- 1 12-pound turkey—thawed if frozen, patted dry, neck reserved, and giblets discarded
- 12 sprigs fresh thyme
- 2 medium onions, cut into wedges
- 2 tablespoons unsalted butter, at room temperature
  Kosher salt
- 2 carrots, cut into 2-inch pieces
- 2 stalks celery, cut into 2-inch pieces
- 1 cup low-sodium chicken broth (if needed)

▶ Heat oven to 375° F. Stuff the turkey cavity with the thyme and half the onions. Tie the legs together with kitchen twine. Tuck the wing tips under the body so they don't burn. Rub the turkey all over (including the crevices of the legs and wings) with the butter and season with 1 teaspoon salt.

▶ Place the turkey neck, carrots, celery, and the remaining onions in a large flameproof roasting pan. Set a roasting rack on top and place the turkey on the rack.

▶ Roast the turkey, basting every 30 minutes with the pan juices, until an instant-read thermometer inserted in the thickest part of a thigh registers 165° F, 2½ to 3 hours. (Tent with foil if the turkey begins to darken well before it is done. If the vegetables begin to scorch, add some broth to the pan.)

▶ Tilt the turkey to empty its juices into the pan, then transfer to a carving board, tent with foil, and let rest for at least 25 minutes before slicing. Reserve the pan and its contents for Classic Gravy (right).

classic gravy

**hands-on time: 20 minutes / total time: 30 minutes
serves 8**

Roasting pan and its contents, from Easy Thanksgiving Turkey (left)
- 1 cup dry white wine
- 1 to 3 cups low-sodium chicken broth
- 4 tablespoons (½ stick) unsalted butter
- ⅓ cup all-purpose flour
  Kosher salt and black pepper

▶ Remove the vegetables and neck from the roasting pan; discard. Carefully strain the pan juices into a fat separator; let stand for 5 minutes, then pour the juices into a large measuring cup, leaving the fat behind.

▶ Place the empty pan across 2 burners over medium-high heat. Add the wine and cook, scraping up the brown bits stuck to the pan, for 1 minute. Pour the contents of the pan into the measuring cup of skimmed juices. Add enough broth to make a total of 4 cups of liquid; set aside.

▶ Melt the butter in a large saucepan over medium heat. Sprinkle with the flour and cook, whisking often, until deep brown, 4 to 5 minutes.

▶ Whisk in the reserved liquid. Bring to a boil; reduce heat and simmer until thickened, 8 to 10 minutes.

▶ Season the gravy with ¾ teaspoon salt and ¼ teaspoon pepper. Strain just before serving.

steak fajitas with sweet potato and poblano
hands-on time: 25 minutes / **total time: 25 minutes** / **serves 4**

2 tablespoons olive oil

1 large sweet potato (about 12 ounces), peeled and cut into 1/4-inch pieces

1 medium onion, thinly sliced

1 small poblano pepper, seeded and thinly sliced

Kosher salt and black pepper

1 1/4 pounds skirt steak, cut into 4 pieces

1/2 cup sour cream

1 to 2 teaspoons chopped chipotle chilies in adobo sauce

8 small flour tortillas, warmed

▸ Heat the oil in a large skillet over medium heat. Add the sweet potato, onion, poblano, 1/2 teaspoon salt, and 1/4 teaspoon black pepper and cook, tossing occasionally, until tender, 10 to 12 minutes.

▸ Meanwhile, heat broiler. Season the steak with 1/2 teaspoon salt and 1/4 teaspoon black pepper. Place on a broilerproof rimmed baking sheet and broil to the desired doneness, 3 to 4 minutes per side for medium-rare. Let rest for at least 5 minutes before slicing.

▸ In a small bowl, combine the sour cream and chipotles. Fill the tortillas with the steak, vegetables, and chipotle sour cream.

TIP
Transform leftovers into a next-day salad: Serve the meat and vegetables over crispy romaine lettuce and dress it with extra chipotle sour cream.

bacon-Gruyère meat loaf with roasted carrots and onions
hands-on time: 15 minutes / total time: 1 hour, 10 minutes / serves 4

1½ pounds ground beef chuck

¼ cup bread crumbs

¼ cup ketchup, plus more for serving

3 small red onions, 1 coarsely grated and 2 cut into wedges

2 slices bacon, chopped

2 cloves garlic, chopped

1 large egg

3 ounces Gruyère or Cheddar, grated (¾ cup)

Kosher salt and black pepper

1¼ pounds carrots (about 12), cut into 3-inch lengths and halved lengthwise if large

2 tablespoons olive oil

▶ Heat oven to 400° F. In a medium bowl, gently combine the beef, bread crumbs, ketchup, grated onion, bacon, garlic, egg, ½ cup of the Gruyère, ½ teaspoon salt, and ¼ teaspoon pepper. Transfer the mixture to an 8-by-4-inch loaf pan and sprinkle with the remaining ¼ cup of Gruyère.

▶ Meanwhile, on a large rimmed baking sheet, toss the onion wedges and carrots with the oil, ½ teaspoon salt, and ¼ teaspoon pepper.

▶ Roast the meat loaf and vegetables until the meat loaf is cooked through, 40 to 45 minutes, and the vegetables are tender, 35 to 40 minutes. Let the meat loaf rest for 10 minutes.

▶ Pour off any accumulated fat from the meat loaf, slice, and serve with the vegetables and additional ketchup.

TIP
Ground chuck— preferably 20 percent fat—is best for meat loaf (and burgers). Chuck is a flavorful cut of beef. It also makes the meat loaf tender and juicy; ground meat from leaner cuts tends to dry out.

beef and bean chili
hands-on time: 30 minutes / **total time: 50 minutes** / **serves 4**

2 tablespoons olive oil

1 medium red onion, chopped, plus more for serving

1 green bell pepper, chopped

2 cloves garlic, chopped

3/4 pound ground beef chuck

2 tablespoons tomato paste

2 teaspoons chili powder

3/4 teaspoon ground cumin

1 28-ounce can diced tomatoes

1 15-ounce can kidney beans, rinsed

1 ounce semisweet chocolate, chopped

  Kosher salt and black pepper

1 tablespoon red wine vinegar

  Sliced avocado, for serving

▸ Heat the oil in a large saucepan over medium-high heat. Add the onion, bell pepper, and garlic and cook, stirring occasionally, until tender, 8 to 10 minutes.

▸ Add the beef to the saucepan and cook, breaking it up with a spoon, until no longer pink, 4 to 6 minutes. Add the tomato paste, chili powder, and cumin and cook, stirring, for 1 minute.

▸ Add the tomatoes (with their juices), beans, chocolate, 1/2 cup water, 1 teaspoon salt, and 1/4 teaspoon black pepper to the saucepan and bring to a boil.

▸ Reduce heat and simmer, stirring occasionally, until thickened, 20 to 25 minutes. Add the vinegar and stir to combine. Serve with avocado and additional onion.

TIP
Draining and rinsing canned beans before cooking with them can reduce the sodium content by about 40 percent.

seared steak with cauliflower puree

hands-on time: 15 minutes / total time: 25 minutes / serves 4

1 small head cauliflower
   (about 1¹/₂ pounds), cored and
   cut into florets

4 tablespoons plus 1 teaspoon
   olive oil

   Kosher salt and black pepper

2 strip steaks (1 inch thick;
   1¹/₂ pounds total)

¹/₄ cup chopped fresh flat-leaf
   parsley

¹/₄ cup pitted green olives,
   chopped

1 shallot, finely chopped

1 tablespoon red wine vinegar

▸ Fill a large saucepan with 1 inch of water and fit with a steamer basket. Bring the water to a boil. Place the cauliflower in the basket, cover, and steam until very tender, 8 to 10 minutes. Drain and transfer to a food processor. Add 2 tablespoons of the oil and ¹/₄ teaspoon each salt and pepper and puree until smooth.

▸ Meanwhile, heat 1 teaspoon of the remaining oil in a large skillet over medium-high heat. Season the steaks with ¹/₂ teaspoon each salt and pepper and cook to the desired doneness, 4 to 6 minutes per side for medium-rare. Let rest for at least 5 minutes before slicing.

▸ In a small bowl, combine the parsley, olives, shallot, vinegar, the remaining 2 tablespoons of oil, and ¹/₄ teaspoon each salt and pepper. Serve with the steak and cauliflower.

TIP
For a tasty, cara-melized crust, take the steaks out of the refrigerator 30 minutes before cooking so they can come to room temperature. Pat dry with a paper towel before seasoning and cooking.

lamb meatballs with couscous and Feta

hands-on time: 25 minutes / total time: 25 minutes / serves 4

- 1 pound ground lamb or beef
- 1/4 cup dried apricots, finely chopped
- 1 small red onion, half finely chopped and half thinly sliced
- 1/2 teaspoon ground coriander
  Kosher salt and black pepper
- 1 cup couscous
- 3 tablespoons olive oil
- 3 tablespoons fresh lemon juice
- 2 plum tomatoes, sliced
- 1/2 English cucumber, halved and thinly sliced
- 4 ounces Feta, crumbled (1 cup)

▶ Heat broiler. In a medium bowl, combine the lamb, apricots, chopped onion, coriander, 1/2 teaspoon salt, and 1/4 teaspoon pepper. Shape into 11/2-inch balls (about 20), place on a broilerproof rimmed baking sheet, and broil until cooked through, 6 to 8 minutes.

▶ Meanwhile, place the couscous in a small bowl. Add 1 cup hot tap water, cover, and let sit for 5 minutes; fluff with a fork.

▶ In a second small bowl, mix together the oil, lemon juice, and 1/4 teaspoon each salt and pepper.

▶ Serve the couscous with the meatballs, tomatoes, cucumber, Feta, and sliced onion. Drizzle with the dressing.

TIP
Crumbled Feta sold in the supermarket is often flavorless, dry, and treated with additives. For tastier results, buy a block of Feta and crumble it yourself. But crumble only as much as you'll use right away. It dries out faster once off the block.

balsamic-glazed pork with lentils
hands-on time: 20 minutes / total time: 40 minutes / serves 4

1 cup lentils, rinsed
  Kosher salt and black pepper
1 apple, cut into ¹/₂-inch pieces
1 celery stalk, thinly sliced
¹/₄ cup fresh flat-leaf parsley leaves
2 tablespoons fresh lemon juice
3 tablespoons olive oil
2 tablespoons balsamic vinegar
2 tablespoons brown sugar
1 1¹/₄-pound pork tenderloin

▸ Heat oven to 400° F. Bring a medium saucepan of water to a boil. Add the lentils and 1 teaspoon salt, reduce heat, and simmer, stirring occasionally, until tender, 20 to 30 minutes; drain and rinse under cold water to cool. In a medium bowl, toss the lentils, apple, and celery with the parsley, lemon juice, 2 tablespoons of the oil, and ¹/₄ teaspoon each salt and pepper.

▸ Meanwhile, in a small bowl, combine the vinegar and sugar; set aside. Heat the remaining tablespoon of oil in a large ovenproof skillet over medium-high heat. Season the pork with ¹/₄ teaspoon each salt and pepper and cook, turning occasionally, until browned, 6 to 8 minutes.

▸ Transfer the pork to oven and roast until cooked through, 10 to 12 minutes, basting with the balsamic glaze twice during the last 5 minutes of cooking. Let rest for at least 5 minutes before slicing. Serve with the lentils and any pan drippings.

TIP
These lentils are also delicious with chicken or a firm white fish, like sea bass or halibut.

roasted sausage and grapes

**hands-on time: 5 minutes / total time: 30 minutes
serves 4**

1½ pounds Italian sausage links (8 small)
2 pounds seedless red grapes
8 sprigs fresh thyme
1 tablespoon olive oil
    Kosher salt and black pepper

▸ Heat oven to 400° F. On a rimmed baking sheet, toss the sausage and grapes with the thyme, oil, ½ teaspoon salt, and ¼ teaspoon pepper.

▸ Roast, tossing occasionally, until the sausage is cooked through, 20 to 25 minutes.

sausage-stuffed zucchini

**hands-on time: 15 minutes / total time: 35 minutes
serves 4**

1 tablespoon olive oil
½ pound Italian sausage links (2 to 3 small), casings removed
1 ounce Asiago or Parmesan, grated (¼ cup)
2 tablespoons pine nuts
2 tablespoons chopped sun-dried tomatoes
2 scallions, chopped
4 medium zucchini, halved lengthwise

▸ Heat oven to 400° F. Heat the oil in a skillet over medium-high heat. Add the sausage and cook, breaking it up with a spoon, until browned, 5 to 7 minutes.

▸ In a medium bowl, mix together the cooked sausage, Asiago, pine nuts, tomatoes, and scallions.

▸ Using a teaspoon, hollow out the zucchini. Place on a rimmed baking sheet and fill the cavities with the sausage mixture. Roast until the zucchini is tender, 12 to 15 minutes.

cauliflower and sausage flat bread

**hands-on time: 10 minutes / total time: 40 minutes
serves 4**

- 1   pound pizza dough, at room temperature
- 1   tablespoon olive oil, plus more for the baking sheet
- 1/2   small head cauliflower, cored and sliced
- 1   red chili pepper, thinly sliced
- 1   cup fresh flat-leaf parsley leaves
   Kosher salt and black pepper
- 8   ounces Gruyère, grated (2 cups)
- 1/2   pound Italian sausage links (2 to 3 small), casings removed and meat broken into small pieces

▶ Heat oven to 425° F. Shape the dough into a large oval and place on an oiled baking sheet.

▶ In a medium bowl, toss the cauliflower and chili with the parsley, oil, 1/2 teaspoon salt, and 1/4 teaspoon black pepper. Scatter over the dough and sprinkle with the Gruyère and sausage.

▶ Bake the flat bread until golden brown and crisp, 25 to 30 minutes.

sausage with white beans

**hands-on time: 30 minutes / total time: 30 minutes
serves 4**

- 2   tablespoons olive oil
- 1 1/2   pounds Italian sausage links (8 small)
- 2   medium carrots, thinly sliced on the bias
- 1   onion, chopped
   Kosher salt and black pepper
- 1   15-ounce can white beans, rinsed
- 3/4   cup dry white wine
- 1   tablespoon fresh tarragon leaves

▶ Heat 1 tablespoon of the oil in a large skillet over medium-high heat. Add the sausage and cook, turning occasionally, until cooked through, 10 to 12 minutes. Remove from skillet, then slice.

▶ Wipe out the skillet. Heat the remaining tablespoon of oil over medium heat. Add the carrots, onion, 1/2 teaspoon salt, and 1/4 teaspoon pepper. Cook, stirring occasionally, until tender, 8 to 10 minutes.

▶ Add the beans and wine; reduce heat and simmer for 5 minutes. Fold in the sausage and tarragon.

pork cutlets with spicy noodles
hands-on time: 30 minutes / total time: 30 minutes / serves 4

4 cups low-sodium chicken broth

1 1½-inch piece fresh ginger, peeled and sliced

½ pound udon noodles

½ pound shiitake mushrooms, stems discarded and caps sliced

1 red jalapeño pepper, sliced

¼ cup all-purpose flour

1 large egg, beaten

¾ cup panko bread crumbs

4 thin pork cutlets (about ¾ pound total)

Kosher salt and black pepper

2 tablespoons canola oil

2 scallions, sliced

▶ In a large pot, bring the broth and ginger to a boil. Add the noodles and cook, stirring often, until the broth is nearly absorbed and the noodles are al dente, 4 to 6 minutes. Add the mushrooms and jalapeño, reduce heat, and simmer until the mushrooms are just tender, 1 to 2 minutes more.

▶ Meanwhile, place the flour, egg, and panko in separate shallow bowls. Season the pork with ½ teaspoon salt and ¼ teaspoon black pepper. Coat with the flour (tapping off any excess), dip in the egg (shaking off any excess), then coat with the panko, pressing gently to help it adhere.

▶ Heat the oil in a large skillet over medium-high heat. Cook the pork until cooked through, 2 to 3 minutes per side. Slice and serve over the noodles; sprinkle with the scallions.

TIP
To tame the heat on this dish, remove the seeds from the jalapeño before slicing. They contain the majority of a chili's fire.

roasted pork chops with polenta
hands-on time: 25 minutes / total time: 25 minutes / serves 4

2 tablespoons olive oil

4 bone-in pork chops (1 inch thick; about 2¹/₂ pounds total)

Kosher salt and black pepper

1 pint grape tomatoes, halved

4 cloves garlic, sliced

¹/₂ cup dry white wine

³/₄ cup instant polenta

6 ounces Gruyère, grated (1¹/₂ cups)

▸ Heat oven to 400° F. Heat 1 tablespoon of the oil in a large ovenproof skillet over medium-high heat. Season the pork with ¹/₂ teaspoon each salt and pepper and cook until browned, 3 to 4 minutes per side; transfer to a plate.

▸ Add the tomatoes, garlic, the remaining tablespoon of oil, and ¹/₄ teaspoon each salt and pepper to the skillet. Cook, tossing, for 2 minutes. Add the wine, reduce heat, and simmer until the tomatoes begin to soften, 2 to 3 minutes more.

▸ Nestle the pork in the tomatoes, transfer the skillet to oven, and roast until the pork is cooked through, 6 to 7 minutes.

▸ Meanwhile, in a medium saucepan, bring 3 cups water to a boil. Whisk in the polenta and cook, whisking often, until thickened, 3 to 4 minutes. Whisk in the Gruyère, ¹/₄ teaspoon salt, and ¹/₈ teaspoon pepper. Serve with the pork and tomatoes.

TIP
Searing, then roasting, produces incredibly moist, juicy chops. You can also use this technique with chicken, beef, or lamb.

shrimp with white beans and toast

hands-on time: 15 minutes / total time: 20 minutes / serves 4

6 tablespoons (³/₄ stick)
   unsalted butter

4 slices country bread

4 cloves garlic, sliced

¹/₂ cup dry white wine

1 pound peeled and deveined
   medium shrimp

   Kosher salt and black pepper

1 15-ounce can cannellini
   beans, rinsed

4 cups baby arugula
   (about 3 ounces)

▸ Dividing evenly, spread 2 tablespoons of the butter on both sides of the bread. In a large skillet, cook the bread over medium heat until browned, 2 to 3 minutes per side; transfer to a plate.

▸ Wipe out the skillet and melt the remaining 4 tablespoons of butter over medium-high heat. Add the garlic and cook, stirring, for 1 minute. Add the wine and bring to a boil. Add the shrimp, ¹/₂ teaspoon salt, and ¹/₄ teaspoon pepper and simmer until opaque throughout, 2 to 3 minutes.

▸ Fold in the beans and arugula and cook just until the beans are heated through, 1 to 2 minutes more. Serve over the toasted bread.

TIP
This hearty shrimp-and-bean combination is also delicious served over pasta.

Dijon tilapia cakes

hands-on time: 15 minutes / total time:
1 hour, 15 minutes (includes chilling) / serves 4

- 4 6-ounce tilapia fillets
   Kosher salt and black pepper
- ¹/₂ cup mayonnaise
- 2 large eggs
- 2 tablespoons chopped fresh dill
- 1 tablespoon Dijon mustard
- ³/₄ cup panko bread crumbs
- 2 tablespoons canola oil
   Salad, for serving

▸ Heat oven to 400° F. Place the tilapia on a rimmed baking sheet; season with ³/₄ teaspoon salt and ¹/₄ teaspoon pepper. Bake until cooked through, 10 to 12 minutes. Let cool, then flake.

▸ In a large bowl, stir together the mayonnaise, eggs, dill, and mustard. Fold in the tilapia and panko. Form 8 cakes; chill for at least 30 minutes.

▸ Heat the oil in a large nonstick skillet over medium heat. Cook the cakes until golden, 3 to 5 minutes per side. Serve with salad.

tilapia tacos with cucumber relish

hands-on time: 20 minutes
total time: 20 minutes / serves 4

- 1 tablespoon olive oil, plus more for the grill
- 4 6-ounce tilapia fillets
- 1 teaspoon ground coriander
   Kosher salt and black pepper
- 6 radishes, sliced
- 1 cucumber, halved and sliced
- 2 tablespoons fresh lime juice, plus lime wedges for serving
- 8 corn tortillas, warmed
- 1 cup fresh cilantro leaves
- ¹/₄ cup sour cream

▸ Heat grill to high; oil grill. Season the tilapia with the coriander, ¹/₂ teaspoon salt, and ¹/₄ teaspoon pepper and grill until cooked through, 1 to 2 minutes per side. Break into pieces.

▸ In a medium bowl, toss the radishes and cucumber with the lime juice, oil, and ¹/₄ teaspoon each salt and pepper. Serve the tilapia in the tortillas with the cucumber relish, cilantro, sour cream, and lime wedges.

tilapia salad with apples

hands-on time: 10 minutes
total time: 25 minutes / serves 4

- 4 tablespoons olive oil, plus more if needed
- 4 6-ounce tilapia fillets
  Kosher salt and black pepper
- 2 tablespoons fresh lime juice
- 1 tablespoon Dijon mustard
- 2 teaspoons honey
- 6 cups arugula, thick stems removed (about 8 ounces)
- 2 heads endive, sliced
- 1 apple, cored and thinly sliced
- ¼ cup sliced almonds, toasted

▸ Heat 2 tablespoons of the oil in a nonstick skillet over medium-high heat. Season the tilapia with ½ teaspoon salt and ¼ teaspoon pepper. Cook in batches until cooked through, 2 to 3 minutes per side (adding more oil to the skillet if necessary). Let cool, then break into pieces.

▸ Meanwhile, in a bowl, whisk the lime juice, mustard, honey, the remaining oil, and ¼ teaspoon each salt and pepper. Add the arugula, endive, apple, and almonds and toss; top with the tilapia.

tilapia po'boys

hands-on time: 20 minutes
total time: 30 minutes / serves 4

- ½ cup all-purpose flour
- 1 tablespoon seafood seasoning
- 3 6-ounce tilapia fillets, cut into strips
- 2 tablespoons canola oil, plus more if needed
- 1 baguette, split horizontally and quartered lengthwise
- ¼ cup mayonnaise
- 1 cup shredded lettuce
- 16 pickle chips
  Hot sauce and potato chips, for serving

▸ In a shallow bowl, combine the flour and seafood seasoning. Coat the tilapia with the flour mixture (tapping off any excess).

▸ Heat the oil in a large nonstick skillet over medium heat. Working in batches, cook the tilapia until cooked through, 3 to 4 minutes per side (adding more oil to the skillet if necessary).

▸ Dividing evenly, spread the bread with the mayonnaise and form sandwiches with the lettuce, pickle chips, and tilapia. Serve with hot sauce and potato chips.

spiced shrimp with green beans and lime

hands-on time: 20 minutes / total time: 20 minutes / serves 4

1 cup long-grain white rice

¹/₂ cup fresh cilantro leaves

2 tablespoons olive oil

¹/₂ pound green beans, trimmed and halved crosswise

4 cloves garlic, chopped

1 to 2 red jalapeño peppers, thinly sliced

  Kosher salt and black pepper

1¹/₂ pounds peeled and deveined large shrimp

1¹/₂ teaspoons chili powder

¹/₄ cup fresh lime juice

▸ Cook the rice according to the package directions; fluff with a fork and fold in the cilantro.

▸ Meanwhile, heat the oil in a large skillet over medium-high heat. Add the green beans, garlic, jalapeños, and ¹/₄ teaspoon each salt and black pepper and cook, tossing frequently, until crisp-tender, 3 to 4 minutes.

▸ Season the shrimp with the chili powder, ¹/₂ teaspoon salt, and ¹/₄ teaspoon black pepper. Add them to the skillet and cook, tossing occasionally, until opaque throughout, 3 to 5 minutes. Stir in the lime juice and serve over the rice.

TIP
To give this dish an Indian accent, use curry powder in place of the chili powder.

spaghetti with meat sauce and mozzarella

hands-on time: 25 minutes / total time: 25 minutes / serves 4

³/₄ pound spaghetti
1 tablespoon olive oil
1 medium onion, chopped
2 cloves garlic, chopped
  Kosher salt and black pepper
³/₄ pound ground beef chuck
1 tablespoon tomato paste
2 pounds beefsteak or plum
  tomatoes, chopped
6 ounces bocconcini (small
  balls of mozzarella), halved
¹/₄ cup chopped fresh basil

▸ Cook the pasta according to the package directions; drain and return it to the pot.

▸ Meanwhile, heat the oil in a large skillet over medium-high heat. Add the onion, garlic, and ¹/₂ teaspoon each salt and pepper and cook, stirring occasionally, until the onion begins to soften, 3 to 5 minutes.

▸ Add the beef to the skillet and cook, breaking it up with a spoon, until browned, 3 to 5 minutes. Add the tomato paste and cook, stirring, for 30 seconds.

▸ Add the tomatoes, ¹/₂ teaspoon salt, and ¹/₄ teaspoon pepper and cook, stirring occasionally, until beginning to soften, 5 to 7 minutes more. (Add up to ¹/₄ cup water if the pan is dry.)

▸ Add the beef mixture, bocconcini, and basil to the pasta and toss to combine.

TIP
If you can't find bocconcini, cubed fresh mozzarella works nicely, too.

rigatoni with roasted sausage and broccoli

hands-on time: 10 minutes / total time: 25 minutes / serves 4

$^{1}/_{2}$ pound rigatoni

1 bunch broccoli, cut into florets

1 small red onion, sliced

3 tablespoons olive oil

 Kosher salt and black pepper

1 pound Italian sausage links (about 5 small), casings removed and meat broken into 1-inch pieces

2 tablespoons unsalted butter

$^{1}/_{4}$ cup grated Parmesan (1 ounce)

▸ Heat oven to 400° F. Cook the pasta according to the package directions. Reserve $^{3}/_{4}$ cup of the cooking water; drain the pasta and return it to the pot.

▸ Meanwhile, on a rimmed baking sheet, toss the broccoli and onion with the oil, $^{1}/_{2}$ teaspoon salt, and $^{1}/_{4}$ teaspoon pepper. Nestle the sausage in the vegetables and roast, tossing once, until the broccoli is tender and the sausage is cooked through, 18 to 20 minutes.

▸ Add the sausage mixture, butter, and $^{1}/_{2}$ cup of the reserved cooking water to the pasta and toss to combine. (Add more cooking water if the pasta seems dry.) Sprinkle with the Parmesan before serving.

TIP
For a meatless meal, omit the sausage, use a large head of broccoli, and roast the vegetables with $^{1}/_{2}$ cup walnuts or pecans.

spicy linguine with clams
hands-on time: 20 minutes / total time: 20 minutes / serves 4

3/4 pound linguine

1/3 cup olive oil

4 cloves garlic, thinly sliced

1 chili pepper (such as serrano or jalapeño), thinly sliced

3/4 cup dry white wine

20 littleneck clams, scrubbed

Kosher salt and black pepper

1/4 cup chopped fresh flat-leaf parsley

▸ Cook the pasta according to the package directions. Reserve 1 cup of the cooking water; drain the pasta and return it to the pot.

▸ Meanwhile, heat the oil in a large skillet over medium-high heat. Add the garlic and chili and cook, stirring, until fragrant, about 30 seconds. Add the wine and cook for 1 minute. Add the clams, 1/2 teaspoon salt, and 1/4 teaspoon black pepper and cook, covered, until the clams open, 6 to 8 minutes. (Discard any clams that remain closed.)

▸ Add the clam mixture, 1/2 cup of the reserved cooking water, and 1/4 teaspoon salt to the pasta and cook over medium heat, tossing gently, until the liquid coats the pasta, 1 to 2 minutes. (Add more cooking water if the pasta seems dry.) Serve sprinkled with the parsley.

TIP
To make sure your clams are alive and fresh, tap each one against your work surface. A live clam will close up tight and is safe to eat. Discard any that remain open before cooking.

whole-grain spaghetti with garlicky kale and tomatoes
hands-on time: 15 minutes / total time: 30 minutes / serves 4

6 ounces whole-grain spaghetti

2 tablespoons olive oil

1 medium red onion, thinly sliced

2 cloves garlic, chopped
Kosher salt and black pepper

1 bunch kale, thick stems removed and leaves torn into bite-size pieces (about 8 cups)

2 pints grape tomatoes, halved

$1/3$ cup chopped roasted almonds

$1/4$ cup grated pecorino (1 ounce), plus more for serving

▸ Cook the pasta according to the package directions. Reserve $1/4$ cup of the cooking water; drain the pasta and return it to the pot.

▸ Meanwhile, heat the oil in a large skillet over medium-high heat. Add the onion, garlic, $1/4$ teaspoon salt, and $1/8$ teaspoon pepper and cook, stirring occasionally, until beginning to brown, 4 to 5 minutes.

▸ Add the kale to the skillet and cook, tossing often, until tender, 2 to 3 minutes. Add the tomatoes and cook, tossing often, until beginning to soften, 1 to 2 minutes more.

▸ Add the kale mixture, almonds, pecorino, and reserved cooking water to the pasta and toss to combine. Serve with additional pecorino.

TIP
Supercharge this good-for-you dinner by adding chopped oil-packed sardines (rich in heart-healthy omega-3 fatty acids) to the pan along with the tomatoes.

sweet potato and Brie flat bread

hands-on time: 15 minutes / total time: 40 minutes / serves 4

1 pound pizza dough, at room temperature

Cornmeal, for the baking sheet

1 medium sweet potato (about ¹/₂ pound)—peeled, halved, and thinly sliced

2 shallots, thinly sliced

8 sprigs fresh thyme

4 tablespoons olive oil

Kosher salt and black pepper

¹/₄ pound Brie, sliced

2 teaspoons red wine vinegar

4 cups mixed greens (about 3 ounces)

▸ Heat oven to 425° F. Shape the dough into a large oval and place on a cornmeal-dusted baking sheet.

▸ In a medium bowl, toss the sweet potato and shallots with the thyme, 3 tablespoons of the oil, ¹/₂ teaspoon salt, and ¹/₄ teaspoon pepper. Scatter over the dough and top with the Brie. Bake until golden brown and crisp, 20 to 25 minutes.

▸ Meanwhile, in a large bowl, whisk together the vinegar, the remaining tablespoon of oil, and ¹/₄ teaspoon each salt and pepper. Add the greens and toss to coat. Serve with the flat bread.

TIP
For variety, try the flat bread with other cheeses, such as buttery Camembert, pungent Taleggio, or nutty Gruyère.

vegetable stir-fry with peanuts

hands-on time: 20 minutes / total time: 20 minutes / serves 4

1 cup long-grain white rice

¼ cup low-sodium soy sauce

2 tablespoons fresh lime juice

½ teaspoon Sriracha or some other hot pepper sauce (such as Tabasco)

1 tablespoon canola oil

2 carrots, cut into very thin strips

1 red bell pepper, thinly sliced

8 ounces shiitake mushrooms, stems removed and caps thinly sliced

2 cups bean sprouts

2 scallions, thinly sliced

¼ cup roasted peanuts, chopped

▸ Cook the rice according to the package directions.

▸ Meanwhile, in a small bowl, whisk together the soy sauce, lime juice, and Sriracha; set aside.

▸ Heat the oil in a large skillet over medium heat. Add the carrots and bell pepper and cook, tossing often, for 3 minutes.

▸ Add the mushrooms and bean sprouts to the skillet and cook, tossing often, until the vegetables are just tender, 2 to 3 minutes more.

▸ Add the soy sauce mixture to the skillet and toss to coat the vegetables. Serve over the rice and sprinkle with the scallions and peanuts.

TIP

For an easy upgrade, make this dish with creamy coconut rice. Cook the white rice as usual but replace 1 cup of the water with a 14-ounce can of coconut milk.

mushroom and herb strata

hands-on time: 20 minutes / total time: 1 hour, 20 minutes / serves 4

4 tablespoons olive oil, plus more for the baking dish

1 medium onion, chopped

1 8- to 10-ounce package button mushrooms, quartered

1/2 cup chopped fresh flat-leaf parsley

6 large eggs

2 cups whole milk

Kosher salt and black pepper

1/2 pound country bread, cut into 1-inch pieces (about 6 cups)

1/2 pound fontina or Cheddar, grated (2 cups)

4 cups mixed greens (about 3 ounces)

2 teaspoons white wine vinegar

▶ Heat oven to 350° F. Oil an 8-inch square baking dish.

▶ Heat 3 tablespoons of the oil in a large skillet over medium-high heat. Add the onion and cook, stirring occasionally, until tender, 3 to 4 minutes. Add the mushrooms and cook, tossing occasionally, until tender and any liquid has cooked off, 4 to 6 minutes more. Remove from heat and mix in the parsley.

▶ Meanwhile, in a large bowl, whisk together the eggs, milk, 3/4 teaspoon salt, and 1/4 teaspoon pepper. Add the mushroom mixture, bread, and fontina and toss; transfer to the prepared baking dish. Bake until golden brown and set, 50 to 60 minutes.

▶ In a second large bowl, toss the greens with the vinegar, the remaining tablespoon of oil, and 1/4 teaspoon each salt and pepper. Serve with the strata.

TIP
This rich, cheesy strata is also tasty served at room temperature on a brunch buffet. It can be prepared (but not baked) up to 12 hours in advance.

creamy broccoli soup

hands-on time: 20 minutes / total time: 40 minutes / serves 4

1 tablespoon olive oil

1 medium onion, chopped

$\frac{1}{8}$ teaspoon crushed red pepper (optional)

2 cups low-sodium vegetable broth

1 bunch broccoli, florets roughly chopped and stems peeled and sliced (about 7 cups)

1 russet potato (about $\frac{1}{2}$ pound), peeled and cut into $\frac{1}{2}$-inch pieces

Kosher salt and black pepper

2 ounces sharp white Cheddar, shaved, for serving

Bagel chips, for serving

▸ Heat the oil in a large saucepan over medium heat. Add the onion and red pepper, if desired, and cook, stirring occasionally, until the onion is soft, 4 to 6 minutes.

▸ Add the broth, broccoli, potato, 2 cups water, $\frac{1}{2}$ teaspoon salt, and $\frac{1}{4}$ teaspoon black pepper to the saucepan and bring to a boil. Reduce heat and simmer, covered, until the vegetables are very tender, 18 to 20 minutes.

▸ In a blender, working in batches, puree the soup until smooth, adjusting the consistency with water as necessary. (Alternatively, use a handheld immersion blender in the saucepan.) Top with Cheddar and bagel chips before serving.

TIP
The potato gives this soup a rich, creamy texture without the calories or fat of heavy cream. Try this trick with other pureed vegetable soups, like cauliflower, carrot, or squash.

greens with fennel and dried apricots

hands-on time: 15 minutes / total time: 15 minutes
serves 8

- 1/2 cup sliced almonds
- 1/4 cup olive oil
- 1/4 cup fresh lemon juice
- 1 tablespoon honey
  Kosher salt and black pepper
- 12 cups torn mixed greens (such as red leaf and green leaf lettuce and frisée; about 9 ounces)
- 2 small bulbs fennel—halved, cored, and thinly sliced
- 4 scallions, thinly sliced
- 1/2 cup dried apricots, quartered
- 2 ounces manchego or pecorino, shaved

▶ Heat oven to 375° F. Spread the almonds on a rimmed baking sheet and toast, tossing occasionally, until golden brown, 4 to 6 minutes.

▶ In a small bowl, whisk together the oil, lemon juice, honey, 1/2 teaspoon salt, and 1/4 teaspoon pepper.

▶ In a large bowl, combine the greens, fennel, scallions, apricots, manchego, and almonds. Toss with the dressing just before serving.

green beans with warm bacon vinaigrette

hands-on time: 15 minutes / total time: 25 minutes
serves 8

- 2 pounds green beans, trimmed
  Kosher salt and black pepper
- 6 slices bacon (about 3 ounces)
- 2 shallots, sliced
- 2 tablespoons cider vinegar
- 2 tablespoons whole-grain mustard
- 2 tablespoons olive oil

▶ Bring a large pot of water to a boil. Add the green beans and 1 tablespoon salt and cook until just tender, 4 to 5 minutes. Drain and run under cold water to cool; transfer to a serving bowl.

▶ Meanwhile, in a medium skillet, cook the bacon over medium heat until crisp, 6 to 8 minutes; transfer to a paper towel–lined plate. Let cool, then break into pieces.

▶ Discard all but 2 tablespoons of the bacon drippings and return the skillet to medium heat. Add the shallots and cook, stirring, for 1 minute. Stir in the vinegar, mustard, oil, 3/4 teaspoon salt, and 1/4 teaspoon pepper.

▶ Add the bacon to the green beans and drizzle with the vinaigrette.

sweet potatoes with pecans and Parmesan
hands-on time: 15 minutes / total time: 1 hour, 15 minutes / serves 8

3 tablespoons olive oil, plus more for the baking dish

2¹/₂ pounds sweet potatoes (about 5), peeled and sliced into ¹/₄-inch-thick rounds

¹/₂ cup grated Parmesan (2 ounces)

Kosher salt and black pepper

³/₄ cup chopped pecans

¹/₄ cup packed light brown sugar

2 teaspoons fresh thyme leaves

Pinch cayenne pepper

▶ Heat oven to 375° F. Oil a shallow 2¹/₂- to 3-quart baking dish.

▶ In a large bowl, toss the sweet potatoes with the Parmesan, 2 tablespoons of the oil, 1 teaspoon salt, and ¹/₄ teaspoon black pepper; transfer to the prepared baking dish. Cover tightly with foil and bake until tender, 45 to 50 minutes.

▶ Meanwhile, in a small bowl, combine the pecans, sugar, thyme, cayenne, the remaining tablespoon of oil, ¹/₄ teaspoon salt, and ¹/₈ teaspoon black pepper.

▶ Remove the foil from the baking dish, sprinkle the pecan mixture over the potatoes, and continue to bake, uncovered, until the pecans are toasted, 10 to 12 minutes more.

TIP
This dish is delicious made with other nuts as well. If you don't like pecans, try almonds, walnuts, hazelnuts, or a combination.

Brie and chive biscuits

hands-on time: 15 minutes
total time: 35 minutes / makes 16

- 2 cups all-purpose flour, spooned and leveled, plus more for the work surface
- 2 teaspoons baking powder
- ³/₄ teaspoon kosher salt
- ¹/₄ teaspoon baking soda
- 6 tablespoons (³/₄ stick) cold unsalted butter, cut into small pieces
- 6 ounces Brie, cut into ¹/₂-inch pieces (including the rind)
- 2 tablespoons chopped fresh chives
- ³/₄ cup buttermilk

▶ Heat oven to 375° F. In a large bowl, whisk together the flour, baking powder, salt, and baking soda. Add the butter and, using a pastry blender or your fingers, cut in until crumbly. Add the Brie and chives and toss to combine. Add the buttermilk and stir just until moistened (do not overmix).

▶ Transfer the dough to a lightly floured surface; knead a few times to bring it together. Shape it into a 1-inch-thick disk. Using a 2-inch round cookie cutter or a small glass, cut out 16 biscuits (flour the cutter and reshape the scraps as needed). Place on a parchment-lined baking sheet and bake until golden, 15 to 18 minutes.

wild rice pilaf

hands-on time: 15 minutes
total time: 55 minutes / serves 8

- 1¹/₂ cups wild and long-grain rice blend (discarding the spice packet, if included)
- ³/₄ cup dried cranberries
- 3 tablespoons olive oil
- 1 large onion, chopped
- 1 pound mixed mushrooms, sliced
  Kosher salt and black pepper
- ¹/₂ cup dry white wine
- ¹/₂ cup chopped fresh flat-leaf parsley
- 2 tablespoons chopped fresh tarragon

▶ Cook the rice according to the package directions. Fold in the cranberries, cover, and let stand for 10 minutes.

▶ Meanwhile, heat the oil in a large skillet over medium-high heat. Add the onion and cook, stirring often, until tender, 5 to 7 minutes. Add the mushrooms, ¹/₂ teaspoon salt, and ¹/₄ teaspoon pepper and cook, tossing often, until tender, 6 to 8 minutes more. Add the wine and simmer for about 1 minute. Stir in the parsley and tarragon. Add the rice and toss to combine.

cauliflower gratin

hands-on time: 20 minutes
total time: 45 minutes / serves 8

- 2 small heads cauliflower (about 3 pounds total), cut into florets
- 4 tablespoons (¹/₂ stick) unsalted butter, plus more for the dish
- ¹/₄ cup all-purpose flour
- 2 cups whole milk
- 6 ounces extra-sharp Cheddar, grated
- ¹/₈ teaspoon ground nutmeg
  Kosher salt and black pepper
- 1 cup panko bread crumbs
- ¹/₂ cup chopped fresh flat-leaf parsley
- 2 tablespoons olive oil

▶ Heat oven to 375° F. Steam the cauliflower until very tender, 12 to 15 minutes; drain.

▶ Meanwhile, melt the butter in a saucepan over medium heat. Add the flour; cook, stirring, for 2 minutes. Whisk in the milk, bring to a boil, then simmer, stirring occasionally, until thickened, 6 to 8 minutes.

▶ Stir in the cauliflower, Cheddar, nutmeg, 1¹/₂ teaspoons salt, and ¹/₄ teaspoon pepper. Transfer to a buttered shallow 2-quart baking dish. Toss the panko with the parsley, oil, and ¹/₄ teaspoon each salt and pepper and sprinkle over the cauliflower. Bake until golden brown, 15 to 20 minutes.

5 IDEAS FOR STUFFING

BASE RECIPE

- 6 tablespoons unsalted butter, plus more for the dish and foil
- 1 large loaf Italian bread (1 pound), cut into ³/₄-inch pieces (about 13 cups)
- 2 medium onions, chopped
- 4 celery stalks, thinly sliced
  Kosher salt and black pepper
- ¹/₂ cup dry white wine
- 2¹/₂ cups low-sodium chicken broth
- 2 large eggs, beaten

1. Heat oven to 375° F. Butter a 9-by-13-inch baking dish. On 2 rimmed baking sheets, bake the bread until dry and crisp, tossing occasionally, 10 to 12 minutes.

2. Meanwhile, melt the butter in a large skillet over medium heat. Add the onions, celery, 1 teaspoon salt, and ¹/₄ teaspoon pepper. Cook, stirring occasionally, until tender and beginning to brown, 10 to 12 minutes.

3. Add the wine and cook until evaporated, 2 to 4 minutes. Transfer the mixture to a large bowl; let cool for 10 minutes.

4. Add the bread, broth, eggs, and ¹/₂ teaspoon salt and toss. Transfer the mixture to the baking dish. Cover with buttered foil and bake for 20 minutes.

5. Uncover the dish and bake the stuffing until browned, 20 to 30 minutes more.

apple, cranberry, and pecan stuffing

hands-on time: 50 minutes
total time: 1 hour, 45 minutes
serves 8

Ingredients for Base Recipe (left)
- 1¹/₂ cups pecan halves
- 2 Gala apples, cored and cut into ¹/₂-inch pieces
- 1 cup dried cranberries
- 1 tablespoon fresh thyme leaves

▸ Heat oven to 375° F. Spread the pecans on a rimmed baking sheet and toast, tossing occasionally, until fragrant, 5 to 6 minutes; chop.

▸ Meanwhile, prepare the Base Recipe, making the following additions: In step 2, add the apples to the skillet along with the onions and celery.

▸ In step 4, add the pecans, cranberries, and thyme to the bread mixture.

oyster and bacon stuffing

hands-on time: 30 minutes
total time: 1 hour, 45 minutes
serves 8

Ingredients for Base Recipe (left)
- 6 slices bacon (about 3 ounces), cut into 1-inch pieces
- 16 oysters, shucked and chopped
- ¹/₂ cup chopped fresh flat-leaf parsley

▸ In a large skillet over medium heat, cook the bacon until crisp, 4 to 6 minutes. Transfer to a paper towel–lined plate.

▸ Meanwhile, prepare the Base Recipe, making the following additions: In step 4, add the bacon, oysters, and parsley to the bread mixture.

sausage and sage stuffing

hands-on time: 35 minutes
total time: 1 hour, 45 minutes
serves 8

Ingredients for Base Recipe (left)
1 tablespoon olive oil
1 pound Italian or breakfast sausage, casings removed
1/2 cup chopped fresh flat-leaf parsley
3 tablespoons chopped fresh sage

▸ Heat the oil in a large skillet over medium-high heat. Cook the sausage, breaking it up with a spoon, until browned, 8 to 10 minutes.

▸ Meanwhile, prepare the Base Recipe, making the following additions: In step 4, add the sausage, parsley, and sage to the bread mixture.

fennel and apricot stuffing

hands-on time: 35 minutes
total time: 1 hour, 45 minutes
serves 8

Ingredients for Base Recipe (left; omitting the celery)
1 bulb fennel—quartered, cored, and thinly sliced—plus 1/4 cup chopped fennel fronds
1 1/2 cups dried apricots, cut in quarters

▸ Prepare the Base Recipe, making the following substitution and additions: In step 2, replace the celery with the sliced fennel.

▸ In step 4, add the apricots and fennel fronds to the bread mixture.

caramelized onion and herb stuffing

hands-on time: 40 minutes
total time: 2 hours, 15 minutes
serves 8

Ingredients for Base Recipe (left; omitting the chopped onions and celery)
6 onions, halved and thinly sliced
1/4 cup chopped fresh chives
1 tablespoon fresh thyme leaves

▸ Prepare the Base Recipe, making the following substitution and additions: In step 2, replace the chopped onions and celery with the 6 halved and thinly sliced onions. Cook over medium-low heat, stirring occasionally, until the onions are deep golden brown, about 1 hour.

▸ In step 4, add the chives and thyme to the bread mixture.

potato and celery root mash

hands-on time: 15 minutes / total time: 45 minutes / serves 8

3 pounds Yukon gold potatoes (about 6 medium), peeled and quartered

1 pound celery root, peeled and cut into 1-inch pieces

Kosher salt and black pepper

1¹/₂ cups half-and-half

4 tablespoons (¹/₂ stick) unsalted butter, cut into pieces

2 tablespoons chopped fresh chives

▸ Place the potatoes and celery root in a large pot and add enough cold water to cover. Bring to a boil and add 2 teaspoons salt.

▸ Reduce heat and simmer until the vegetables are very tender, 18 to 20 minutes. Drain and return the vegetables to the pot.

▸ Add the half-and-half, butter, 1 teaspoon salt, and ¹/₄ teaspoon pepper to the vegetables and mash to the desired consistency. Sprinkle with the chives.

TIP
This dish can be made up to 1 day in advance; refrigerate, covered. Reheat it in a heatproof bowl set over (but not in) a pot of boiling water before serving.

honeyed carrots and oranges

hands-on time: 15 minutes / total time: 50 minutes / serves 8

2 pounds very slender carrots, scrubbed,
   or 2 pounds regular carrots—trimmed, peeled,
   and cut into thin sticks

1 orange, cut into 8 pieces

2 tablespoons olive oil

2 tablespoons honey
   Kosher salt and black pepper

2 tablespoons small fresh dill sprigs

▶ Heat oven to 375° F. On a large rimmed baking sheet, toss the carrots and orange with the oil, honey, 1 teaspoon salt, and ¼ teaspoon pepper.

▶ Roast, tossing once, until tender, 30 to 35 minutes. Sprinkle with the dill before serving.

butternut squash bread pudding

hands-on time: 30 minutes / total time: 1½ hours / serves 8

2 tablespoons olive oil, plus more for the baking dish

2 medium onions, chopped

1½ pounds butternut squash (about half a medium
   squash)—peeled, seeded, and cut into ½-inch pieces
   Kosher salt and black pepper

2 tablespoons chopped fresh sage

6 large eggs

2 cups whole milk

¾ pound soft French or Italian bread, cut into 1-inch
   pieces (about 8 cups)

½ pound Gruyère, grated (2 cups)

▶ Heat oven to 375° F. Oil a shallow 2½- to 3-quart baking dish.

▶ Heat the oil in a large skillet over medium-high heat. Add the onions and cook, stirring often, until beginning to soften, 4 to 5 minutes.

▶ Add the squash to the skillet, season with ½ teaspoon salt and ¼ teaspoon pepper, and cook, tossing often, until just tender, 8 to 10 minutes more. Stir in the sage. Let cool for 10 minutes.

▶ In a large bowl, whisk together the eggs, milk, and ¼ teaspoon each salt and pepper. Add the bread, Gruyère, and cooled squash mixture and toss to combine.

▶ Transfer the bread mixture to the prepared baking dish and bake until golden brown and set, 55 to 60 minutes.

peanut M&M's and jelly cookies

hands-on time: 5 minutes
total time: 20 minutes
makes 16

1 1-pound log store-bought sugar cookie dough
¹/₃ cup grape jelly
1 cup crushed Peanut M&M's

▶ Cut the dough into 16 slices and bake according to the package directions; let cool.

▶ Dividing evenly, spread the cookies with the jelly and sprinkle with the M&M's.

caramel-cookie cheesecake pie

hands-on time: 20 minutes
total time: 10 hours (includes chilling)
serves 8

2 8-ounce bars cream cheese, at room temperature
¹/₂ cup sugar
2 large eggs
22 Twix Fun Size Bars (16 grams each), chopped
1 8-inch chocolate cookie piecrust

▶ Heat oven to 325° F. With an electric mixer, beat the cream cheese, sugar, and eggs on medium-high until smooth. Mix in 2 cups of the chopped Twix bars. Pour the mixture into the piecrust.

▶ Bake the pie until set, 40 to 45 minutes; let cool.

▶ Sprinkle the pie with the remaining Twix bars and chill until firm, 8 to 10 hours.

candy corn and pretzel bark

hands-on time: 15 minutes
total time: 1 hour, 15 minutes (includes chilling) / serves 8

¹/₂ pound white chocolate, chopped
1 cup miniature pretzels
¹/₂ cup candy corn
¹/₃ cup dried cranberries

▶ Line an 8-inch square baking pan with parchment, leaving an overhang on two sides.

▶ Heat the chocolate in a double boiler or medium heatproof bowl set over (but not in) a saucepan of simmering water, stirring often, until melted and smooth.

▶ Spread the chocolate in the prepared pan and sprinkle with the pretzels, candy corn, and dried cranberries. Chill until firm, about 1 hour.

▶ Remove the bark from the pan and break into pieces.

peppermint patty brownies

hands-on time: 25 minutes
total time: 2 hours (includes cooling)
makes 16

  Canola oil, for pan
 1 19-ounce box brownie mix
16 York Miniatures Peppermint Patties
    (13.6 grams each)

▸ Oil an 8-inch square pan. Prepare the brownie batter according to the package directions.

▸ Spread half the batter in the prepared pan. Top with the peppermint patties, leaving an even border of batter all around the edges of the pan.

▸ Spread the remaining batter on top and bake according to the package directions. Let cool, then cut into 16 squares.

dulce de leche candy bar terrine

hands-on time: 15 minutes
total time: 6 hours, 15 minutes
(includes freezing) / serves 8

14 Snickers Fun Size Bars
    (17 grams each), cut in thirds
 2 pints dulce de leche ice cream,
    softened

▸ Line an 8-by-4½-inch loaf pan with parchment. Arrange the Snickers bars on the bottom of the pan.

▸ Top the Snickers bars with the ice cream and press in gently. Freeze until firm, about 6 hours. Invert onto a plate and slice.

frozen peanut butter cup banana pops

hands-on time: 15 minutes
total time: 2 hours, 10 minutes
(includes freezing) / makes 4

2 bananas, peeled and halved
   crosswise
4 Reese's Peanut Butter Cups
   (21 grams each)
6 ounces chocolate, chopped

▸ Insert a wooden stick into each banana half. Freeze the bananas and the peanut butter cups for 2 hours.

▸ Meanwhile, heat the chocolate in a double boiler or medium heatproof bowl set over (but not in) a saucepan of simmering water, stirring often, until melted and smooth.

▸ Chop the frozen peanut butter cups. Line a plate with parchment.

▸ Coat the frozen bananas in the melted chocolate. Sprinkle with the chopped peanut butter cups. Freeze on the prepared plate until firm, 4 to 5 minutes.

pecan and walnut pie

hands-on time: 10 minutes / total time: 4 hours (includes cooling) / serves 8

1¼ cups light corn syrup

½ cup packed dark brown sugar

¼ cup granulated sugar

3 large eggs

2 tablespoons unsalted butter, melted

2 teaspoons pure vanilla extract

¼ teaspoon kosher salt

1 cup pecan halves

1 cup walnut halves

1 refrigerated rolled piecrust, fitted into a 9-inch pie plate

▶ Heat oven to 350° F. In a large bowl, whisk together the corn syrup, sugars, eggs, butter, vanilla, and salt. Mix in the pecans and walnuts.

▶ Place the pie plate on a rimmed baking sheet. Fill the crust with the nut mixture and bake until the center is set, 45 to 50 minutes. Let cool completely before serving.

TIP
This pie can be baked up to 1 day in advance. Store, covered, at room temperature.

gingersnap cherry cheesecake
hands-on time: 20 minutes / total time: 5 hours (includes chilling) / serves 12

3 cups ground gingersnap
  cookies

1/2 cup (1 stick) unsalted butter,
  melted

3 8-ounce bars cream cheese,
  at room temperature

1 1/4 cups sugar

2 large eggs

2 cups sour cream

2 teaspoons pure vanilla
  extract

1/2 cup cherry preserves

▸ Heat oven to 350° F. In a medium bowl, combine the cookies and butter. Using a straight-sided dry measuring cup, press the mixture into the bottom and 2 inches up the side of a 9-inch springform pan.

▸ Using an electric mixer, beat the cream cheese and 1 cup of the sugar on medium-high until smooth. One at a time, beat in the eggs. Beat in 1/2 cup of the sour cream and 1 teaspoon of the vanilla.

▸ Pour the cream cheese mixture into the crust and bake until just set, 40 to 45 minutes.

▸ In a small bowl, combine the remaining 1 1/2 cups of sour cream, 1/4 cup of sugar, and teaspoon of vanilla. Spread over the hot cheesecake and bake until set, 3 to 5 minutes more. Let cool in the pan, then refrigerate for at least 4 hours.

▸ Run a knife around the edge of the cheesecake and unmold. Before serving, bring the cake to room temperature and spoon the preserves on top.

TIP
The cheesecake can be baked up to 2 days in advance; refrigerate in the pan, loosely covered.

pear and apricot tart

hands-on time: 20 minutes / total time: 1 hour, 45 minutes (includes cooling) / serves 8

½ cup (1 stick) unsalted butter, at room temperature, plus more for the pan

½ cup almonds

½ cup plus 1 tablespoon sugar

1 large egg

½ teaspoon pure almond extract

1 cup all-purpose flour, spooned and leveled

½ teaspoon baking powder

½ teaspoon kosher salt

2 pears (such as Bosc or Bartlett)—peeled, quartered, and cored

½ cup dried apricots, halved

1 tablespoon fresh lemon juice

¼ cup apricot preserves

▶ Heat oven to 350° F. Butter a 9-inch removable-bottom fluted tart pan.

▶ In a food processor, process the almonds and ½ cup of the sugar until finely ground. Add the butter, egg, and almond extract and blend until smooth. Add the flour, baking powder, and salt and pulse a few times just to combine (the dough will be soft). Spread the dough in the bottom of the prepared pan.

▶ In a small bowl, toss the pears and apricots with the lemon juice and the remaining tablespoon of sugar. Arrange the pears on top of the dough. Scatter the apricots over the dough, pressing them in gently.

▶ Bake until the pears are tender and the center is firm, 50 to 55 minutes. (Cover the edge with foil if it browns too quickly.)

▶ In a small bowl, combine the preserves and 1 tablespoon water. Brush over the warm tart. Let cool in the pan before unmolding.

TIP
The tart can be baked and glazed up to 1 day in advance. Store, covered, at room temperature.

spiced pumpkin cake

hands-on time: 20 minutes / total time: 4 hours (includes cooling) / serves 12

1 cup (2 sticks) unsalted butter, at room temperature, plus more for the pan

3 cups all-purpose flour, spooned and leveled, plus more for the pan

5 teaspoons pumpkin pie spice

1½ teaspoons baking powder

¾ teaspoon baking soda

½ teaspoon kosher salt

1½ cups granulated sugar

3 large eggs

1 15-ounce can pumpkin puree (about 1½ cups)

½ cup whole milk

¼ cup molasses

1¼ cups confectioners' sugar

2 tablespoons fresh lemon juice

▶ Heat oven to 350° F. Butter and flour a 12-cup Bundt pan.

▶ In a large bowl, whisk together the flour, pumpkin pie spice, baking powder, baking soda, and salt.

▶ Using an electric mixer, beat the butter and granulated sugar on medium-high until fluffy, 2 to 3 minutes. One at a time, beat in the eggs. Beat in the pumpkin puree, milk, and molasses (the mixture may appear curdled). Reduce the mixer speed to low; gradually add the flour mixture and mix until just combined (do not overmix).

▶ Pour the batter into the prepared pan and bake until a toothpick inserted in the center comes out clean, 55 to 65 minutes. Let cool in the pan for 30 minutes, then invert onto a wire rack to cool completely.

▶ In a small bowl, whisk together the confectioners' sugar and lemon juice until smooth. Drizzle over the cake. Let set before serving.

TIP
The cake can be baked and glazed up to 1 day in advance. Store, covered, at room temperature.

winter

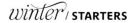

hot ricotta dip
hands-on time: 10 minutes / **total time: 10 minutes** / **serves 20**

2   15-ounce containers ricotta

¼   cup chopped fresh flat-leaf parsley

2   teaspoons fresh thyme leaves

¼   teaspoon crushed red pepper

½   cup plus 1 tablespoon grated Parmesan (2 ounces)

    Kosher salt and black pepper

1   tablespoon olive oil

8   heads green and red endive, ends trimmed and leaves separated

▸ Heat broiler. In a medium bowl, mix together the ricotta, parsley, thyme, red pepper, ½ cup of the Parmesan, ½ teaspoon salt, and ¼ teaspoon black pepper.

▸ Transfer the ricotta mixture to a shallow, broiler-proof 1-quart baking dish, drizzle with the oil, and sprinkle with the remaining tablespoon of Parmesan. Broil until the top browns in spots, 3 to 5 minutes. Serve warm with the endive leaves.

TIP
The dip can be prepared (but not broiled) up to 1 day in advance. Refrigerate, covered, until ready to cook.

5 IDEAS FOR CROSTINI

BASIC CROSTINI

hands-on time: 5 minutes
total time: 15 minutes / makes 24

- 24 thin slices baguette (from 1 small loaf)
- 2 tablespoons olive oil

▸ Heat oven to 400° F. Place the baguette slices on a baking sheet and brush both sides of the bread with the oil.

▸ Bake until golden brown, 4 to 5 minutes per side. Top as desired. (For the following recipes, use 1 batch of these Basic Crostini.)

smoked salmon crostini

hands-on time: 10 minutes
total time: 25 minutes / makes 24

Ingredients for Basic Crostini (left)
- 4 ounces cream cheese
- 1 tablespoon prepared horseradish
- 2 tablespoons chopped fresh dill
  Kosher salt and black pepper
- ¼ pound smoked salmon

▸ Make the Basic Crostini.

▸ Meanwhile, in a small bowl, mix together the cream cheese, horseradish, 1 tablespoon of the dill, and ¼ teaspoon each salt and pepper.

▸ Dividing evenly, spread the cream cheese mixture on the crostini, top with the salmon, and sprinkle with the remaining tablespoon of dill.

mushroom and herb crostini

hands-on time: 15 minutes
total time: 25 minutes / makes 24

Ingredients for Basic Crostini (left)
- 1 tablespoon olive oil
- ¾ pound assorted mushrooms, thinly sliced
  Kosher salt and black pepper
- ½ cup white wine
- 1 tablespoon chopped fresh chives

▸ Make the Basic Crostini.

▸ Meanwhile, heat the oil in a large skillet over medium-high heat. Add the mushrooms and ¼ teaspoon each salt and pepper and cook, stirring occasionally, until tender, 4 to 5 minutes. Add the wine and simmer until evaporated, 3 to 4 minutes.

▸ Dividing evenly, top the crostini with the mushrooms and sprinkle with the chives.

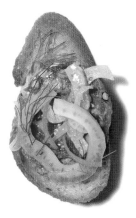

roast beef and pomegranate crostini
hands-on time: 10 minutes
total time: 25 minutes / makes 24

    Ingredients for Basic Crostini (left)
¼ pound thinly sliced roast beef
¼ cup sour cream
½ cup pomegranate seeds
1 scallion, thinly sliced
    Kosher salt and black pepper

▸ Make the Basic Crostini.

▸ Dividing evenly, top the crostini with the roast beef, sour cream, pomegranate seeds, and scallion; season with ½ teaspoon each salt and pepper.

artichoke and olive crostini
hands-on time: 10 minutes
total time: 25 minutes / makes 24

    Ingredients for Basic Crostini (left)
1 14-ounce can artichoke hearts, rinsed and chopped
½ cup pitted kalamata olives, chopped
1 tablespoon chopped fresh flat-leaf parsley
3 tablespoons olive oil
    Kosher salt and black pepper
2 ounces Parmesan, shaved

▸ Make the Basic Crostini.

▸ In a small bowl, toss the artichoke hearts and olives with the parsley, oil, and ¼ teaspoon each salt and pepper.

▸ Dividing evenly, top the crostini with the artichoke mixture and the Parmesan.

salami and fennel crostini
hands-on time: 10 minutes
total time: 25 minutes / makes 24

    Ingredients for Basic Crostini (left)
½ bulb fennel, thinly sliced, plus 1 tablespoon chopped fronds
½ teaspoon grated orange zest, plus 2 tablespoons fresh orange juice
1 tablespoon olive oil
    Kosher salt and black pepper
3 ounces thinly sliced salami

▸ Make the Basic Crostini.

▸ In a medium bowl, toss the sliced fennel with the orange zest and juice, oil, and ¼ teaspoon each salt and pepper.

▸ Dividing evenly, top the crostini with the salami and the fennel mixture and sprinkle with the fennel fronds.

crab and chive puffs
hands-on time: 10 minutes / total time: 35 minutes / serves 20 (makes 60 puffs)

2 sheets frozen puff pastry (one 17.3-ounce box), thawed

4 ounces cream cheese, at room temperature

1/2 cup mayonnaise

1/4 cup chopped fresh chives, plus more for garnish

1 tablespoon fresh lemon juice
Kosher salt and black pepper

1 pound lump crabmeat

▸ Heat oven to 400° F. Line 2 baking sheets with parchment. Unfold the pastry and, using a 2-inch cookie cutter, cut out rounds. Place them on the prepared baking sheets.

▸ In a medium bowl, mix together the cream cheese, mayonnaise, chives, lemon juice, 1/2 teaspoon salt, and 1/4 teaspoon pepper. Fold in the crabmeat.

▸ Dividing evenly, spoon the crab mixture onto the pastry rounds (about 2 teaspoons each). Bake, rotating the baking sheets halfway through, until the puffs are golden and crisp, 20 to 25 minutes. Sprinkle with additional chives and serve.

TIP
The puffs can be assembled (but not baked) up to 1 day in advance. Refrigerate, covered, until ready to bake.

slow-cooker creamy chicken with biscuits
hands-on time: 15 minutes / total time: 3 to 6¹/₂ hours
serves 6

- ³/₄ pound medium carrots (about 7), cut into 1-inch pieces
- 2 stalks celery, thinly sliced
- 1 small onion, chopped
- ¹/₄ cup all-purpose flour
- 1¹/₂ pounds boneless, skinless chicken thighs (about 8)
- ¹/₂ teaspoon poultry seasoning
  Kosher salt and black pepper
- ¹/₂ cup dry white wine
- ¹/₂ cup low-sodium chicken broth
- 6 biscuits (store-bought or Easy Drop Biscuits, right), split
- 1 cup frozen peas
- ¹/₂ cup heavy cream

▸ In a 4- to 6-quart slow cooker, toss together the carrots, celery, onion, and flour. Place the chicken on top and season with the poultry seasoning, 1 teaspoon salt, and ¹/₄ teaspoon pepper. Add the wine and broth. Cover and cook until the chicken and vegetables are tender, on low for 5 to 6 hours or on high for 2¹/₂ to 3 hours.

▸ Thirty minutes before serving, prepare the Easy Drop Biscuits (if using).

▸ Ten minutes before serving, add the peas, cream, and ¹/₂ teaspoon salt to the chicken and stir to combine. Cover and cook until heated through, 5 to 10 minutes more.

▸ To serve, place the bottom halves of the biscuits in shallow bowls, then top with the chicken mixture and the remaining biscuit halves.

easy drop biscuits
hands-on time: 10 minutes / total time: 30 minutes
makes 6 biscuits

- 2 cups all-purpose flour, spooned and leveled
- 8 tablespoons (1 stick) cold unsalted butter, cut into small pieces
- 1 tablespoon baking powder
- 1 teaspoon kosher salt
- 1 cup whole milk

▸ Heat oven to 400° F. In a food processor, combine the flour, butter, baking powder, and salt. Pulse until pea-size clumps form. Add the milk and pulse just until moistened.

▸ Drop 6 large mounds of the dough (about ¹/₂ cup each) onto a baking sheet. Bake until golden, 18 to 20 minutes.

yogurt-marinated chicken with mushrooms and sweet potatoes

hands-on time: 10 minutes / **total time: 55 minutes (includes marinating)** / **serves 4**

- 1/2 cup plain nonfat Greek yogurt
- 4 cloves garlic, crushed
- 1 tablespoon fresh lemon juice
  Kosher salt and black pepper
- 4 4-ounce chicken cutlets
- 1/4 cup walnuts
- 2/3 cup quinoa, rinsed
- 1/4 cup chopped fresh flat-leaf parsley
- 1 tablespoon plus 3 teaspoons olive oil
- 1 large sweet potato (about 3/4 pound), peeled and thinly sliced
- 1/2 pound shiitake mushrooms, stems discarded
- 1/2 pound cremini mushrooms, halved if large
- 2 sprigs fresh thyme
- 2 teaspoons sherry vinegar or red wine vinegar

▸ Heat oven to 450° F. In a medium bowl, mix together the yogurt, garlic, lemon juice, 1/4 teaspoon salt, and 1/8 teaspoon pepper. Add the chicken and turn to coat. Refrigerate for at least 30 minutes and up to 2 hours.

▸ Meanwhile, spread the walnuts on a rimmed baking sheet and toast in oven, tossing occasionally, until fragrant, 4 to 5 minutes. Let cool and coarsely chop.

▸ Cook the quinoa according to the package directions. Fold in the walnuts, parsley, 2 teaspoons of the oil, 1/2 teaspoon salt, and 1/8 teaspoon pepper.

▸ Divide the potato, mushrooms, and thyme between 2 rimmed baking sheets; toss with 1 tablespoon of the remaining oil, 1/2 teaspoon salt, and 1/4 teaspoon pepper. Roast, rotating the sheets halfway through, until tender, 13 to 15 minutes. Drizzle with the vinegar.

▸ Heat the remaining teaspoon of oil in a large cast-iron or other nonstick skillet over medium heat. Wipe the excess marinade off the chicken and cook until golden brown and cooked through, 3 to 4 minutes per side. Serve with the quinoa and vegetables.

TIP
The yogurt in the marinade not only flavors the chicken but also acts as a tenderizer. Try it with lamb, too.

slow-cooker curried chicken with ginger and yogurt
hands-on time: 15 minutes / total time: 3¹/₂ to 8¹/₂ hours / serves 6

¹/₃ cup tomato paste

4 cloves garlic, chopped

2 tablespoons curry powder

1 tablespoon grated
 fresh ginger

1 teaspoon ground cumin

1 medium onion, chopped

2 pounds boneless, skinless
 chicken thighs (about 10)

 Kosher salt and black pepper

1¹/₂ cups long-grain white rice

¹/₂ cup plain whole-milk
 Greek yogurt

2 scallions, thinly sliced

▶ In a 4- to 6-quart slow cooker, stir together the tomato paste, garlic, curry powder, ginger, cumin, and ³/₄ cup water. Add the onion and stir to combine. Place the chicken on top and season with 1 teaspoon salt and ¹/₄ teaspoon pepper.

▶ Cover and cook until the chicken is tender, on low for 7 to 8 hours or on high for 3 to 4 hours.

▶ Twenty minutes before serving, cook the rice according to the package directions.

▶ Just before serving, add the yogurt and ¹/₂ teaspoon salt to the chicken and stir to combine. Serve over the rice and sprinkle with the scallions.

TIP
Like your curry spicy? Turn up the heat by adding ¹/₄ to ¹/₂ teaspoon cayenne pepper along with the curry powder.

roasted chicken, potatoes, and fennel
hands-on time: 10 minutes / total time: 1 hour, 40 minutes / serves 4

1 pound baby potatoes
(about 16)

4 small bulbs fennel, quartered

8 cloves garlic (unpeeled)

2 tablespoons olive oil
Kosher salt and black pepper

1 3 1/2- to 4-pound chicken,
legs tied

1/4 cup fresh flat-leaf parsley
leaves

▸ Heat oven to 425° F. On a large rimmed baking sheet, toss the potatoes, fennel, and garlic with 1 tablespoon of the oil, 1/2 teaspoon salt, and 1/4 teaspoon pepper.

▸ Rub the chicken with the remaining tablespoon of oil, 1 teaspoon salt, and 1/2 teaspoon pepper and nestle among the vegetables.

▸ Roast, tossing the vegetables and basting the chicken once, until the vegetables are tender and an instant-read thermometer inserted in the thickest part of a thigh registers 165° F, 65 to 75 minutes. Let rest for at least 10 minutes before carving.

▸ Toss the vegetables with the parsley and serve with the chicken.

TIP
For extra flavor, reserve some fennel fronds, chop, and toss with the vegetables, along with the parsley.

Greek lemon soup with chicken
hands-on time: 15 minutes / **total time: 30 minutes** / **serves 4**

6 cups low-sodium chicken broth

1/3 cup orzo

6 large egg yolks

1 1/2 cups shredded rotisserie chicken

1/4 cup fresh lemon juice

Kosher salt and black pepper

▸ In a large saucepan, bring the broth to a boil. Add the pasta and boil until tender, 8 to 9 minutes.

▸ In a large bowl, beat the egg yolks. Gradually whisk in 1 cup of the hot broth. Add the egg mixture to the saucepan, reduce heat to medium, and cook, stirring, until thickened, 5 to 7 minutes.

▸ Add the chicken and lemon juice to the saucepan. Season with 1/2 teaspoon salt and 1/4 teaspoon pepper.

TIP
To shred a rotisserie chicken, first pull off the breasts and legs with your hands or cut them off with a knife. Remove the skin and bones and, using 2 forks, pull the meat apart.

spicy Asian chicken with Brussels sprouts
hands-on time: 35 minutes / total time: 35 minutes / serves 4

1 cup long-grain white rice

1/2 cup cornstarch

1 large egg

1 pound boneless, skinless chicken breasts (2 large), thinly sliced

3 tablespoons canola oil, plus more if needed

1/2 pound Brussels sprouts, thinly sliced

1 1-inch piece fresh ginger, peeled and cut into matchsticks

2 cloves garlic, thinly sliced

3 tablespoons low-sodium soy sauce

3 tablespoons rice vinegar

2 tablespoons light brown sugar

1 red chili pepper, thinly sliced

1 teaspoon toasted sesame oil

2 scallions, thinly sliced

2 tablespoons chopped roasted peanuts

▸ Cook the rice according to the package directions.

▸ Meanwhile, place the cornstarch in a shallow bowl. In a large bowl, beat the egg; add the chicken and toss to coat. A few pieces at a time, lift the chicken out of the egg and coat in the cornstarch, tapping off the excess; transfer to a plate.

▸ Heat 2 tablespoons of the canola oil in a large nonstick skillet over medium-high heat. In 2 batches, cook the chicken, turning occasionally, until golden, 3 to 5 minutes (add more oil for the second batch if necessary); transfer to a plate.

▸ Reduce heat to medium and heat the remaining tablespoon of canola oil in the skillet. Add the Brussels sprouts, ginger, and garlic and cook, tossing occasionally, until beginning to soften, 2 to 3 minutes. Add the soy sauce, vinegar, sugar, and 3/4 cup water and cook, stirring occasionally, until the Brussels sprouts are crisp-tender and the liquid begins to thicken, 2 to 3 minutes more.

▸ Return the chicken to the skillet, add the chili, and cook, tossing, until heated through, about 1 minute. Toss with the sesame oil and scallions. Serve over the rice and sprinkle with the peanuts.

TIP
To make quick work of preparing the Brussels sprouts, slice them in a food processor fitted with the slicing blade.

steak with roasted carrots and onions

hands-on time: 30 minutes / total time: 30 minutes / serves 4

1½ pounds medium carrots (about 15), halved crosswise and thick pieces halved lengthwise

2 small red onions, quartered and stem ends left intact

3 tablespoons olive oil

Kosher salt and black pepper

4 small Newport or sirloin steaks (1 inch thick; about 1½ pounds total)

½ cup dry white wine

2 tablespoons Dijon mustard

2 tablespoons chopped fresh tarragon

▶ Heat oven to 425° F. On a large rimmed baking sheet, toss the carrots and onions with 2 table-spoons of the oil, ¾ teaspoon salt, and ¼ teaspoon pepper. Roast, tossing once, until tender, 20 to 25 minutes.

▶ Meanwhile, heat the remaining tablespoon of oil in a large skillet over medium-high heat. Season the steaks with ½ teaspoon each salt and pepper and cook to the desired doneness, 4 to 5 minutes per side for medium-rare; transfer to plates.

▶ Add the wine to the skillet and whisk in the mustard. Simmer until slightly thickened, 1 to 2 minutes; stir in the tarragon. Serve the steaks with the sauce and the vegetables.

TIP
Also try this easy wine and Dijon sauce with seared lamb or pork chops.

chipotle meatballs with rice

hands-on time: 25 minutes / total time: 40 minutes / serves 4

1 tablespoon olive oil

1 medium onion, chopped

6 cloves garlic, finely chopped

1 28-ounce can whole peeled tomatoes

2 to 3 teaspoons chopped chipotle chilies in adobo sauce

1 cup long-grain white rice

1 1/2 pounds ground beef chuck

1/2 cup chopped fresh cilantro, plus more for serving

1/4 cup bread crumbs

1 large egg, beaten

1 teaspoon ground cumin

Kosher salt and black pepper

▸ Heat the oil in a large skillet over medium heat. Add the onion and half the garlic and cook, stirring occasionally, until beginning to brown, 5 to 7 minutes.

▸ Add the tomatoes (with their juices) and chipotles to the skillet; using a potato masher, break up the tomatoes. Reduce heat and simmer, partially covered, until the sauce has thickened, 15 to 20 minutes. (If it becomes too thick, add up to 1/2 cup water.)

▸ Meanwhile, cook the rice according to the package directions.

▸ While the rice is cooking, in a medium bowl, mix together the beef, cilantro, bread crumbs, egg, cumin, the remaining garlic, 1 1/2 teaspoons salt, and 1/4 teaspoon black pepper. Form the mixture into 16 meatballs (about 2 heaping tablespoons each).

▸ Heat broiler. Place the meatballs on a foil-lined broilerproof baking sheet and broil, turning once, until cooked through, 8 to 12 minutes. Add the meatballs to the sauce. Serve over the rice and sprinkle with additional cilantro.

TIP
The meatballs and sauce can be cooked and combined up to 2 days in advance and refrigerated, covered. Or freeze in an airtight container for up to 3 months.

LEG OF LAMB DINNER

roasted leg of lamb with carrots and honey-mint sauce

hands-on time: 15 minutes / total time: 2 hours, 15 minutes
serves 8 (with leftovers)

- 1 lemon, strips of zest removed with a vegetable peeler and juice squeezed
- 6 cloves garlic
- 1/2 cup plus 3 tablespoons olive oil
  Kosher salt and black pepper
- 1 6- to 7-pound bone-in leg of lamb, at room temperature
- 3 pounds very slender carrots, scrubbed
- 2 cups fresh flat-leaf parsley
- 1 cup fresh mint leaves
- 6 scallions, chopped
- 2 teaspoons honey

▸ Heat oven to 400° F. In a food processor, pulse the lemon zest, garlic, 2 tablespoons of the oil, and 1 teaspoon each salt and pepper until coarsely chopped. Place the lamb in a large roasting pan and rub with the lemon mixture.

▸ In a large bowl, toss the carrots, 1 tablespoon of the remaining oil, 1/2 teaspoon salt, and 1/4 teaspoon pepper; set aside.

▸ Roast the lamb until an instant-read thermometer inserted in the thickest part registers 130° F for medium-rare. Add the carrots to the pan after the lamb has cooked for 50 minutes. Let the lamb rest, tented with foil, for at least 15 minutes before slicing.

▸ Meanwhile, in the food processor, puree the parsley, mint, scallions, honey, lemon juice, the remaining 1/2 cup of oil, 3/4 teaspoon salt, and 1/2 teaspoon pepper. Serve with the lamb and carrots.

rice pilaf with almonds and dill

hands-on time: 15 minutes / total time: 50 minutes
serves 8

- 2 tablespoons olive oil
- 2 large onions, chopped
  Kosher salt and black pepper
- 2 cups long-grain white rice
- 1/2 cup sliced almonds
- 2 tablespoons chopped fresh dill

▸ Heat oven to 400° F. Heat the oil in a large saucepan over medium heat. Add the onions, 1/2 teaspoon salt, and 1/4 teaspoon pepper and cook, stirring occasionally, until soft and beginning to brown, 12 to 15 minutes.

▸ Add the rice and cook, stirring, for 2 minutes. Add 3 1/2 cups water and 1 1/2 teaspoons salt and bring to a boil. Reduce heat to low and cook, covered, until the rice is tender, 18 to 20 minutes. Let sit off the heat for 5 minutes.

▸ Meanwhile, spread the almonds on a baking sheet. Toast in oven, tossing occasionally, until golden brown, 4 to 6 minutes. Fluff the rice with a fork and fold in the almonds and dill.

burgers with balsamic shallots and vegetable fries

hands-on time: 30 minutes / total time: 30 minutes / serves 4

1 small rutabaga (about
 1 pound), peeled and cut
 into ¹/₂-inch-thick sticks

4 medium carrots (about
 ¹/₂ pound), peeled and cut
 into ¹/₂-inch-thick sticks

4 tablespoons plus 1 teaspoon
 olive oil

 Kosher salt and black pepper

4 large shallots, sliced

¹/₄ cup balsamic vinegar

1¹/₄ pounds ground beef chuck

4 soft sandwich buns

 Mayonnaise and lettuce, for
 serving

▸ Heat oven to 450° F. On a rimmed baking sheet, toss the rutabaga and carrots with 2 tablespoons of the oil, ¹/₂ teaspoon salt, and ¹/₄ teaspoon pepper. Roast, tossing once, until golden brown and tender, 20 to 25 minutes.

▸ Meanwhile, heat 2 tablespoons of the remaining oil in a large skillet over medium-high heat. Add the shallots and cook, stirring often, until tender, 3 to 4 minutes. Stir in the vinegar and transfer the shallots to a bowl. Wipe out the skillet.

▸ Form the beef into four ¹/₂-inch-thick patties. Use your fingers to make a shallow well in the top of each. (This will prevent overplumping during cooking.) Dividing evenly, season the patties with ¹/₂ teaspoon salt and ¹/₄ teaspoon pepper.

▸ Heat the remaining teaspoon of oil in the skillet over medium-high heat. Cook the patties with the wells facing up until the burgers release easily, 3 to 4 minutes. Flip and cook until an instant-read thermometer inserted in the center registers 160° F for medium, 3 to 4 minutes more.

▸ Serve the burgers on the buns with the mayonnaise, lettuce, and shallots, accompanied by the fries.

TIP
Almost any kind of root vegetable can be turned into oven fries. Also try parsnips, turnips, or sweet potatoes.

ROAST BEEF DINNER

peppered roast beef with horseradish sauce

hands-on time: 10 minutes
total time: 2 hours / serves 8

- 2 tablespoons mixed-color peppercorns
- 1 4-pound boneless beef rib roast, at room temperature
  Kosher salt and black pepper
- ³/₄ cup sour cream
- ¹/₄ cup prepared horseradish

▸ Heat oven to 375° F. Place the peppercorns in a plastic bag and crush with the bottom of a skillet.

▸ Place the beef in a large roasting pan. Season with the peppercorns and 1¹/₂ teaspoons salt, pressing gently to help the peppercorns adhere.

▸ Roast the beef to the desired doneness, 85 to 95 minutes for medium-rare (an instant-read thermometer inserted in the center registers 130° F). Tent with foil and let rest for at least 15 minutes before slicing.

▸ Meanwhile, in a small bowl, combine the sour cream, horseradish, and ¹/₂ teaspoon each salt and pepper. Serve with the beef.

sour cream mashed potatoes

hands-on time: 10 minutes
total time: 40 minutes / serves 8

- 4 pounds red potatoes (about 8), halved
  Kosher salt and black pepper
- 2 cups sour cream
- ¹/₂ cup milk
- 4 tablespoons (¹/₂ stick) unsalted butter
- 2 scallions, chopped

▸ Place the potatoes in a large pot and add enough cold water to cover. Add 2 teaspoons salt and bring to a boil. Reduce heat and simmer until tender, 15 to 18 minutes. Drain the potatoes and return them to the pot.

▸ Add the sour cream, milk, butter, 1 teaspoon salt, and ¹/₄ teaspoon pepper to the potatoes and mash to the desired consistency. Sprinkle with the scallions.

broccoli rabe with red currant sauce

hands-on time: 10 minutes
total time: 15 minutes / serves 8

  Kosher salt and black pepper
- 3 bunches broccoli rabe (about 3 pounds), trimmed
- ¹/₄ cup red currant jelly
- ¹/₄ cup olive oil
- ¹/₂ teaspoon Dijon mustard
- ¹/₄ teaspoon crushed red pepper

▸ Bring a large saucepan of salted water to a boil. Add the broccoli rabe and cook until tender, about 3 minutes. Drain, squeezing to remove any excess water, and transfer to a serving bowl.

▸ Heat the jelly in a small saucepan over low heat for 2 to 3 minutes. Remove from heat and whisk in the oil, mustard, red pepper, ¹/₂ teaspoon salt, and ¹/₈ teaspoon black pepper.

▸ Drizzle the broccoli rabe with the sauce. Serve warm or at room temperature.

slow-cooker white bean soup with andouille and collards
hands-on time: 10 minutes / total time: 4¹/₂ to 8 hours / serves 6

1 pound dried white beans
   (such as cannellini or
   great Northern)

8 cups low-sodium
   chicken broth

¹/₂ pound andouille sausage links,
   halved lengthwise
   and sliced crosswise

1 large onion, chopped

2 stalks celery, chopped

4 sprigs fresh thyme

1 bunch collard greens,
   stems discarded and leaves
   cut into bite-size pieces
   (about 8 cups)

1 tablespoon red wine vinegar

Kosher salt and black pepper

Olive oil and bread sticks,
   for serving

▸ In a 4- to 6-quart slow cooker, combine the beans, broth, sausage, onion, celery, and thyme. Cover and cook until the beans are tender, on low for 7 to 8 hours or on high for 4 to 5 hours.

▸ Twenty minutes before serving, discard the thyme stems, add the collard greens, cover, and cook until the greens are tender, 15 to 20 minutes. Add the vinegar and ¹/₂ teaspoon each salt and pepper.

▸ Drizzle with oil and serve with bread sticks.

TIP
If you can't find collard greens, try mustard greens or kale.

crispy pork cutlets with arugula and apple salad

hands-on time: 25 minutes / total time: 25 minutes / serves 4

1/4 cup all-purpose flour

2 large eggs, beaten

2/3 cup panko bread crumbs

4 thin pork cutlets
(about 1 pound total)

Kosher salt and black pepper

5 tablespoons olive oil

1/4 cup sour cream

1 tablespoon fresh lemon juice,
plus lemon wedges for
serving

1 bunch arugula, thick stems
removed (about 4 cups)

1 apple, thinly sliced

▸ Place the flour, eggs, and panko in separate shallow bowls. Season the pork with 1/2 teaspoon salt and 1/4 teaspoon pepper. Coat the pork in the flour (tapping off any excess), dip in the eggs (shaking off any excess), then coat in the panko, pressing gently to help them adhere.

▸ Heat 3 tablespoons of the oil in a large skillet over medium-high heat. Cook the pork until golden and cooked through, 2 to 3 minutes per side; transfer to a paper towel–lined plate.

▸ Meanwhile, in a large bowl, whisk together the sour cream, lemon juice, the remaining 2 tablespoons of oil, 1/2 teaspoon salt, and 1/4 teaspoon pepper. Add the arugula and apple and toss to coat. Serve with the pork and lemon wedges.

TIP

Japanese panko bread crumbs, lighter and coarser than the usual variety, add a delicious crunch to meat and seafood. At the market, you'll find them next to regular dried bread crumbs or in the international aisle.

slow-cooker Asian pork with snow peas, peppers, and noodles

hands-on time: 10 minutes / total time: 4$\frac{1}{2}$ to 8$\frac{1}{2}$ hours / serves 6

$\frac{1}{2}$ cup low-sodium soy sauce

$\frac{1}{2}$ cup dark brown sugar

2 tablespoons rice vinegar

1 teaspoon toasted sesame oil

1 1-inch piece fresh ginger, peeled and sliced

$\frac{1}{4}$ to $\frac{1}{2}$ teaspoon crushed red pepper

2$\frac{1}{2}$ pounds pork shoulder, trimmed and cut into 2-inch pieces

$\frac{3}{4}$ pound soba noodles

2 red bell peppers, thinly sliced

$\frac{1}{2}$ pound snow peas, trimmed

Chopped roasted peanuts, for serving

▸ In a 4- to 6-quart slow cooker, stir together the soy sauce, sugar, vinegar, oil, ginger, and red pepper. Add the pork and toss to coat. Cover and cook until the pork is tender, on low for 7 to 8 hours or on high for 4 to 5 hours.

▸ Fifteen minutes before serving, cook the noodles according to the package directions, adding the bell peppers and snow peas to the water during the last minute of cooking.

▸ Transfer the pork to a medium bowl; set aside. Pour the cooking liquid into a large skillet and boil until slightly thickened, 4 to 5 minutes. Add the pork and toss to coat. Serve over the noodles and vegetables and sprinkle with peanuts.

TIP
For extra flavor, sprinkle the cooked pork with toasted sesame seeds and more crushed red pepper in addition to the peanuts.

roasted pork chops and butternut squash with kale

hands-on time: 30 minutes / total time: 55 minutes / serves 4

1 small butternut squash (about 2 pounds)—peeled, seeded, and cut into 1½-inch pieces

¼ cup fresh sage leaves

2 tablespoons plus 1 teaspoon olive oil

Kosher salt and black pepper

4 bone-in pork chops (1 inch thick; about 2 pounds total)

2 cloves garlic, thinly sliced

1 large bunch kale, thick ribs removed and leaves roughly chopped (about 14 cups)

▸ Heat oven to 400° F. On a large rimmed baking sheet, toss the squash with the sage, 1 tablespoon of the oil, ½ teaspoon salt, and ¼ teaspoon pepper. Roast, tossing once, until tender, 30 to 35 minutes.

▸ After the squash has cooked for 20 minutes, heat 1 teaspoon of the remaining oil in a large skillet over high heat. Season the pork with ½ teaspoon salt and ¼ teaspoon pepper. Cook until browned, 3 to 5 minutes per side.

▸ Transfer the pork to the baking sheet with the squash and roast until the pork is cooked through, 6 to 8 minutes more.

▸ Meanwhile, heat the remaining tablespoon of oil in the skillet over medium heat. Add the garlic and cook, stirring, until fragrant, about 30 seconds. Add the kale, ¼ cup water, and ¼ teaspoon salt. Cook, tossing the kale and scraping up any brown bits on the bottom of the skillet, until the kale is tender, 5 to 7 minutes. Serve with the pork and squash.

TIP
When peeling butternut squash, be sure to get all the way down to the bright orange interior. Otherwise the squash may be a little tough once it's roasted.

PORK ROAST DINNER

mustard-crusted pork roast with shallots and wine sauce
hands-on time: 15 minutes / total time: 2 hours / serves 8

16 shallots, unpeeled
 3 tablespoons olive oil
    Kosher salt and black pepper
 1 6-pound bone-in center-cut pork rib roast
    (8 ribs)—chine bone removed, bones Frenched,
    at room temperature
¼ cup whole-grain mustard
 2 tablespoons Dijon mustard
 2 tablespoons chopped fresh sage
 2 cups dry white wine
½ cup sour cream
 2 tablespoons chopped fresh chives

▶ Heat oven to 400° F. In a large flameproof roasting pan, toss the shallots with 1 tablespoon of the oil and ¼ teaspoon each salt and pepper. Push toward the edges of the pan.

▶ Place the pork in the center of the roasting pan and season with 1 teaspoon salt and ½ teaspoon pepper. In a small bowl, combine the mustards, sage, and the remaining 2 tablespoons of oil; spread over the pork.

▶ Roast the pork until an instant-read thermometer inserted in the thickest part registers 145° F, 85 to 95 minutes. Transfer the shallots to a platter. Tent the pork with foil and let rest for at least 15 minutes before slicing.

▶ Place the empty roasting pan across 2 burners over medium-high heat. Add the wine and simmer, scraping up any browned bits, until syrupy, 5 to 6 minutes. Whisk in the sour cream and chives. Serve with the pork and shallots.

Parmesan polenta
hands-on time: 10 minutes / total time: 10 minutes / serves 8

    Kosher salt
 2 cups instant polenta
 1 cup grated Parmesan (4 ounces)
½ cup (1 stick) unsalted butter, cut into pieces

▶ In a large saucepan, bring 8 cups water to a boil. Add 1 tablespoon salt. Gradually whisk in the polenta.

▶ Cook over medium heat, whisking constantly, until the polenta thickens, 3 to 4 minutes. Remove from heat and stir in the Parmesan and butter.

sautéed collard greens and garlic
hands-on time: 10 minutes / total time: 25 minutes / serves 8

    Kosher salt and black pepper
 3 bunches collard greens, stems discarded and leaves
    cut into 1-inch strips
½ cup olive oil
 3 cloves garlic, thinly sliced

▶ Bring a large pot of salted water to a boil. Add the collard greens in batches and cook until just tender, about 10 minutes. Drain the greens in a colander and rinse under cold water to cool; squeeze to remove any excess water.

▶ Heat the oil in a large saucepan over medium heat. Add the garlic and cook, stirring, for 1 minute. Add the greens, 1 teaspoon salt, and ½ teaspoon pepper. Cook, tossing often, until wilted and tender, 3 to 4 minutes.

seafood chowder with crispy bread crumbs

hands-on time: 25 minutes / total time: 25 minutes / serves 4

1   slice sandwich bread, torn into pieces

3   tablespoons olive oil

2   leeks (light green and white parts only), thinly sliced

1/2   cup dry white wine

1   8-ounce bottle clam juice

1 1/2   pounds skinless cod, halibut, or sea bass fillet, cut into 2-inch pieces

12   littleneck clams and/or 1/2 pound cockles

1   cup half-and-half

Kosher salt and black pepper

2   tablespoons chopped fresh flat-leaf parsley

▸ Heat oven to 400° F. In a food processor, pulse the bread and 2 tablespoons of the oil to form coarse crumbs. Spread on a rimmed baking sheet and toast, tossing once, until golden, 6 to 8 minutes.

▸ Meanwhile, heat the remaining tablespoon of oil in a large saucepan or Dutch oven over medium-high heat. Add the leeks and cook, stirring occasionally, until tender, 4 to 5 minutes.

▸ Add the wine to the saucepan and cook until reduced by half, about 2 minutes more. Add the clam juice and 1 1/2 cups water and bring to a boil.

▸ Add the cod and clams to the saucepan, reduce heat, and simmer gently, covered, until the cod is opaque throughout and the clams have opened, 4 to 6 minutes. (Discard clams that remain closed.)

▸ Stir the half-and-half, 1/2 teaspoon salt, and 1/4 teaspoon pepper into the chowder and cook until heated through, 1 to 2 minutes. Serve sprinkled with the parsley and bread crumbs.

TIP
Before using clams or cockles, rid them of sand and grit by scrubbing them well with a stiff brush under cold running water.

roasted cod and scallions with spiced potatoes

hands-on time: 15 minutes / total time: 30 minutes / serves 4

1 pound small red potatoes (about 12), sliced $1/4$ inch thick

2 tablespoons olive oil

$1/2$ teaspoon chili powder

Kosher salt and black pepper

$1\frac{1}{2}$ pounds skinless cod, halibut, or striped bass fillet, cut into 4 pieces

2 bunches scallions, trimmed

1 lemon

▸ Heat oven to 425° F. On a rimmed baking sheet, toss the potatoes with 1 tablespoon of the oil, the chili powder, $1/2$ teaspoon salt, and $1/4$ teaspoon pepper. Roast, tossing once, until golden brown and tender, 20 to 25 minutes.

▸ Meanwhile, place the cod and scallions on a second rimmed baking sheet. Drizzle with the remaining tablespoon of oil and season with $1/2$ teaspoon salt and $1/4$ teaspoon pepper. Using a vegetable peeler, peel strips of zest from the lemon. Thinly slice the strips and sprinkle them on the cod (reserve the lemon).

▸ After the potatoes have been cooking for 10 minutes, place the baking sheet with the cod and scallions in oven and roast until the cod is opaque throughout and the scallions are tender, 12 to 15 minutes.

▸ Cut the reserved lemon in half and squeeze over the cod. Serve the cod and scallions with the potatoes.

TIP
Fresh cod should have a minimal fishy smell and be firm and springy to the touch. It keeps in the refrigerator, tightly wrapped, for up to 2 days. (Freezing cod will result in a mushy texture.)

spinach salad with salmon, barley, and oranges
hands-on time: 20 minutes / total time: 30 minutes / serves 4

$2/3$ cup quick-cooking barley

2 tablespoons plus 1 teaspoon olive oil

1 pound skinless salmon fillet, cut into 4 pieces

Kosher salt and black pepper

2 navel or blood oranges

2 tablespoons red wine vinegar

6 cups baby spinach (about 5 ounces)

$1/2$ cup fresh cilantro sprigs

$1/2$ avocado, sliced

2 scallions, thinly sliced

▸ Cook the barley according to the package directions. Spread on a plate and refrigerate until cool.

▸ Meanwhile, heat 1 teaspoon of the oil in a large cast-iron or other nonstick skillet over medium heat. Season the salmon with $1/4$ teaspoon salt and $1/8$ teaspoon pepper and cook until opaque through-out, 3 to 5 minutes per side. Transfer to a plate and refrigerate until cool. Using a fork, flake the salmon into bite-size pieces.

▸ Cut away the peel and pith of the oranges. Working over a small bowl, cut along both sides of each orange segment, releasing the segments and juice into the bowl.

▸ Transfer 2 tablespoons of the juice to a large bowl and whisk in the vinegar, the remaining 2 table-spoons of oil, $1/4$ teaspoon salt, and $1/8$ teaspoon pepper. Add the spinach, cilantro, avocado, scallions, orange segments, and cooked barley and toss to combine. Serve topped with the salmon.

TIP
Rich in fiber, barley is a delicious side dish with fish, poultry, or meat. Make a double batch and keep it in the refrigerator, covered, for up to 3 days.

creamy seafood casserole

hands-on time: 30 minutes / total time: 55 minutes / serves 4

$1/4$ cup plus 3 tablespoons olive oil

1 large onion, chopped

$1/2$ pound medium carrots (about 5), halved lengthwise and thinly sliced

$1/2$ pound medium parsnips (about 4), halved lengthwise and thinly sliced

2 stalks celery, thinly sliced

Kosher salt and black pepper

2 tablespoons all-purpose flour

$1/2$ cup dry white wine

1 cup heavy cream

$1/4$ cup chopped fresh flat-leaf parsley

$1^1/_2$ pounds waxy potatoes, peeled and quartered

$3/4$ pound skinless tilapia fillets (about 3), cut into 1-inch pieces

$1/2$ pound peeled and deveined medium shrimp (about 18), tails removed

$1/2$ cup coarse fresh bread crumbs

▸ Heat oven to 375° F. Heat 2 tablespoons of the oil in a large pot over medium heat. Add the onion, carrots, parsnips, celery, and $1/2$ teaspoon salt and cook, stirring occasionally, until tender, 15 to 18 minutes.

▸ Sprinkle the vegetables with the flour and cook, stirring, for 1 minute (do not let darken). Add the wine and cook, stirring, until nearly evaporated, 1 to 2 minutes more.

▸ Add the cream, $1/2$ teaspoon salt, and $1/4$ teaspoon pepper and bring to a boil. Remove from heat, stir in the parsley, and transfer the vegetable mixture to an 8-inch square baking dish.

▸ Meanwhile, place the potatoes in a medium saucepan and add enough cold water to cover. Add 1 teaspoon salt and bring to a boil. Reduce heat and simmer until tender, 15 to 18 minutes. Reserve $3/4$ cup of the cooking water; drain the potatoes and return them to the pot. Add $1/4$ cup of the remaining oil, $1/2$ teaspoon salt, $1/4$ teaspoon pepper, and $1/4$ cup of the reserved cooking water and mash (adding more cooking water if necessary) until smooth.

▸ Nestle the tilapia and shrimp in the vegetable mixture and top with the mashed potatoes.

▸ In a small bowl, combine the bread crumbs and the remaining tablespoon of oil; sprinkle over the potatoes. Place the baking dish on a rimmed baking sheet and bake until golden brown, 20 to 25 minutes.

TIP
To make $1/2$ cup coarse fresh bread crumbs, pulse 1 slice sandwich bread in a food processor until the crumbs have reached the right consistency.

pappardelle with beef and mushroom ragù

hands-on time: 35 minutes / total time: 1 hour, 45 minutes / serves 4

2 tablespoons olive oil

1 pound beef chuck, cut into 1-inch pieces

Kosher salt and black pepper

1 large onion, chopped

2 carrots, chopped

4 cloves garlic, smashed

1 teaspoon chopped fresh rosemary

1 tablespoon tomato paste

2 cups low-sodium chicken broth

1 15-ounce can crushed tomatoes

1 pound assorted mushrooms (such as button, cremini, and shiitake), sliced

³/₄ pound pappardelle or fettuccine

¹/₂ cup grated Parmesan (2 ounces), plus more for serving

▶ Heat 1 tablespoon of the oil in a large saucepan or Dutch oven over medium-high heat. Season the beef with ¹/₂ teaspoon salt and ¹/₄ teaspoon pepper and cook, turning occasionally, until browned on all sides, 3 to 5 minutes. Transfer to a plate.

▶ Return the saucepan to medium-high heat and heat the remaining tablespoon of oil. Add the onion, carrots, garlic, rosemary, and ¹/₄ teaspoon each salt and pepper and cook, stirring occasionally, until softened, 6 to 8 minutes. Add the tomato paste and cook, stirring, until slightly darkened, about 1 minute more.

▶ Return the beef to the saucepan and add the chicken broth and tomatoes. Reduce heat and simmer, covered, stirring occasionally, until the beef is fork-tender, 60 to 75 minutes.

▶ Add the mushrooms to the saucepan and cook, covered, stirring occasionally, until tender, 10 to 12 minutes more. If the sauce is too thin, simmer, uncovered, until thickened to the desired consistency.

▶ Meanwhile, cook the pasta according to the package directions; drain and return it to the pot. Add the beef ragù and Parmesan and toss to combine. Serve sprinkled with additional Parmesan.

TIP
The ragù can be refrigerated, covered, for up to 3 days or frozen for up to 3 months.

slow-cooker spinach and ricotta lasagna with romaine salad

hands-on time: 15 minutes / total time: 4 hours, 15 minutes / serves 6

2 10-ounce packages chopped frozen spinach, thawed and squeezed to remove excess moisture

1 cup ricotta

3/4 cup grated Parmesan (3 ounces)

3 cups marinara sauce

6 lasagna noodles (not no-boil)

1 1/2 cups grated mozzarella (6 ounces)

2 tablespoons olive oil

2 teaspoons red wine vinegar

Kosher salt and black pepper

1 small head romaine lettuce, cut into strips (about 8 cups)

1 cucumber, thinly sliced

1/2 small red onion, thinly sliced

▸ In a medium bowl, mix together the spinach, ricotta, and 1/2 cup of the Parmesan. In a second medium bowl, mix together the marinara sauce and 1/2 cup water.

▸ Spread 3/4 cup of the marinara mixture in the bottom of a 4- to 6-quart slow cooker. Top with 2 of the noodles (breaking to fit), 3/4 cup of the remaining marinara mixture, half the spinach mixture, and 1/2 cup of the mozzarella; repeat. Top with the remaining noodles, marinara mixture, mozzarella, and Parmesan. Cover and cook on low until the noodles are tender, 3 1/2 to 4 hours.

▸ In a large bowl, whisk together the oil, vinegar, 1/2 teaspoon salt, and 1/4 teaspoon pepper. Add the lettuce, cucumber, and onion and toss to coat. Serve with the lasagna.

TIP

If your slow-cooker insert is broiler-safe, try this finishing touch: Pop the cooked lasagna under the broiler until the cheese is golden, 3 to 5 minutes.

spaghetti with herbs, chilies, and fried eggs

hands-on time: 10 minutes / total time: 20 minutes / serves 4

3/4 pound spaghetti
4 tablespoons olive oil
2 cloves garlic, sliced
1 red chili pepper, sliced
1/2 cup chopped fresh herbs
4 large eggs
1/4 cup shaved Parmesan

▸ Cook the spaghetti according to the package directions. Drain and return it to the pot.

▸ Meanwhile, in a small saucepan, warm 3 tablespoons of the oil with the garlic and chili over medium-low heat until the garlic begins to sizzle, 2 to 3 minutes. Add the garlic-chili oil and herbs to the pasta and toss to combine.

▸ Heat the remaining tablespoon of oil in a large nonstick skillet over medium heat. Add the eggs and cook until the whites are set, 2 to 3 minutes. Serve on the spaghetti and sprinkle with the Parmesan.

TIP
Use your favorite herbs to dress the spaghetti, or try parsley, basil, and chives—a particularly nice combination.

ravioli with Brussels sprouts and bacon

hands-on time: 20 minutes / total time: 20 minutes / serves 4

1 pound cheese ravioli (fresh or frozen)

6 slices bacon (about 3 ounces)

3 tablespoons olive oil

1/2 cup pecans, coarsely chopped

1/2 pound Brussels sprouts, thinly sliced

Kosher salt and black pepper

1 tablespoon white wine vinegar

Grated Parmesan, for serving

▸ Cook the ravioli according to the package directions.

▸ Meanwhile, cook the bacon in a large skillet over medium-high heat until crisp, 6 to 8 minutes. Transfer to a paper towel–lined plate. Let cool, then break into pieces.

▸ Wipe out the skillet and heat 2 tablespoons of the oil over medium heat. Add the pecans and cook, stirring often, until lightly toasted, 2 to 4 minutes.

▸ Add the Brussels sprouts, 1/2 teaspoon salt, and 1/4 teaspoon pepper to the skillet and cook, tossing occasionally, until just tender, 3 to 4 minutes; stir in the vinegar. Add the bacon and toss to combine.

▸ Top the ravioli with the Brussels sprouts mixture, the remaining tablespoon of oil, and Parmesan.

TIP
When shopping for Brussels sprouts, look for clean stem ends and compact, blemish-free bright green heads no larger than an inch in diameter. (The bigger the sprout, the more bitter it tends to be.)

parsnip and fennel soup with dill

hands-on time: 30 minutes / total time: 35 minutes / serves 4

2 tablespoons olive oil

2 leeks (white and light green parts), halved lengthwise and sliced crosswise

2 medium parsnips, peeled and cut into 1/4-inch pieces

1 large bulb fennel, cored and cut into 1/4-inch pieces

Kosher salt and black pepper

1/2 cup dry white wine

2 Yukon gold potatoes (about 1 pound), peeled and cut into 1/2-inch pieces

5 cups low-sodium vegetable or chicken broth

1 small baguette, split horizontally

2 ounces grated Gruyère or Swiss cheese (1/2 cup)

1/4 cup chopped fresh dill

▸ Heat the oil in a large pot or Dutch oven over medium heat. Add the leeks, parsnips, fennel, 3/4 teaspoon salt, and 1/4 teaspoon pepper and cook, stirring occasionally, until the vegetables begin to soften, 6 to 8 minutes.

▸ Add the wine, reduce heat, and simmer until evaporated, 1 to 2 minutes.

▸ Add the potatoes and broth and bring to a boil. Reduce heat and simmer until the potatoes are tender, 12 to 15 minutes. Transfer half the mixture to a blender and puree until smooth; return it to the pot.

▸ Meanwhile, heat broiler. Place the baguette, cut-side up, on a baking sheet and sprinkle with the Gruyère. Broil until the cheese has melted, then cut the baguette into pieces. Sprinkle the soup with the dill and serve with the cheese toast.

TIP
The soup can be refrigerated for up to 3 days or frozen for up to 3 months.

cauliflower and chickpea stew with couscous

hands-on time: 25 minutes / total time: 35 minutes / serves 4

2 tablespoons olive oil

1 medium onion, chopped

1½ teaspoons ground cumin

½ teaspoon ground ginger

Kosher salt and black pepper

1 28-ounce can whole peeled tomatoes

1 15-ounce can chickpeas, rinsed

1 head cauliflower, cored and cut into small florets

½ cup raisins

1 5-ounce package baby spinach, chopped

1 cup couscous

▶ Heat the oil in a large saucepan or Dutch oven over medium heat. Add the onion and cook, stirring occasionally, until beginning to soften, 4 to 5 minutes. Add the cumin, ginger, ½ teaspoon salt, and ¼ teaspoon pepper and cook, stirring, until fragrant, 1 minute more.

▶ Add the tomatoes and their juices (crush the tomatoes with your hands as you add them), chickpeas, cauliflower, raisins, and ½ cup water to the saucepan and bring to a boil.

▶ Reduce heat and simmer the vegetables, stirring occasionally, until they are tender and the liquid has thickened slightly, 15 to 20 minutes. Fold in the spinach and cook until just wilted, 1 to 2 minutes more.

▶ Meanwhile, place the couscous in a large bowl. Add 1 cup hot tap water, cover, and let sit for 5 minutes; fluff with a fork. Serve with the stew.

TIP
To add extra protein to this satisfying stew, sprinkle it with sliced almonds.

black bean and sweet potato enchiladas
hands-on time: 30 minutes / total time: 45 minutes / serves 4

1 28-ounce can whole peeled tomatoes

2 teaspoons chili powder

1 large onion, chopped

3 tablespoons canola oil
   Kosher salt and black pepper

2 cloves garlic, chopped

1 15.5-ounce can black beans, rinsed

1 medium sweet potato (about $^1/_2$ pound), peeled and coarsely grated

2 teaspoons dried oregano

8 ounces Cheddar, grated (2 cups)

8 6-inch flour tortillas

2 scallions, thinly sliced and white and green parts separated

2 cups frozen corn

▶ Heat oven to 450° F. In a blender, puree the tomatoes (and their juices), chili powder, half the onion, 1 tablespoon of the oil, $^1/_2$ teaspoon salt, and $^1/_4$ teaspoon pepper until smooth.

▶ Heat 1 tablespoon of the remaining oil in a large skillet over medium-high heat. Add the remaining onion and half the garlic and cook until softened, 2 to 3 minutes. Add the beans, sweet potato, oregano, and $^1/_4$ teaspoon each salt and pepper and cook, tossing frequently, until the sweet potatoes are tender, 4 to 6 minutes. Transfer to a large bowl and let cool. Fold in 1 cup of the Cheddar.

▶ Spread 1 cup of the tomato mixture in the bottom of a 9-by-13-inch baking dish. Roll up the bean mixture in the tortillas (about $^1/_2$ cup each) and place the rolls seam-side down in the dish. Top with the remaining tomato sauce and Cheddar. Bake on the top rack of oven until the Cheddar is brown and bubbly, 10 to 15 minutes.

▶ Meanwhile, wipe out the skillet and heat the remaining tablespoon of oil over medium-high heat. Add the remaining garlic and the scallion whites and cook, stirring, until fragrant, about 1 minute. Add the corn and $^1/_4$ teaspoon each salt and pepper and cook, tossing frequently, until tender, 3 to 5 minutes more. Sprinkle the enchiladas with the scallion greens and serve with the corn.

TIP
For a bit of heat, serve the enchiladas with some chopped pickled jalapeño peppers and a dash of hot sauce.

flaky mushroom and Gruyère tarts
hands-on time: 20 minutes / total time: 45 minutes / serves 4

1 sheet frozen puff pastry (half a 17.3-ounce package), thawed

4 tablespoons olive oil

10 ounces assorted mushrooms (such as button, cremini, shiitake, and oyster), sliced

1 shallot, sliced

Kosher salt and black pepper

¹/₄ cup dry white wine

4 ounces Gruyère or sharp white Cheddar, grated (1 cup)

1 teaspoon Dijon mustard

1 teaspoon white wine vinegar

6 cups mixed greens (about ¹/₄ pound)

2 radishes, thinly sliced

1 tablespoon chopped fresh chives

▶ Heat oven to 400° F. Line a baking sheet with parchment. Unfold the pastry and cut it into 4 squares. Place the squares on the prepared baking sheet and, using a fork, prick the dough all over.

▶ Heat 2 tablespoons of the oil in a large skillet over medium-high heat. Add the mushrooms, shallot, ¹/₂ teaspoon salt, and ¹/₄ teaspoon pepper and cook, tossing occasionally, until the mushrooms are browned and tender, 4 to 5 minutes. Add the wine and cook until it has nearly evaporated, about 1 minute more.

▶ Dividing evenly, sprinkle the pastry squares with half the Gruyère, leaving a ¹/₂-inch border on each. Top with the mushroom mixture and the remaining Gruyère. Bake until the pastry is golden brown, 20 to 25 minutes.

▶ In a large bowl, whisk together the mustard, vinegar, the remaining 2 tablespoons of oil, and ¹/₄ teaspoon each salt and pepper. Add the greens and radishes and toss to coat. Sprinkle the tarts with the chives and serve with the salad.

TIP
To clean mushrooms, trim the ends, then rinse them briefly, stem-side down, under cold running water. (Do not let them soak or they will become soggy.) Pat dry with a paper towel or a clean dishcloth.

sautéed escarole and leeks

hands-on time: 20 minutes / total time: 20 minutes / serves 8

¼ cup olive oil

4 leeks (white and light green parts), halved lengthwise and sliced crosswise

4 cloves garlic, sliced

¼ teaspoon crushed red pepper

Kosher salt and black pepper

2 heads escarole, torn into 3-inch pieces (about 20 cups)

▶ Heat the oil in a large pot over medium-high heat. Add the leeks and garlic and cook, stirring often, until softened, 6 to 8 minutes.

▶ Season with the red pepper, ¾ teaspoon salt, and ¼ teaspoon black pepper. Add the escarole to the pot in batches, tossing and adding more as room becomes available, and cook until tender and beginning to wilt, 3 to 4 minutes.

TIP

Leeks can be gritty. To clean them thoroughly, halve the stalks and thinly slice, then swish them around in a bowl of cold water a few times. Lift them out with loosely cupped hands (leaving the sand behind), change the water, and repeat until the water is clear.

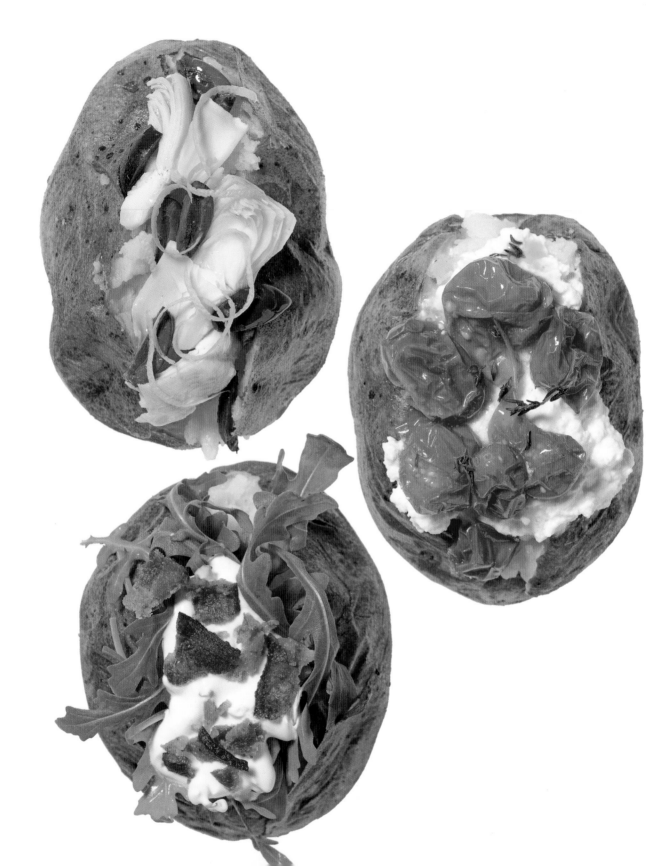

3 IDEAS FOR BAKED POTATOES

baked potatoes with artichokes, olives, and lemon

hands-on time: 10 minutes
total time: 1 hour, 25 minutes
serves 4

- 4 medium russet potatoes (about 2 pounds)
- 1 teaspoon olive oil
- 1 cup oil-packed artichoke hearts, quartered, plus $1/4$ cup of the packing oil
- $1^1/4$ cup kalamata olives, slivered
- $1^1/2$ teaspoons grated lemon zest

▸ Heat oven to 400° F. Rub the potatoes with the oil. Place them on a rimmed baking sheet and bake, turning occasionally, until tender and easily pierced with a paring knife, 65 to 75 minutes.

▸ In a small bowl, combine the artichoke hearts and their oil, the olives, and lemon zest. Split the potatoes and, dividing evenly, top with the artichoke mixture.

baked potatoes with ricotta and roasted tomatoes

hands-on time: 10 minutes
total time: 1 hour, 25 minutes
serves 4

- 4 medium russet potatoes (about 2 pounds)
- 1 tablespoon plus 1 teaspoon olive oil
- 1 pint grape tomatoes
- 4 sprigs fresh thyme
  Kosher salt and black pepper
- $1/2$ cup ricotta

▸ Heat oven to 400° F. Rub the potatoes with 1 teaspoon of the oil. Place them on a rimmed baking sheet and bake, turning occasionally, until tender and easily pierced with a paring knife, 65 to 75 minutes.

▸ Fifteen minutes before the potatoes are done, on a large rimmed baking sheet, toss the tomatoes with the thyme, the remaining tablespoon of oil, 1 teaspoon salt, and $1/4$ teaspoon pepper. Roast, tossing occasionally, until the tomatoes have burst, 12 to 15 minutes.

▸ Split the potatoes and, dividing evenly, top with the ricotta and the tomato mixture.

baked potatoes with arugula, sour cream, and bacon

hands-on time: 10 minutes
total time: 1 hour, 25 minutes
serves 4

- 4 medium russet potatoes (about 2 pounds)
- 1 teaspoon olive oil
- 8 slices bacon (about $1/4$ pound)
- 1 cup baby arugula leaves
- $1/2$ cup sour cream

▸ Heat oven to 400° F. Rub the potatoes with the oil. Place them on a rimmed baking sheet and bake, turning occasionally, until tender and easily pierced with a paring knife, 65 to 75 minutes.

▸ Meanwhile, in a medium skillet, cook the bacon over medium heat until crisp, 6 to 8 minutes. Transfer to a paper towel–lined plate. Let cool, then crumble.

▸ Split the potatoes and, dividing evenly, top with the arugula, sour cream, and bacon.

spinach and Gruyère gratin

hands-on time: 30 minutes / total time: 1 hour, 25 minutes / serves 8

1 tablespoon olive oil, plus more for the baking dish

6 shallots, thinly sliced

Kosher salt and black pepper

1 cup dry white wine

6 large eggs

1 cup heavy cream

1 cup whole milk

1/4 teaspoon ground nutmeg

4 10-ounce packages frozen spinach, thawed and squeezed to remove excess moisture

8 ounces Gruyère, grated (2 cups)

1/2 cup grated Parmesan (2 ounces)

▸ Heat oven to 400° F. Coat a shallow 2 1/2- to 3-quart baking dish with oil; set aside.

▸ Heat the oil in a large skillet over medium-high heat. Add the shallots, 1/2 teaspoon salt, and 1/4 teaspoon pepper. Cook, stirring occasionally, until soft, 6 to 8 minutes. Add the wine and simmer until evaporated, 4 to 6 minutes.

▸ In a large bowl, whisk together the eggs, cream, milk, nutmeg, 1/2 teaspoon salt, and 1/4 teaspoon pepper. Stir in the spinach, shallot mixture, Gruyère, and Parmesan. Transfer to the prepared baking dish.

▸ Bake until the spinach mixture is bubbling and the top is golden brown, 45 to 55 minutes.

TIP
The gratin can be prepared (but not baked) and refrigerated, covered, up to 1 day in advance. Bring to room temperature, then bake as directed, adding 5 to 10 minutes to the cooking time.

6 IDEAS FOR BIG-BATCH HOLIDAY COCKTAILS

vodka cranberry cooler
hands-on time: 15 minutes
total time: 40 minutes / serves 20

4 12-ounce bags cranberries
   (fresh or frozen)
4 cups sugar
3 liters tonic water
1 liter vodka
1 cup fresh lime juice
2 cups cream soda (optional)

▸ In a large saucepan, combine
the cranberries, sugar, and 2 cups
water; bring to a boil. Reduce
heat and simmer for 5 minutes.

▸ Using a slotted spoon, transfer
3 cups of the cranberries to a large
bowl, then strain the remaining
syrup into the bowl; let cool.

▸ Add the tonic water, vodka, and
lime juice to the cranberry syrup.
Serve over ice and top off with
a splash of cream soda, if desired.

tequila grapefruit splash
hands-on time: 5 minutes
total time: 5 minutes / serves 20

2 quarts fresh pink grapefruit juice
2 liters ginger ale
1 liter tequila
³/₄ cup Campari
¹/₄ cup Triple Sec

▸ In a large bowl, combine the
grapefruit juice, ginger ale,
tequila, Campari, and Triple Sec.
Serve over ice.

pineapple mint punch
hands-on time: 10 minutes
total time: 35 minutes / serves 20

¹/₂ cup sugar
3 quarts pineapple juice
1 liter gin
1 liter club soda
1 cup fresh lime juice
1 cup fresh mint leaves

▸ In a small saucepan, combine
the sugar and ¹/₂ cup water;
bring to a boil. Reduce heat and
simmer until the sugar dissolves,
1 to 2 minutes; let cool.

▸ In a large bowl, combine the
sugar syrup, pineapple juice, gin,
club soda, lime juice, and mint.
Serve over ice.

bourbon ginger snap

hands-on time: 10 minutes
total time: 35 minutes / serves 20

1 cup fresh lemon juice, plus
  2 lemons, thinly sliced

1 cup honey

1 3-inch piece fresh ginger, peeled
  and sliced

6 cups fresh orange juice

4 cups pear nectar

1 liter bourbon

  Orange zest twists, for serving

▸ In a large saucepan, combine
the lemon juice, honey, ginger,
and 2 quarts water; bring to
a boil.

▸ Reduce heat and simmer
for 5 minutes. Strain into a large
bowl; let cool.

▸ Add the orange juice, pear nectar, bourbon, and lemons to the
bowl. Serve over ice, garnished
with orange zest twists.

spiked sparkling cider

hands-on time: 5 minutes
total time: 5 minutes / serves 20

4 bottles cold Prosecco (or some
  other dry sparkling wine)

6 cups cold apple juice

³/₄ cup cinnamon schnapps
  (such as Goldschlager)

▸ In a large bowl, combine the
Prosecco, apple juice, and
cinnamon schnapps. Serve
immediately.

winter sangria

hands-on time: 20 minutes
total time: 20 minutes / serves 20

3 bottles fruity red wine
  (such as Pinot Noir or
  Cabernet Sauvignon)

2 liters black cherry soda

1¹/₂ cups pomegranate juice

³/₄ cup brandy

¹/₂ cup Triple Sec

4 pears, cored and thinly sliced

2 oranges, thinly sliced

▸ In a large bowl, combine the
wine, cherry soda, pomegranate
juice, brandy, Triple Sec, pears,
and oranges. Serve over ice.

hazelnut ganache tart with sea salt
hands-on time: 25 minutes / total time: 3 hours (includes chilling) / serves 10

¾ cup hazelnuts

1½ cups crushed chocolate wafer cookies (from about 30 cookies)

6 tablespoons (¾ stick) unsalted butter, melted

1½ cups heavy cream

¾ pound semisweet chocolate, chopped

1 teaspoon flaky sea salt

▸ Heat oven to 350° F. Spread the hazelnuts on a large rimmed baking sheet and toast, tossing occasionally, until fragrant, 10 to 12 minutes. Rub the warm nuts in a clean dish towel to remove the skins (discard the skins). Let cool.

▸ In a food processor, finely grind ½ cup of the hazelnuts. Add the crushed cookies and butter and pulse until moistened. Press the mixture into the bottom and up the sides of a 9-inch removable-bottom fluted tart pan.

▸ Place the tart pan on a rimmed baking sheet and bake until the crust is dry, 10 to 12 minutes. (If it puffs up during baking, gently press it down with the back of a spoon.) Let cool in the pan on a wire rack.

▸ Meanwhile, in a medium saucepan, bring the cream just to a boil. Remove from heat and whisk in the chocolate until smooth. Pour into the cooled tart shell. Refrigerate until set, about 2 hours.

▸ Coarsely chop the remaining ¼ cup of hazelnuts and sprinkle on the tart.

▸ Just before serving, sprinkle the tart with the salt. For the easiest slicing, use a thin, sharp knife, wiping it clean and running it under hot water between slices.

TIP
The tart can be made up to 2 days in advance (omit the sea salt). Refrigerate, covered. Bring to room temperature and sprinkle with the salt before serving.

chewy spice cookies
hands-on time: 30 minutes / total time: 1 hour, 15 minutes (includes cooling) / makes 42 cookies

2 cups all-purpose flour, spooned and leveled

2 teaspoons ground ginger

1½ teaspoons baking soda

½ teaspoon ground cinnamon

½ teaspoon kosher salt

¼ teaspoon black pepper

¼ teaspoon ground nutmeg

⅛ teaspoon ground cloves

¾ cup vegetable shortening (preferably trans fat–free)

⅔ cup packed light brown sugar

1 large egg

½ cup molasses

1 teaspoon pure vanilla extract

¼ cup granulated sugar, plus more for sprinkling

▶ Heat oven to 350° F. Line 2 baking sheets with parchment. In a medium bowl, whisk together the flour, ginger, baking soda, cinnamon, salt, pepper, nutmeg, and cloves; set aside.

▶ Using an electric mixer, beat the shortening and brown sugar on medium-high speed until fluffy, 2 to 3 minutes. Reduce speed to low and beat in the egg, molasses, and vanilla. Gradually add the flour mixture and mix just until combined (do not overmix).

▶ Place the granulated sugar on a plate. Shape the dough into balls (about a heaping tablespoon each). A few at a time, roll in the sugar to coat. Place the balls 2 inches apart on the prepared baking sheets. Using a glass, press the balls to a ⅜-inch thickness and sprinkle with more granulated sugar.

▶ Bake the cookies, rotating the baking sheets halfway through, until the edges are firm, 10 to 12 minutes. Cool slightly on the baking sheets, then transfer to wire racks to cool completely. Store in an airtight container at room temperature for up to 5 days.

TIP
For extra sparkle and texture, sprinkle the unbaked cookies with turbinado sugar—sometimes labeled raw sugar—in place of granulated.

praline-topped blondies

hands-on time: 15 minutes / total time: 2 hours, 15 minutes (includes cooling) / makes 16

BLONDIES

Nonstick cooking spray

1 cup all-purpose flour, spooned and leveled

1 teaspoon baking powder

1 teaspoon kosher salt

8 tablespoons (1 stick) unsalted butter

1 cup packed light brown sugar

1 teaspoon pure vanilla extract

2 large eggs

TOPPING

3 tablespoons light brown sugar

2 tablespoons unsalted butter

1 cup confectioners' sugar

1 teaspoon pure vanilla extract

½ cup chopped pecans

▸ Heat oven to 350° F. Spray an 8-inch square baking pan with the cooking spray. Line the pan with 2 crisscrossed strips of parchment, spraying between the layers (to hold them in place) and leaving an overhang on each side.

▸ Make the blondies: In a medium bowl, whisk together the flour, baking powder, and salt; set aside.

▸ In a medium saucepan, melt the butter over medium-low heat. Remove from heat and mix in the brown sugar and vanilla. One at a time, mix in the eggs. Gradually add the flour mixture and mix until just combined (do not overmix).

▸ Spread the batter in the prepared pan and bake until a toothpick inserted in the center comes out with moist crumbs clinging to it, 25 to 28 minutes. Cool completely in the pan.

▸ Make the topping: In a small saucepan, heat the brown sugar and butter over medium heat, stirring occasionally, until bubbling, about 2 minutes. Remove from heat and whisk in the confectioners' sugar, vanilla, and 1 tablespoon water until smooth. Spread over the cooled blondies and sprinkle with the pecans. Let the topping set, 10 to 15 minutes.

▸ Holding both sides of the paper overhang, lift the blondies out of the pan and transfer to a cutting board. Cut into 16 squares. Store in an airtight container at room temperature for up to 5 days.

TIP
Chocolate lover? Mix 1 cup chocolate chips into the batter.

double-chocolate profiteroles

hands-on time: 20 minutes / total time: 1 hour, 20 minutes (includes cooling) / serves 8

$1/2$ cup (1 stick) unsalted butter, cut into pieces
1 tablespoon sugar
$1/4$ teaspoon kosher salt
1 cup all-purpose flour, spooned and leveled
5 large eggs
2 pints chocolate ice cream
    Dark Chocolate Sauce (right)

▸ Heat oven to 400° F. In a medium saucepan, combine the butter, sugar, salt, and 1 cup water. Bring to a boil, stirring to melt the butter. Remove from heat and stir in the flour.

▸ Cook the flour mixture over medium heat, stirring constantly, until it pulls away from the sides of the pan, about 1 minute. Let cool for 5 minutes.

▸ One at a time, add 4 of the eggs to the saucepan, mixing well after each addition. The batter should be shiny and smooth and hold its shape on a spoon.

▸ Using one soup spoon to scoop the dough and another to scrape it off, drop mounds of dough (about 1 tablespoon each) 2 inches apart on parchment-lined baking sheets (you should get about 24). In a small bowl, beat the remaining egg; brush it over the dough.

▸ Bake the profiteroles, rotating the baking sheets halfway through, until puffed and golden, 25 to 30 minutes. Let cool completely on the baking sheets.

▸ Cut the profiteroles in half horizontally, fill with the ice cream, and drizzle with the Dark Chocolate Sauce. (They can be baked up to 1 day in advance and kept in an airtight container at room temperature.)

dark chocolate sauce

hands-on time: 5 minutes / total time: 5 minutes makes 1 cup

$1/2$ cup sugar
$1/4$ cup unsweetened cocoa powder
$1/4$ pound semisweet chocolate, chopped

▸ In a small saucepan, whisk together the sugar, cocoa powder, and $1/2$ cup water. Bring to a boil.

▸ Remove the pan from heat and whisk in the chocolate until smooth. (The sauce can be made up to 2 weeks in advance. Refrigerate, covered; reheat before serving.)

raspberry-almond Linzer cookies
hands-on time: 1 hour / total time: 5 hours (includes chilling) / makes 36

²/₃ cup almonds

¹/₂ cup packed light brown sugar

2¹/₂ cups all-purpose flour, spooned and leveled, plus more for the work surface

¹/₂ teaspoon baking powder

¹/₂ teaspoon kosher salt

¹/₄ teaspoon ground cinnamon

1 cup (2 sticks) unsalted butter, at room temperature

1 large egg

1 teaspoon pure vanilla extract

1 tablespoon confectioners' sugar

1 12-ounce jar raspberry jam

▸ Heat oven to 350° F. Spread the almonds on a baking sheet and toast, tossing occasionally, until fragrant, 6 to 8 minutes; let cool. In a food processor, finely grind the almonds with ¹/₄ cup of the brown sugar. In a medium bowl, whisk together the flour, baking powder, salt, and cinnamon; set aside.

▸ Using an electric mixer, beat the butter and the remaining ¹/₄ cup of brown sugar on medium-high speed until fluffy, 2 to 3 minutes. Beat in the egg and vanilla. Reduce speed to low and gradually add the almond mixture, then the flour mixture, mixing until just combined (do not overmix). Shape the dough into two disks, tightly wrap, and refrigerate until firm, at least 3 hours.

▸ Heat oven to 350° F. Line 2 baking sheets with parchment. On a lightly floured surface, roll each disk of dough to a ¹/₈-inch thickness. Using a 2- to 2¹/₂-inch round cookie cutter, cut out rounds and place 1 inch apart on the prepared baking sheets. Using a ³/₄- to 1-inch round cookie cutter, cut the centers out of half the cookies. Reroll and cut the scraps as necessary.

▸ Bake the cookies, rotating the baking sheets halfway through, until the edges are golden, 10 to 12 minutes. Cool slightly on the baking sheets, then transfer to wire racks to cool completely.

▸ Sprinkle the confectioners' sugar on the cookies with the holes. Spread 1 teaspoon of the jam on each of the remaining cookies; top with the sugared cookies. Store in an airtight container at room temperature for up to 5 days.

TIP
Giving these treats as a present? To keep the confectioners' sugar from getting all over the gift tin, line the tin with wax paper and use more to separate the layers of cookies.

helpful info

A by-the-numbers guide to what's in every recipe.

RECIPE KEY

🕐 30 MINUTES OR LESS
❤ HEART-HEALTHY
🍲 ONE-POT MEAL
🌱 VEGETARIAN
✖ NO-COOK
🧸 FAMILY-FRIENDLY

spring

STARTERS

9 shrimp with tarragon mayonnaise
PER SERVING: 252 calories; 18g fat (3g saturated fat); 146mg cholesterol; 810mg sodium; 15g protein; 7g carbohydrates; 5g sugar; 1g fiber; 2mg iron; 34mg calcium.
🕐 ✖

10 tomatillo and avocado dip
PER TABLESPOON: 11 calories; 1g fat (0g saturated fat); 0mg cholesterol; 61mg sodium; 0g protein; 1g carbohydrates; 0g sugar; 0g fiber; 0mg iron; 2mg calcium.
🕐 ❤ 🌱 ✖

10 lemon, pepper, and pecorino dip
PER TABLESPOON: 35 calories; 3g fat (2g saturated fat); 10mg cholesterol; 74mg sodium; 1g protein; 0g carbohydrates; 0g sugar; 0g fiber; 0mg iron; 44mg calcium.
🕐 ❤ 🌱 ✖

10 spinach and white bean dip
PER TABLESPOON: 29 calories; 2g fat (0g saturated fat); 0mg cholesterol; 77mg sodium; 0g protein; 2g carbohydrates; 0g sugar; 0g fiber; 0mg iron; 5mg calcium.
🕐 ❤ 🌱 🧸

11 Feta and sun-dried tomato dip
PER TABLESPOON: 34 calories; 3g fat (1g saturated fat); 5mg cholesterol; 102mg sodium; 2g protein; 1g carbohydrates; 1g sugar; 0g fiber; 0mg iron; 35mg calcium.
🕐 ❤ 🌱 ✖ 🧸

11 roasted eggplant and basil dip
PER TABLESPOON: 15 calories; 1g fat (0g saturated fat); 0mg cholesterol; 46mg sodium; 0g protein; 2g carbohydrates; 1g sugar; 1g fiber; 0mg iron; 4mg calcium.
❤ 🌱

11 curried yogurt and lime dip
PER TABLESPOON: 10 calories; 0g fat (0g saturated fat); 1mg cholesterol; 44mg sodium; 1g protein; 1g carbohydrates; 1g sugar; 0g fiber; 0mg iron; 17mg calcium.
❤ 🌱 ✖

13 roasted red pepper canapés
PER 3-CHIP SERVING: 108 calories; 9g fat (1g saturated fat); 0mg cholesterol; 243mg sodium; 2g protein; 5g carbohydrates; 1g sugar; 1g fiber; 1mg iron; 15mg calcium.
🕐 🌱

13 goat cheese and red pepper quesadillas
PER 2-WEDGE SERVING: 226 calories; 13g fat (7g saturated fat); 22mg cholesterol; 706mg sodium; 9g protein; 18g carbohydrates; 3g sugar; 1g fiber; 2mg iron; 129mg calcium.
🕐 🌱 🧸

13 crudités with red pepper aïoli
PER ¼-CUP SERVING: 55 calories; 1g fat (1g saturated fat); 4mg cholesterol; 207mg sodium; 6g protein; 5g carbohydrates; 4g sugar; 0g fiber; 0mg iron; 69mg calcium.
🕐 🌱 ✖

POULTRY

15 roasted turkey with Cheddar-stuffed potatoes
PER SERVING (INCLUDES 5 OUNCES OF COOKED TURKEY): 597 calories; 27g fat (15g saturated fat); 175mg cholesterol; 778mg sodium; 54g protein; 34g carbohydrates; 4g sugar; 7g fiber; 5mg iron; 403mg calcium.
🧸

17 chicken with white beans and tomatoes
PER SERVING: 624 calories; 35g fat (9g saturated fat); 168mg cholesterol; 808mg sodium; 51g protein; 22g carbohydrates; 2g sugar; 6g fiber; 5mg iron; 85mg calcium.
🍲 🧸

19 oven-"fried" chicken with crunchy broccoli slaw
PER SERVING: 566 calories; 24g fat (6g saturated fat); 158mg cholesterol; 1,075mg sodium; 54g protein; 31g carbohydrates; 9g sugar; 4g fiber; 4mg iron; 201mg calcium.
🧸

21 red curry chicken skewers
PER SERVING: 454 calories; 10g fat (3g saturated fat); 94mg cholesterol; 495mg sodium; 40g protein; 47g carbohydrates; 3g sugar; 3g fiber; 4mg iron; 87mg calcium.

23 sweet and spicy chicken with soba salad
PER SERVING: 541 calories; 12g fat (2g saturated fat); 94mg cholesterol; 576mg sodium; 44g protein; 65g carbohydrates; 32g sugar; 5g fiber; 3mg iron; 35mg calcium.

25 turkey burgers with creamy romaine slaw
PER SERVING: 376 calories; 19g fat (4g saturated fat); 69mg cholesterol; 750mg sodium; 27g protein; 25g carbohydrates; 4g sugar; 2g fiber; 4mg iron; 92mg calcium.

BEEF & LAMB

27 beef quesadillas with watercress and corn salad
PER SERVING: 612 calories; 37g fat (13g saturated fat); 88mg cholesterol; 965mg sodium; 32g protein; 37g carbohydrates; 2g sugar; 3g fiber; 4mg iron; 442mg calcium.

29 steak salad with bacon, potatoes, and blue cheese dressing
PER SERVING: 539 calories; 31g fat (13g saturated fat); 108mg cholesterol; 1,004mg sodium; 45g protein; 17g carbohydrates; 5g sugar; 3g fiber; 4mg iron; 234mg calcium.

31 lamb kebabs with lima bean salad
PER SERVING: 409 calories; 19g fat (4g saturated fat); 54mg cholesterol; 688mg sodium; 25g protein; 33g carbohydrates; 2g sugar; 8g fiber; 3mg iron; 124mg calcium.

33 slow-cooker chipotle beef tacos with cabbage-radish slaw
PER SERVING: 431 calories; 12g fat (4g saturated fat); 95mg cholesterol; 573mg sodium; 51g protein; 30g carbohydrates; 3g sugar; 6g fiber; 5mg iron; 98mg calcium.

35 spicy hoisin skirt steak with cucumber salad
PER SERVING: 444 calories; 20g fat (6g saturated fat); 79mg cholesterol; 458mg sodium; 40g protein; 26g carbohydrates; 5g sugar; 3g fiber; 5mg iron; 50mg calcium.

PORK

37 chipotle pork loin with black bean salad
PER SERVING: 511 calories; 27g fat (5g saturated fat); 98mg cholesterol; 1,106mg sodium; 44g protein; 27g carbohydrates; 2g sugar; 11g fiber; 5mg iron; 68mg calcium.

39 oven-"fried" pork cutlets with fennel-chickpea slaw
PER SERVING: 420 calories; 19g fat (4g saturated fat); 65mg cholesterol; 850mg sodium; 35g protein; 32g carbohydrates; 2g sugar; 7g fiber; 3mg iron; 127mg calcium.

41 deep-dish pepperoni pizza with arugula salad
PER SERVING: 528 calories; 29g fat (10g saturated fat); 50mg cholesterol; 1,356mg sodium; 23g protein; 44g carbohydrates; 5g sugar; 3g fiber; 4mg iron; 364mg calcium.

43 pork chops with tangy rhubarb chutney
PER SERVING: 381 calories; 20g fat (5g saturated fat); 92mg cholesterol; 674mg sodium; 36g protein; 15g carbohydrates; 11g sugar; 2g fiber; 2mg iron; 104mg calcium.

SEAFOOD

45 seared salmon with potato and watercress salad
PER SERVING: 497 calories; 26g fat (4g saturated fat); 108mg cholesterol; 723mg sodium; 42g protein; 22g carbohydrates; 1g sugar; 2g fiber; 3mg iron; 54mg calcium.

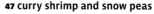

47 curry shrimp and snow peas
PER SERVING: 621 calories; 29g fat (20g saturated fat); 259mg cholesterol; 722mg sodium; 42g protein; 49g carbohydrates; 1g sugar; 3g fiber; 10mg iron; 146mg calcium.

49 roasted tilapia, potatoes, and lemons
PER SERVING: 374 calories; 15g fat (3g saturated fat); 85mg cholesterol; 567mg sodium; 37g protein; 23g carbohydrates; 0g sugar; 2g fiber; 3mg iron; 34mg calcium.

51 lemony baked salmon with asparagus and bulgur
PER SERVING: 375 calories; 11g fat (2g saturated fat); 90mg cholesterol; 491mg sodium; 38g protein; 32g carbohydrates; 2g sugar; 8g fiber; 4mg iron; 58mg calcium.

PASTA

53 shrimp, leek, and spinach pasta
PER SERVING: 691 calories; 26g fat (15g saturated fat); 249mg cholesterol; 791mg sodium; 38g protein; 80g carbohydrates; 5g sugar; 7g fiber; 9mg iron; 184mg calcium.

55 pesto orecchiette with chicken sausage
PER SERVING: 666 calories; 26g fat (7g saturated fat); 67mg cholesterol; 913mg sodium; 32g protein; 76g carbohydrates; 5g sugar; 9g fiber; 4mg iron; 291mg calcium.

56 spaghetti primavera with basil
PER SERVING: 484 calories; 16g fat (2g saturated fat); 0mg cholesterol; 264mg sodium; 15g protein; 72g carbohydrates; 3g sugar; 7g fiber; 4mg iron; 64mg calcium.

56 peanut noodles with snap peas and cabbage
PER SERVING: 529 calories; 22g fat (4g saturated fat); 0mg cholesterol; 1,561mg sodium; 21g protein; 66g carbohydrates; 15g sugar; 7g fiber; 4mg iron; 66mg calcium.

57 spaghetti with ricotta and roasted tomatoes
PER SERVING: 492 calories; 12g fat (6g saturated fat); 32mg cholesterol; 427mg sodium; 21g protein; 73g carbohydrates; 3g sugar; 5g fiber; 4mg iron; 154mg calcium.

57 spaghetti with pesto and shrimp
PER SERVING: 678 calories; 27g fat (5g saturated fat); 228mg cholesterol; 822mg sodium; 41g protein; 67g carbohydrates; 1g sugar; 5g fiber; 7mg iron; 211mg calcium.

59 pappardelle with Swiss chard, onions, and goat cheese
PER SERVING: 419 calories; 13g fat (5g saturated fat); 13mg cholesterol; 765mg sodium; 18g protein; 57g carbohydrates; 3g sugar; 7g fiber; 7mg iron; 140mg calcium.

VEGETARIAN

61 quinoa and vegetable salad with tahini dressing
PER SERVING: 376 calories; 15g fat (2g saturated fat); 0mg cholesterol; 345mg sodium; 17g protein; 48g carbohydrates; 9g sugar; 8g fiber; 7mg iron; 157mg calcium.

63 asparagus and ricotta pizzas
PER PIZZA: 621 calories; 29g fat (11g saturated fat); 57mg cholesterol; 1,335mg sodium; 29g protein; 62g carbohydrates; 4g sugar; 4g fiber; 5mg iron; 433mg calcium.

65 baked spinach and pea risotto
PER SERVING: 309 calories; 8g fat (5g saturated fat); 20mg cholesterol; 774mg sodium; 10g protein; 48g carbohydrates; 4g sugar; 5g fiber; 2mg iron; 154mg calcium.

67 Thai curry vegetable and tofu soup
PER SERVING: 348 calories; 26g fat (19g saturated fat); 0mg cholesterol; 729mg sodium; 14g protein; 17g carbohydrates; 4g sugar; 5g fiber; 7mg iron; 258mg calcium.

SIDE DISHES

69 baked stuffed artichokes with pecorino
PER SERVING: 225 calories; 11g fat (4g saturated fat); 9mg cholesterol; 712mg sodium; 9g protein; 23g carbohydrates; 2g sugar; 4g fiber; 2mg iron; 218mg calcium.

70 pea, Feta, and crispy prosciutto salad
PER SERVING: 188 calories; 12g fat (4g saturated fat); 24mg cholesterol; 805mg sodium; 10g protein; 13g carbohydrates; 5g sugar; 4g fiber; 2mg iron; 94mg calcium.

70 roasted potatoes and lemon with dill
PER SERVING: 250 calories; 7g fat (1g saturated fat); 0mg cholesterol; 374mg sodium; 5g protein; 41g carbohydrates; 0g sugar; 3g fiber; 2mg iron; 2mg calcium.

71 roasted asparagus with olive vinaigrette
PER SERVING: 162 calories; 14g fat (2g saturated fat); 0mg cholesterol; 595mg sodium; 3g protein; 6g carbohydrates; 2g sugar; 3g fiber; 3mg iron; 38mg calcium.

71 gingery sautéed watercress and shiitakes
PER SERVING: 94 calories; 8g fat (1g saturated fat); 0mg cholesterol; 262mg sodium; 3g protein; 4g carbohydrates; 0g sugar; 0g fiber; 1mg iron; 67mg calcium.

73 tomato and Parmesan rice
PER SERVING: 260 calories; 4g fat (2g saturated fat); 10mg cholesterol; 654mg sodium; 11g protein; 43g carbohydrates; 2g sugar; 1g fiber; 2mg iron; 218mg calcium.

73 apricot and almond rice
PER SERVING: 160 calories; 6g fat (1g saturated fat); 0mg cholesterol; 242mg sodium; 4g protein; 24g carbohydrates; 9g sugar; 3g fiber; 1mg iron; 44mg calcium.

73 broccoli and sesame rice
PER SERVING: 104 calories; 4g fat (0g saturated fat); 0mg cholesterol; 251mg sodium; 3g protein; 15g carbohydrates; 0g sugar; 1g fiber; 7mg iron; 26mg calcium.

DESSERTS

75 yellow cake with pastry cream filling, chocolate ganache frosting, and shaved chocolate
PER SERVING: 1,036 calories; 58g fat (34g saturated fat); 304mg cholesterol; 475mg sodium; 14g protein; 121g carbohydrates; 75g sugar; 2g fiber; 4mg iron; 158mg calcium.

75 yellow cake with lemon curd filling, lemon frosting, chopped pistachios, and candied lemons
PER SERVING: 1,077 calories; 68g fat (37g saturated fat); 268mg cholesterol; 255mg sodium; 12g protein; 112g carbohydrates; 85g sugar; 3g fiber; 3mg iron; 99mg calcium.

75 chocolate cake with caramel frosting and gumdrop roses
PER SERVING: 844 calories; 50g fat (31g saturated fat); 182mg cholesterol; 376mg sodium; 7g protein; 97g carbohydrates; 74g sugar; 2g fiber; 2mg iron; 108mg calcium.

75 yellow cake with vanilla frosting and white chocolate chips
PER SERVING: 937 calories; 58g fat (36g saturated fat); 182mg cholesterol; 243mg sodium; 7g protein; 101g carbohydrates; 80g sugar; 1g fiber; 2mg iron; 117mg calcium.

75 yellow cupcake with vanilla frosting and chocolate nonpareils
PER SERVING: 402 calories; 24g fat (15g saturated fat); 88mg cholesterol; 109mg sodium; 3g protein; 46g carbohydrates; 35g sugar; 0g fiber; 1mg iron; 30mg calcium.

75 chocolate cupcake with chocolate sour cream frosting and M&M's Minis
PER SERVING: 447 calories; 27g fat (17g saturated fat); 84mg cholesterol; 184mg sodium; 5g protein; 50g carbohydrates; 39g sugar; 1g fiber; 1mg iron; 46mg calcium.

75 chocolate cupcake with vanilla frosting and colored sprinkles
PER SERVING: 407 calories; 25g fat (15g saturated fat); 88mg cholesterol; 179mg sodium; 3g protein; 45g carbohydrates; 35g sugar; 1g fiber; 1mg iron; 37mg calcium.

75 chocolate cupcake with chocolate ganache frosting and mini marshmallows
PER SERVING: 359 calories; 22g fat (13g saturated fat); 75mg cholesterol; 190mg sodium; 5g protein; 39g carbohydrates; 27g sugar; 1g fiber; 1mg iron; 45mg calcium.

75 yellow cupcake with chocolate sour cream frosting and toasted sliced almonds
PER SERVING: 435 calories; 26g fat (16g saturated fat); 83mg cholesterol; 111mg sodium; 4g protein; 48g carbohydrates; 36g sugar; 1g fiber; 1mg iron; 39mg calcium.

75 chocolate cake with coffee frosting and crushed cookies
PER SERVING: 866 calories; 52g fat (32g saturated fat); 179mg cholesterol; 469mg sodium; 8g protein; 97g carbohydrates; 69g sugar; 3g fiber; 3mg iron; 80mg calcium.

75 yellow cake with fresh strawberry filling, chocolate sour cream frosting, and a strawberry fan
PER SERVING: 918 calories; 52g fat (32g saturated fat); 168mg cholesterol; 233mg sodium; 8g protein; 110g carbohydrates; 84g sugar; 2g fiber; 3mg iron; 81mg calcium.

summer

STARTERS

89 flaky tomato and mozzarella tart
PER SERVING: 253 calories; 18g fat (6g saturated fat); 22mg cholesterol; 569mg sodium; 9g protein; 14g carbohydrates; 2g sugar; 1g fiber; 1mg iron; 148mg calcium.

90 hummus and cucumber crostini
PER SERVING: 141 calories; 9g fat (2g saturated fat); 0mg cholesterol; 367mg sodium; 4g protein; 12g carbohydrates; 1g sugar; 2g fiber; 1mg iron; 15mg calcium.

90 Mexican grilled corn with cilantro
PER SERVING: 70 calories; 4g fat (1g saturated fat); 0mg cholesterol; 127mg sodium; 1g protein; 9g carbohydrates; 1g sugar; 1g fiber; 0mg iron; 2mg calcium.

91 roast beef and horseradish canapés
PER SERVING: 55 calories; 2g fat (1g saturated fat); 12mg cholesterol; 209mg sodium; 5g protein; 5g carbohydrates; 1g sugar; 1g fiber; 1mg iron; 4mg calcium.

91 grilled spiced chicken wings
PER SERVING: 282 calories; 23g fat (9g saturated fat); 80mg cholesterol; 377mg sodium; 18g protein; 0g carbohydrates; 0g sugar; 0g fiber; 1mg iron; 13mg calcium.

93 grilled Feta with thyme
PER SERVING: 144 calories; 12g fat (7g saturated fat); 38mg cholesterol; 475mg sodium; 6g protein; 2g carbohydrates; 2g sugar; 0g fiber; 1mg iron; 217mg calcium.

POULTRY

95 chicken and orange skewers with zucchini rice
PER SERVING: 473 calories; 17g fat (4g saturated fat); 93mg cholesterol; 454mg sodium; 30g protein; 48g carbohydrates; 5g sugar; 2g fiber; 3mg iron; 55mg calcium.

97 grilled chicken and corn salad with avocado and Parmesan
PER SERVING: 427 calories; 27g fat (6g saturated fat); 57mg cholesterol; 725mg sodium; 27g protein; 23g carbohydrates; 3g sugar; 7g fiber; 3mg iron; 254mg calcium.

99 lemon and olive chicken with arugula and white bean salad
PER SERVING: 376 calories; 26g fat (6g saturated fat); 111mg cholesterol; 569mg sodium; 32g protein; 3g carbohydrates; 0g sugar; 1g fiber; 2mg iron; 24mg calcium.

101 chicken pitas with tzatziki
PER SERVING: 461 calories; 21g fat (5g saturated fat); 115mg cholesterol; 761mg sodium; 40g protein; 27g carbohydrates; 7g sugar; 3g fiber; 5mg iron; 180mg calcium.

103 grilled hoisin chicken and scallions with sweet potatoes
PER SERVING: 375 calories; 9g fat (2g saturated fat); 94mg cholesterol; 863mg sodium; 38g protein; 34g carbohydrates; 13g sugar; 5g fiber; 5mg iron; 91mg calcium.

105 chicken niçoise salad
PER SERVING: 299 calories; 12g fat (3g saturated fat); 254mg cholesterol; 460mg sodium; 25g protein; 22g carbohydrates; 5g sugar; 5g fiber; 3mg iron; 75mg calcium.

BEEF & LAMB
107 grilled steak with caper sauce
PER SERVING: 665 calories; 54g fat (18g saturated fat); 114mg cholesterol; 1,005mg sodium; 42g protein; 1g carbohydrates; 0g sugar; 1g fiber; 7mg iron; 37mg calcium.

107 grilled asparagus with manchego
PER SERVING: 61 calories; 4g fat (2g saturated fat); 8mg cholesterol; 164mg sodium; 3g protein; 2g carbohydrates; 1g sugar; 1g fiber; 1mg iron; 90mg calcium.

107 tomato salad with pickled onion
PER SERVING: 69 calories; 5g fat (1g saturated fat); 0mg cholesterol; 245mg sodium; 1g protein; 5g carbohydrates; 3g sugar; 1g fiber; 0mg iron; 14mg calcium.

109 lamb chops with orzo and cucumber salad
PER SERVING: 602 calories; 29g fat (7g saturated fat); 128mg cholesterol; 745mg sodium; 47g protein; 37g carbohydrates; 3g sugar; 3g fiber; 5mg iron; 76mg calcium.

110 burger master recipe
PER SERVING: 272 calories; 18g fat (7g saturated fat); 88mg cholesterol; 312mg sodium; 25g protein; 0g carbohydrates; 0g sugar; 0g fiber; 2mg iron; 24mg calcium.

110 Cheddar, avocado, and sprouts burgers
PER SERVING: 936 calories; 65g fat (18g saturated fat); 167mg cholesterol; 976mg sodium; 53g protein; 35g carbohydrates; 4g sugar; 9g fiber; 6mg iron; 283mg calcium.

110 ricotta salata and pickled zucchini burgers
PER SERVING: 591 calories; 31g fat (14g saturated fat); 162mg cholesterol; 1,242mg sodium; 38g protein; 39g carbohydrates; 8g sugar; 2g fiber; 6mg iron; 136mg calcium.

111 celery, olive, and blue cheese burgers
PER SERVING: 602 calories; 39 fat (10g saturated fat); 92mg cholesterol; 1,172mg sodium; 31g protein; 31g carbohydrates; 2g sugar; 0g fiber; 3mg iron; 150mg calcium.

111 onion dip and potato chip burgers
PER SERVING: 510 calories; 26g fat (10g saturated fat); 88mg cholesterol; 883mg sodium; 31g protein; 36g carbohydrates; 9g sugar; 1g fiber; 4mg iron; 97mg calcium.

111 chipotle mayo and grilled onion burgers
PER SERVING: 629 calories; 40g fat (9g saturated fat); 97mg cholesterol; 965mg sodium; 30g protein; 34g carbohydrates; 4g sugar; 3g fiber; 5mg iron; 117mg calcium.

113 Asian steak salad with mango
PER SERVING: 287 calories; 15g fat (2g saturated fat); 31mg cholesterol; 377mg sodium; 19g protein; 21g carbohydrates; 15g sugar; 4g fiber; 4mg iron; 69mg calcium.
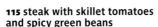

115 steak with skillet tomatoes and spicy green beans
PER SERVING: 325 calories; 13g fat (4g saturated fat); 74mg cholesterol; 863mg sodium; 37g protein; 15g carbohydrates; 4g sugar; 6g fiber; 4mg iron; 86mg calcium.

PORK
117 Thai pork salad with chilies and mint
PER SERVING: 434 calories; 31g fat (10g saturated fat); 82mg cholesterol; 1,902mg sodium; 25g protein; 16g carbohydrates; 8g sugar; 3g fiber; 3mg iron; 90mg calcium.

119 pork and pineapple kebabs
PER SERVING: 468 calories; 6g fat (2g saturated fat); 82mg cholesterol; 306mg sodium; 34g protein; 69g carbohydrates; 25g sugar; 3g fiber; 4mg iron; 43mg calcium.

121 chorizo and potato tacos with black bean salsa
PER SERVING: 871 calories; 61g fat (21g saturated fat); 110mg cholesterol; 2,004mg sodium; 36g protein; 47g carbohydrates; 2g sugar; 10g fiber; 4mg iron; 100mg calcium.

123 apricot-glazed pork chops with brown rice–pecan pilaf
PER SERVING: 724 calories; 30g fat (9g saturated fat); 130mg cholesterol; 574mg sodium; 48g protein; 64g carbohydrates; 26g sugar; 4g fiber; 2mg iron; 74mg calcium.

125 pork loin with mustard sauce and sautéed squash
PER SERVING: 315 calories; 13g fat (3g saturated fat); 98mg cholesterol; 689mg sodium; 37g protein; 10g carbohydrates; 3g sugar; 2g fiber; 3mg iron; 41mg calcium.

SEAFOOD
127 red curry salmon with bok choy and pineapple slaw
PER SERVING: 409 calories; 25g fat (3g saturated fat); 90mg cholesterol; 717mg sodium; 34g protein; 12g carbohydrates; 8g sugar; 2g fiber; 3mg iron; 150mg calcium.

129 grilled halibut with salt-and-vinegar potatoes
PER SERVING: 372 calories; 12g fat (2g saturated fat); 59mg cholesterol; 468mg sodium; 41g protein; 24g carbohydrates; 3g sugar; 2g fiber; 2mg iron; 117mg calcium.

131 grilled shrimp panzanella with basil
PER SERVING: 521 calories; 18g fat (3g saturated fat); 259mg cholesterol; 996mg sodium; 44g protein; 46g carbohydrates; 9g sugar; 6g fiber; 8mg iron; 176mg calcium.

133 plank-grilled salmon with lemon and fennel
PER SERVING: 280 calories; 13g fat (2g saturated fat); 99mg cholesterol; 456mg sodium; 36g protein; 3g carbohydrates; 0g sugar; 1g fiber; 2mg iron; 41mg calcium.

133 wild rice and pine nut salad
PER SERVING: 312 calories; 14g fat (2g saturated fat); 0mg cholesterol; 250mg sodium; 6g protein; 41g carbohydrates; 0g sugar; 4g fiber; 2mg iron; 18mg calcium.

133 greens with radishes and snap peas
PER SERVING: 74 calories; 5g fat (1g saturated fat); 0mg cholesterol; 277mg sodium; 2g protein; 5g carbohydrates; 2g sugar; 2g fiber; 1mg iron; 50mg calcium.

PASTA
135 basil spaghetti with cheesy broiled tomatoes
PER SERVING: 663 calories; 29g fat (11g saturated fat); 50mg cholesterol; 850mg sodium; 29g protein; 72g carbohydrates; 5g sugar; 6g fiber; 4mg iron; 431mg calcium.
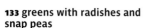

137 campanelle with roasted red peppers and almonds
PER SERVING: 558 calories; 24g fat (3g saturated fat); 0mg cholesterol; 469mg sodium; 16g protein; 75g carbohydrates; 9g sugar; 8g fiber; 5mg iron; 78mg calcium.

139 bucatini with turkey sausage and zucchini
PER SERVING: 581 calories; 13g fat (4g saturated fat); 98mg cholesterol; 1,355mg sodium; 41g protein; 74g carbohydrates; 5g sugar; 6g fiber; 5mg iron; 289mg calcium.

141 pasta with goat cheese and basil oil
PER SERVING: 660 calories; 37g fat (10g saturated fat); 22mg cholesterol; 392mg sodium; 18g protein; 65g carbohydrates; 4g sugar; 4g fiber; 4mg iron; 146mg calcium.

VEGETARIAN
143 chopped Greek salad with pita chips
PER SERVING: 380 calories; 21g fat (6g saturated fat); 25mg cholesterol; 865mg sodium; 12g protein; 37g carbohydrates; 7g sugar; 6g fiber; 3mg iron; 226mg calcium.

145 lentil fritter pitas with red cabbage slaw
PER SERVING: 384 calories; 12g fat (2g saturated fat); 2mg cholesterol; 652mg sodium; 19g protein; 53g carbohydrates; 7g sugar; 12g fiber; 5mg iron; 122mg calcium.

147 cool gazpacho
PER SERVING: 177 calories; 14g fat (2g saturated fat); 0mg cholesterol; 735mg sodium; 3g protein; 12g carbohydrates; 8g sugar; 4g fiber; 1mg iron; 37mg calcium.

149 grilled Mediterranean vegetables
PER SERVING: 347 calories; 15g fat (2g saturated fat); 0mg cholesterol; 269mg sodium; 10g protein; 49g carbohydrates; 8g sugar; 7g fiber; 2mg iron; 72mg calcium.

149 spiced chili oil
PER TABLESPOON: 84 calories; 9g fat (1g saturated fat); 0mg cholesterol; 81mg sodium; 0g protein; 1g carbohydrates; 0g sugar; 0g fiber; 0mg iron; 3mg calcium.

149 chickpea and raisin salad
PER SERVING: 237 calories; 10g fat (1g saturated fat); 0mg cholesterol; 336mg sodium; 6g protein; 31g carbohydrates; 13g sugar; 5g fiber; 2mg iron; 52mg calcium.

SIDE DISHES
151 corn salad with Feta and walnuts
PER SERVING: 259 calories; 19g fat (3g saturated fat); 8mg cholesterol; 280mg sodium; 7g protein; 22g carbohydrates; 4g sugar; 4g fiber; 1mg iron; 66mg calcium.

153 grilled zucchini salad with lemon and scallions
PER SERVING: 57 calories; 3g fat (0g saturated fat); 0mg cholesterol; 258mg sodium; 2g protein; 7g carbohydrates; 3g sugar; 2g fiber; 1mg iron; 34mg calcium.

155 potato salad with bacon and parsley
PER SERVING: 167 calories; 9g fat (2g saturated fat); 5mg cholesterol; 444mg sodium; 4g protein; 19g carbohydrates; 1g sugar; 2g fiber; 2mg iron; 26mg calcium.

157 baked beans
PER SERVING: 299 calories; 5g fat (1g saturated fat); 7mg cholesterol; 442mg sodium; 13g protein; 52g carbohydrates; 14g sugar; 14g fiber; 5mg iron; 141mg calcium.

DRINKS
159 spicy cayenne shandy
PER SERVING: 79 calories; 0g fat (0g saturated fat); 0mg cholesterol; 127mg sodium; 0g protein; 10g carbohydrates; 7g sugar; 0g fiber; 0mg iron; 8mg calcium.

159 thyme and lime lemonade
PER SERVING: 185 calories; 0g fat (0g saturated fat); 0mg cholesterol; 1mg sodium; 0g protein; 24g carbohydrates; 20g sugar; 0g fiber; 0mg iron; 9mg calcium.

159 hibiscus and mint lemonade
PER SERVING: 79 calories; 0g fat (0g saturated fat); 0mg cholesterol; 4mg sodium; 1g protein; 21g carbohydrates; 17g sugar; 1g fiber; 1mg iron; 34mg calcium.

DESSERTS

161 nectarine galette
PER SERVING: 371 calories; 20g fat (10g saturated fat); 25mg cholesterol; 201mg sodium; 3g protein; 46g carbohydrates; 19g sugar; 2g fiber; 0mg iron; 8mg calcium.

162 strawberry sorbet with balsamic syrup
PER SERVING: 201 calories; 1g fat (0g saturated fat); 0mg cholesterol; 19mg sodium; 1g protein; 48g carbohydrates; 42g sugar; 4g fiber; 1mg iron; 35mg calcium.

162 chocolate pound cake with ricotta
PER SERVING: 385 calories; 18g fat (10g saturated fat); 64mg cholesterol; 235mg sodium; 9g protein; 49g carbohydrates; 40g sugar; 1g fiber; 1mg iron; 138mg calcium.

163 cantaloupe parfait with salted pistachios
PER SERVING: 264 calories; 16g fat (6g saturated fat); 25mg cholesterol; 111mg sodium; 7g protein; 25g carbohydrates; 20g sugar; 2g fiber; 1mg iron; 104mg calcium.

163 blackberry and granola crisp
PER SERVING: 433 calories; 18g fat (8g saturated fat); 30mg cholesterol; 228mg sodium; 7g protein; 68g carbohydrates; 34g sugar; 11g fiber; 3mg iron; 82mg calcium.

165 dulce de leche mousse
PER SERVING: 289 calories; 25g fat (16g saturated fat); 87mg cholesterol; 90mg sodium; 2g protein; 16g carbohydrates; 12g sugar; 0g fiber; 0mg iron; 90mg calcium.

167 ballpark cone
PER SERVING: 286 calories; 13g fat (8g saturated fat); 20mg cholesterol; 96mg sodium; 5g protein; 39g carbohydrates; 30g sugar; 2g fiber; 1mg iron; 80mg calcium.

167 tropical cone
PER SERVING: 272 calories; 12g fat (6g saturated fat); 29mg cholesterol; 127mg sodium; 3g protein; 39g carbohydrates; 29g sugar; 1g fiber; 1mg iron; 101mg calcium.

167 nutty crunch cone
PER SERVING: 284 calories; 13g fat (5g saturated fat); 20mg cholesterol; 204mg sodium; 5g protein; 38g carbohydrates; 22g sugar; 1g fiber; 2mg iron; 80mg calcium.

fall

STARTERS

171 stuffed mushrooms with spinach
PER 3-PIECE SERVING: 104 calories; 6g fat (2g saturated fat); 7mg cholesterol; 121mg sodium; 5g protein; 8g carbohydrates; 1g sugar; 2g fiber; 1mg iron; 84mg calcium.

172 goat cheese with pistachios and cranberries
PER SERVING: 163 calories; 10g fat (5g saturated fat); 23mg cholesterol; 200mg sodium; 7g protein; 12g carbohydrates; 3g sugar; 0g fiber; 1mg iron; 42mg calcium.

172 spiced pickled carrots with mint
PER SERVING: 49 calories; 0g fat (0g saturated fat); 0mg cholesterol; 158mg sodium; 1g protein; 12g carbohydrates; 9g sugar; 2g fiber; 1mg iron; 22mg calcium.

173 Parmesan-scallion pastry pinwheels
PER 3-PIECE SERVING: 55 calories; 4g fat (1g saturated fat); 30mg cholesterol; 188mg sodium; 4g protein; 2g carbohydrates; 0g sugar; 0g fiber; 0mg iron; 82mg calcium.

173 caramelized onion dip
PER ¼-CUP SERVING: 196 calories; 18g fat (11g saturated fat); 58mg cholesterol; 282mg sodium; 3g protein; 5g carbohydrates; 3g sugar; 0g fiber; 0mg iron; 28mg calcium.

175 chocolate-drizzled nuts with sea salt
PER ¼-CUP SERVING: 252 calories; 20g fat (4g saturated fat); 0mg cholesterol; 179mg sodium; 8g protein; 13g carbohydrates; 8g sugar; 2g fiber; 2mg iron; 46mg calcium.

175 buttered nuts with rosemary and orange
PER ⅓-CUP SERVING: 216 calories; 18g fat (3g saturated fat); 3mg cholesterol; 64mg sodium; 7g protein; 8g carbohydrates; 4g sugar; 2g fiber; 2mg iron; 48mg calcium.

175 sweet and spicy candied nuts
PER ¼-CUP SERVING: 219 calories; 17g fat (2g saturated fat); 0mg cholesterol; 71mg sodium; 7g protein; 11g carbohydrates; 7g sugar; 3g fiber; 2mg iron; 52mg calcium.

SANDWICHES

176 chipotle turkey club
PER SERVING: 530 calories; 31g fat (9g saturated fat); 72mg cholesterol; 1,408mg sodium; 3g protein; 35g carbohydrates; 4g sugar; 6g fiber; 3mg iron; 257mg calcium.

176 ham banh mi sandwich
PER SERVING: 388 calories; 18g fat (3g saturated fat); 22mg cholesterol; 1,057mg sodium; 16g protein; 41g carbohydrates; 7g sugar; 3g fiber; 3mg iron; 89mg calcium.

176 roast beef, Gouda, and apple sandwich
PER SERVING: 529 calories; 18g fat (7g saturated fat); 174mg cholesterol; 1,174mg sodium; 31g protein; 63g carbohydrates; 13g sugar; 2g fiber; 5mg iron; 27mg calcium.

177 double-onion turkey sandwich
PER SERVING: 322 calories; 11g fat (2g saturated fat); 27mg cholesterol; 1,145mg sodium; 18g protein; 40g carbohydrates; 8g sugar; 2g fiber; 3mg iron; 97mg calcium.

177 peanut butter, celery, and raisin sandwich
PER SERVING: 347 calories; 18g fat (4g saturated fat); 0mg cholesterol; 398mg sodium; 15g protein; 44g carbohydrates; 16g sugar; 8g fiber; 5mg iron; 317mg calcium.

177 ham and pineapple sandwich
PER SERVING: 578 calories; 33g fat (14g saturated fat); 82mg cholesterol; 1,225mg sodium; 30g protein; 43g carbohydrates; 15g sugar; 5g fiber; 3mg iron; 522mg calcium.

POULTRY
179 red currant–glazed chicken with spinach
PER SERVING: 536 calories; 26g fat (6g saturated fat); 119mg cholesterol; 541mg sodium; 40g protein; 38g carbohydrates; 30g sugar; 3g fiber; 3mg iron; 137mg calcium.

181 chicken enchiladas verdes
PER SERVING: 969 calories; 36g fat (20g saturated fat); 182mg cholesterol; 1,511mg sodium; 59g protein; 93g carbohydrates; 10g sugar; 5g fiber; 6mg iron; 563mg calcium.

183 Colombian chicken and potato soup
PER SERVING: 405 calories; 14g fat (3g saturated fat); 79mg cholesterol; 463mg sodium; 30g protein; 40g carbohydrates; 6g sugar; 4g fiber; 2mg iron; 31mg calcium.

185 chicken paprikash
PER SERVING: 613 calories; 30g fat (9g saturated fat); 164mg cholesterol; 867mg sodium; 39g protein; 44g carbohydrates; 10g sugar; 4g fiber; 5mg iron; 53mg calcium.

187 chicken skewers with bean salad and parsley pesto
PER SERVING: 466 calories; 28g fat (4g saturated fat); 95mg cholesterol; 560mg sodium; 39g protein; 14g carbohydrates; 2g sugar; 4g fiber; 5mg iron; 116mg calcium.

189 easy Thanksgiving turkey
PER SERVING: 342 calories; 17g fat (6g saturated fat); 125mg cholesterol; 359mg sodium; 40g protein; 5g carbohydrates; 2g sugar; 1g fiber; 3mg iron; 62mg calcium.

189 classic gravy
PER SERVING: 114 calories; 9g fat (5g saturated fat); 20mg cholesterol; 217mg sodium; 2g protein; 5g carbohydrates; 0g sugar; 0g fiber; 0mg iron; 4mg calcium.

BEEF & LAMB
191 steak fajitas with sweet potato and poblano
PER SERVING: 693 calories; 35g fat (13g saturated fat); 105mg cholesterol; 1,081mg sodium; 37g protein; 53g carbohydrates; 8g sugar; 6g fiber; 6mg iron; 134mg calcium.

193 bacon-Gruyère meat loaf with roasted carrots and onions
PER SERVING: 504 calories; 30g fat (11g saturated fat); 146mg cholesterol; 1,019mg sodium; 33g protein; 27g carbohydrates; 12g sugar; 5g fiber; 3mg iron; 314mg calcium.

195 beef and bean chili
PER SERVING: 300 calories; 10g fat (3g saturated fat); 45mg cholesterol; 797mg sodium; 24g protein; 28g carbohydrates; 13g sugar; 7g fiber; 4mg iron; 57mg calcium.

197 seared steak with cauliflower puree
PER SERVING: 372 calories; 23g fat (5g saturated fat); 63mg cholesterol; 737mg sodium; 35g protein; 6g carbohydrates; 2g sugar; 2g fiber; 3mg iron; 44mg calcium.

199 lamb meatballs with couscous and Feta
PER SERVING: 689 calories; 44g fat (17g saturated fat); 108mg cholesterol; 752mg sodium; 30g protein; 46g carbohydrates; 9g sugar; 4g fiber; 4mg iron; 195mg calcium.

PORK
201 balsamic-glazed pork with lentils
PER SERVING: 477 calories; 16g fat (3g saturated fat); 92mg cholesterol; 449mg sodium; 43g protein; 42g carbohydrates; 14g sugar; 12g fiber; 7mg iron; 54mg calcium.

202 roasted sausage and grapes
PER SERVING: 481 calories; 27g fat (9g saturated fat); 49mg cholesterol; 1,292mg sodium; 18g protein; 44g carbohydrates; 34g sugar; 2g fiber; 2mg iron; 48mg calcium.

202 sausage-stuffed zucchini
PER SERVING: 254 calories; 20g fat (5g saturated fat); 23mg cholesterol; 473mg sodium; 10g protein; 10g carbohydrates; 5g sugar; 3g fiber; 2mg iron; 94mg calcium.

203 cauliflower and sausage flat bread
PER SERVING: 639 calories; 31g fat (13g saturated fat); 76mg cholesterol; 1,312mg sodium; 34g protein; 57g carbohydrates; 5g sugar; 4g fiber; 5mg iron; 593mg calcium.

203 sausage with white beans
PER SERVING: 447 calories; 31g fat (9g saturated fat); 49mg cholesterol; 1,396mg sodium; 20g protein; 19g carbohydrates; 4g sugar; 4g fiber; 2mg iron; 59mg calcium.

205 pork cutlets with spicy noodles
PER SERVING: 494 calories; 15g fat (3g saturated fat); 100mg cholesterol; 531mg sodium; 35g protein; 53g carbohydrates; 4g sugar; 4g fiber; 4mg iron; 46mg calcium.

207 roasted pork chops with polenta
PER SERVING: 687 calories; 35g fat (14g saturated fat); 172mg cholesterol; 993mg sodium; 61g protein; 28g carbohydrates; 4g sugar; 3g fiber; 5mg iron; 529mg calcium.

SEAFOOD

209 shrimp with white beans and toast
PER SERVING: 458 calories; 20g fat (11g saturated fat); 218mg cholesterol; 704mg sodium; 30g protein; 32g carbohydrates; 4g sugar; 5g fiber; 6mg iron; 166mg calcium.

210 Dijon tilapia cakes
PER SERVING: 504 calories; 35g fat (5g saturated fat); 188mg cholesterol; 662mg sodium; 38g protein; 10g carbohydrates; 1g sugar; 0g fiber; 2mg iron; 32mg calcium.

210 tilapia tacos with cucumber relish
PER SERVING: 363 calories; 12g fat (4g saturated fat); 83mg cholesterol; 466mg sodium; 38g protein; 28g carbohydrates; 3g sugar; 4g fiber; 2mg iron; 89mg calcium.

211 tilapia salad with apples
PER SERVING: 395 calories; 21g fat (3g saturated fat); 73mg cholesterol; 517mg sodium; 39g protein; 18g carbohydrates; 7g sugar; 10g fiber; 4mg iron; 218mg calcium.

211 tilapia po'boys
PER SERVING: 821 calories; 39g fat (7g saturated fat); 60mg cholesterol; 1,567mg sodium; 39g protein; 80g carbohydrates; 7g sugar; 4g fiber; 4mg iron; 54mg calcium.

213 spiced shrimp with green beans and lime
PER SERVING: 461 calories; 11g fat (2g saturated fat); 259mg cholesterol; 633mg sodium; 40g protein; 50g carbohydrates; 2g sugar; 3g fiber; 7mg iron; 139mg calcium.

PASTA

215 spaghetti with meat sauce and mozzarella
PER SERVING: 677 calories; 24g fat (10g saturated fat); 84mg cholesterol; 606mg sodium; 38g protein; 78g carbohydrates; 8g sugar; 7g fiber; 5mg iron; 302mg calcium.

217 rigatoni with roasted sausage and broccoli
PER SERVING: 634 calories; 35g fat (12g saturated fat); 53mg cholesterol; 1,118mg sodium; 26g protein; 57g carbohydrates; 6g sugar; 6g fiber; 4mg iron; 200mg calcium.

219 spicy linguine with clams
PER SERVING: 551 calories; 20g fat (3g saturated fat); 33mg cholesterol; 409mg sodium; 19g protein; 69g carbohydrates; 5g sugar; 3g fiber; 6mg iron; 64mg calcium.

221 whole-grain spaghetti with garlicky kale and tomatoes
PER SERVING: 413 calories; 16g fat (3g saturated fat); 5mg cholesterol; 313mg sodium; 17g protein; 56g carbohydrates; 6g sugar; 8g fiber; 5mg iron; 335mg calcium.

VEGETARIAN

223 sweet potato and Brie flat bread
PER SERVING: 531 calories; 26g fat (7g saturated fat); 28mg cholesterol; 968mg sodium; 16g protein; 66g carbohydrates; 8g sugar; 5g fiber; 4mg iron; 100mg calcium.

225 vegetable stir-fry with peanuts
PER SERVING: 363 calories; 11g fat (1g saturated fat); 0mg cholesterol; 435mg sodium; 14g protein; 54g carbohydrates; 3g sugar; 3g fiber; 4mg iron; 64mg calcium.

227 mushroom and herb strata
PER SERVING: 734 calories; 45g fat (18g saturated fat); 395mg cholesterol; 1,416mg sodium; 36g protein; 45g carbohydrates; 16g sugar; 5g fiber; 5mg iron; 570mg calcium.
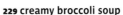

229 creamy broccoli soup
PER SERVING: 200 calories; 8g fat (3.5g saturated fat); 15mg cholesterol; 436mg sodium; 8g protein; 25g carbohydrates; 4g sugar; 4g fiber; 2mg iron; 164mg calcium.

SIDE DISHES

231 greens with fennel and dried apricots
PER SERVING: 189 calories; 12g fat (3g saturated fat); 8mg cholesterol; 225mg sodium; 5g protein; 18g carbohydrates; 9g sugar; 5g fiber; 2mg iron; 129mg calcium.

231 green beans with warm bacon vinaigrette
PER SERVING: 121 calories; 8g fat (2g saturated fat); 8mg cholesterol; 516mg sodium; 4g protein; 9g carbohydrates; 2g sugar; 4g fiber; 1mg iron; 43mg calcium.

233 sweet potatoes with pecans and Parmesan
PER SERVING: 297 calories; 16g fat (3g saturated fat); 5mg cholesterol; 504mg sodium; 6g protein; 34g carbohydrates; 15g sugar; 6g fiber; 1mg iron; 137mg calcium.

235 Brie and chive biscuits
PER SERVING: 136 calories; 8g fat (5g saturated fat); 22mg cholesterol; 258mg sodium; 4g protein; 13g carbohydrates; 1g sugar; 0g fiber; 1mg iron; 49mg calcium.

235 wild rice pilaf
PER SERVING: 222 calories; 6g fat (1g saturated fat); 0mg cholesterol; 127mg sodium; 5g protein; 40g carbohydrates; 9g sugar; 3g fiber; 1mg iron; 23mg calcium.

235 cauliflower gratin
PER SERVING: 292 calories; 20g fat (10g saturated fat); 46mg cholesterol; 618mg sodium; 11g protein; 18g carbohydrates; 6g sugar; 4g fiber; 1mg iron; 263mg calcium.

236 apple, cranberry, and pecan stuffing
PER SERVING: 485 calories; 28g fat (8g saturated fat); 80mg cholesterol; 771mg sodium; 10g protein; 52g carbohydrates; 17g sugar; 6g fiber; 3mg iron; 86mg calcium.

236 oyster and bacon stuffing
PER SERVING: 321 calories; 15g fat (8g saturated fat); 97mg cholesterol; 919mg sodium; 12g protein; 33g carbohydrates; 3g sugar; 2g fiber; 4mg iron; 84mg calcium.

237 sausage and sage stuffing
PER SERVING: 398 calories; 23g fat (10g saturated fat); 96mg cholesterol; 1,122mg sodium; 14g protein; 34g carbohydrates; 3g sugar; 2g fiber; 3mg iron; 84mg calcium.

237 fennel and apricot stuffing
PER SERVING: 347 calories; 13g fat (7g saturated fat); 80mg cholesterol; 774mg sodium; 9g protein; 49g carbohydrates; 15g sugar; 5g fiber; 3mg iron; 90mg calcium.

237 caramelized onion and herb stuffing
PER SERVING: 293 calories; 13g fat (7g saturated fat); 78mg cholesterol; 714mg sodium; 8g protein; 36g carbohydrates; 4g sugar; 3g fiber; 2mg iron; 76mg calcium.

239 potato and celery root mash
PER SERVING: 273 calories; 11g fat (7g saturated fat); 32mg cholesterol; 446mg sodium; 6g protein; 37g carbohydrates; 1g sugar; 3g fiber; 2mg iron; 74mg calcium.

241 honeyed carrots and oranges
PER SERVING: 94 calories; 4g fat (1g saturated fat); 0mg cholesterol; 329mg sodium; 1g protein; 16g carbohydrates; 11g sugar; 4g fiber; 1mg iron; 44mg calcium.

241 butternut squash bread pudding
PER SERVING: 411 calories; 20g fat (9g saturated fat); 196mg cholesterol; 633mg sodium; 21g protein; 38g carbohydrates; 7g sugar; 4g fiber; 3mg iron; 434mg calcium.

DESSERTS
242 peanut M&M's and jelly cookies
PER SERVING: 209 calories; 9g fat (3g saturated fat); 10mg cholesterol; 138mg sodium; 2g protein; 29g carbohydrates; 16g sugar; 1g fiber; 1mg iron; 36mg calcium.

242 caramel-cookie cheesecake pie
PER SERVING: 583 calories; 37g fat (22g saturated fat); 116mg cholesterol; 410mg sodium; 8g protein; 57g carbohydrates; 42g sugar; 1g fiber; 2mg iron; 53mg calcium.

242 candy corn and pretzel bark
PER SERVING: 234 calories; 9g fat (6g saturated fat); 10mg cholesterol; 105mg sodium; 2g protein; 35g carbohydrates; 30g sugar; 0g fiber; 0mg iron; 41mg calcium.

243 peppermint patty brownies
PER SERVING: 264 calories; 12g fat (1g saturated fat); 27mg cholesterol; 111mg sodium; 2g protein; 40g carbohydrates; 29g sugar; 1g fiber; 1mg iron; 5mg calcium.
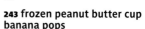

243 dulce de leche candy bar terrine
PER SERVING: 285 calories; 13g fat (7g saturated fat); 23mg cholesterol; 145mg sodium; 4g protein; 37g carbohydrates; 32g sugar; 1g fiber; 0mg iron; 104mg calcium.

243 frozen peanut butter cup banana pops
PER SERVING: 353 calories; 18g fat (9g saturated fat); 1mg cholesterol; 54mg sodium; 5g protein; 50g carbohydrates; 40g sugar; 2g fiber; 1mg iron; 16mg calcium.

245 pecan and walnut pie
PER SERVING: 571 calories; 30g fat (7g saturated fat); 92mg cholesterol; 224mg sodium; 7g protein; 76g carbohydrates; 35g sugar; 2g fiber; 1mg iron; 51mg calcium.

247 gingersnap cherry cheesecake
PER SERVING: 675 calories; 39g fat (23g saturated fat); 142mg cholesterol; 489mg sodium; 8g protein; 70g carbohydrates; 49g sugar; 2g fiber; 3mg iron; 67mg calcium.

249 pear and apricot tart
PER SERVING: 357 calories; 18g fat (8g saturated fat); 59mg cholesterol; 167mg sodium; 5g protein; 48g carbohydrates; 30g sugar; 4g fiber; 2mg iron; 47mg calcium.

251 spiced pumpkin cake
PER SERVING: 453 calories; 17g fat (10g saturated fat); 94mg cholesterol; 256mg sodium; 6g protein; 71g carbohydrates; 43g sugar; 3g fiber; 2mg iron; 65mg calcium.

winter

STARTERS
255 hot ricotta dip
PER 3-TABLESPOON SERVING: 129 calories; 8g fat (4g saturated fat); 24mg cholesterol; 186mg sodium; 9g protein; 8g carbohydrates; 1g fiber; 6g fiber; 2mg iron; 241mg calcium.

256 basic crostini
PER PIECE: 37 calories; 1g fat (0g saturated fat); 0mg cholesterol; 61mg sodium; 1g protein; 5g carbohydrates; 0g sugar; 0g fiber; 0mg iron; 4mg calcium.

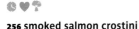

256 smoked salmon crostini
PER PIECE: 70 calories; 3g fat (1g saturated fat); 12mg cholesterol; 145mg sodium; 4g protein; 6g carbohydrates; 0g sugar; 0g fiber; 0mg iron; 10mg calcium.

256 mushroom and herb crostini
PER PIECE: 47 calories; 2g fat (0g saturated fat); 0mg cholesterol; 82mg sodium; 2g protein; 6g carbohydrates; 1g sugar; 0g fiber; 0mg iron; 5mg calcium.

257 roast beef and pomegranate crostini
PER PIECE: 52 calories; 2g fat (1g saturated fat); 4mg cholesterol; 129mg sodium; 2g protein; 7g carbohydrates; 1g sugar; 0g fiber; 0mg iron; 7mg calcium.

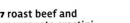

257 artichoke and olive crostini
PER PIECE: 74 calories; 4g fat (1g saturated fat); 2mg cholesterol; 201mg sodium; 3g protein; 7g carbohydrates; 0g sugar; 1g fiber; 0mg iron; 39mg calcium.

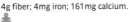

257 salami and fennel crostini
PER PIECE: 62 calories; 3g fat (1g saturated fat); 5mg cholesterol; 140mg sodium; 2g protein; 6g carbohydrates; 0g sugar; 0g fiber; 0mg iron; 7mg calcium.

259 crab and chive puffs
PER 3-PIECE SERVING: 99 calories; 8g fat (2g saturated fat); 24mg cholesterol; 198mg sodium; 6g protein; 2g carbohydrates; 0g sugar; 0g fiber; 0mg iron; 21mg calcium.

POULTRY
261 slow-cooker creamy chicken with biscuits
PER SERVING (INCLUDES 1 EASY DROP BISCUIT): 616 calories; 33g fat (18g saturated fat); 146mg cholesterol; 1,255mg sodium; 29g protein; 49g carbohydrates; 7g sugar; 4g fiber; 4mg iron; 161mg calcium.

261 easy drop biscuits
PER BISCUIT: 315 calories; 17g fat (10g saturated fat); 44mg cholesterol; 614mg sodium; 6g protein; 35g carbohydrates; 2g sugar; 1g fiber; 2mg iron; 106mg calcium.

263 yogurt-marinated chicken with mushrooms and sweet potatoes
PER SERVING: 470 calories; 15g fat (2g saturated fat); 63mg cholesterol; 739mg sodium; 35g protein; 47g carbohydrates; 9g sugar; 6g fiber; 6mg iron; 108mg calcium.

265 slow-cooker curried chicken with ginger and yogurt
PER SERVING: 463 calories; 14g fat (5g saturated fat); 102mg cholesterol; 591mg sodium; 34g protein; 48g carbohydrates; 3g sugar; 2g fiber; 4mg iron; 68mg calcium.

267 roasted chicken, potatoes, and fennel
PER SERVING: 674 calories; 33g fat (8g saturated fat); 166mg cholesterol; 1,007mg sodium; 57g protein; 38g carbohydrates; 2g sugar; 10g fiber; 5mg iron; 172mg calcium.

269 Greek lemon soup with chicken
PER SERVING: 274 calories; 11g fat (4g saturated fat); 361mg cholesterol; 508mg sodium; 27g protein; 14g carbohydrates; 3g sugar; 1g fiber; 2mg iron; 45mg calcium.

271 spicy Asian chicken with Brussels sprouts
PER SERVING: 440 calories; 18g fat (2g saturated fat); 116mg cholesterol; 383mg sodium; 29g protein; 40g carbohydrates; 8g sugar; 3g fiber; 3mg iron; 57mg calcium.

BEEF & LAMB
273 steak with roasted carrots and onions
PER SERVING: 392 calories; 17g fat (4g saturated fat); 63mg cholesterol; 837mg sodium; 35g protein; 19g carbohydrates; 9g sugar; 5g fiber; 3mg iron; 88mg calcium.

275 chipotle meatballs with rice
PER SERVING: 633 calories; 25g fat (8g saturated fat); 153mg cholesterol; 1,320mg sodium; 39g protein; 57g carbohydrates; 8g sugar; 3g fiber; 8mg iron; 83mg calcium.

277 roasted leg of lamb with carrots and honey-mint sauce
PER SERVING: 477 calories; 37g fat (14g saturated fat); 101mg cholesterol; 336mg sodium; 26g protein; 9g carbohydrates; 5g sugar; 2g fiber; 3mg iron; 48mg calcium.

277 rice pilaf with almonds and dill
PER SERVING: 261 calories; 7g fat (1g saturated fat); 0mg cholesterol; 423mg sodium; 5g protein; 44g carbohydrates; 2g sugar; 2g fiber; 2mg iron; 36mg calcium.

279 burgers with balsamic shallots and vegetable fries
PER SERVING: 597 calories; 33g fat (9g saturated fat); 83mg cholesterol; 836mg sodium; 32g protein; 43g carbohydrates; 14g sugar; 5g fiber; 5mg iron; 156mg calcium.

281 peppered roast beef with horseradish sauce
PER SERVING: 395 calories; 21g fat (10g saturated fat); 149mg cholesterol; 610mg sodium; 45g protein; 2g carbohydrates; 1g sugar; 0g fiber; 5mg iron; 37mg calcium.

281 sour cream mashed potatoes
PER SERVING: 333 calories; 16g fat (11g saturated fat); 54mg cholesterol; 400mg sodium; 7g protein; 39g carbohydrates; 5g sugar; 4g fiber; 2mg iron; 82mg calcium.

281 broccoli rabe with red currant sauce
PER SERVING: 135 calories; 7g fat (1g saturated fat); 0mg cholesterol; 178mg sodium; 6mg protein; 15g carbohydrates; 8g sugar; 0g fiber; 1mg iron; 80mg calcium.

PORK

283 slow-cooker white bean soup with andouille and collards
PER SERVING: 393 calories; 8g fat (4g saturated fat); 28mg cholesterol; 670mg sodium; 30g protein; 51g carbohydrates; 4g sugar; 14g fiber; 9mg iron; 212mg calcium.

285 crispy pork cutlets with arugula and apple salad
PER SERVING: 477 calories; 29g fat (7g saturated fat); 181mg cholesterol; 600mg sodium; 31g protein; 22g carbohydrates; 7g sugar; 3g fiber; 3mg iron; 161mg calcium.

287 slow-cooker Asian pork with snow peas, peppers, and noodles
PER SERVING: 675 calories; 22g fat (7g saturated fat); 148mg cholesterol; 745mg sodium; 51g protein; 65g carbohydrates; 25g sugar; 4g fiber; 7mg iron; 93mg calcium.

289 roasted pork chops and butternut squash with kale
PER SERVING: 477 calories; 19g fat (4.6g saturated fat); 92mg cholesterol; 775mg sodium; 43g protein; 40g carbohydrates; 3g sugar; 9g fiber; 6mg iron; 425mg calcium.

291 mustard-crusted pork roast with shallots and wine sauce
PER SERVING: 556 calories; 25g fat (8g saturated fat); 156mg cholesterol; 554mg sodium; 60g protein; 12g carbohydrates; 3g sugar; 0g fiber; 3mg iron; 34mg calcium.

291 Parmesan polenta
PER SERVING: 290 calories; 16g fat (9g saturated fat); 40mg cholesterol; 972mg sodium; 9g protein; 27g carbohydrates; 0g sugar; 2g fiber; 1mg iron; 203mg calcium.

291 sautéed collard greens and garlic
PER SERVING: 198 calories; 15g fat (2g saturated fat); 0mg cholesterol; 360mg sodium; 6g protein; 15g carbohydrates; 1g sugar; 8g fiber; 4mg iron; 417mg calcium.

SEAFOOD

293 seafood chowder with crispy bread crumbs
PER SERVING: 390 calories; 19g fat (6g saturated fat); 108mg cholesterol; 562mg sodium; 37g protein; 14g carbohydrates; 2g sugar; 1g fiber; 10mg iron; 154mg calcium.

295 roasted cod and scallions with spiced potatoes
PER SERVING: 293 calories; 8g fat (1g saturated fat); 65mg cholesterol; 589mg sodium; 30g protein; 24g carbohydrates; 1g sugar; 3g fiber; 2mg iron; 52mg calcium.

297 spinach salad with salmon, barley, and oranges
PER SERVING: 456 calories; 19g fat (3g saturated fat); 72mg cholesterol; 360mg sodium; 31g protein; 41g carbohydrates; 7g sugar; 9g fiber; 4mg iron; 85mg calcium.

299 creamy seafood casserole
PER SERVING: 789 calories; 49g fat (18g saturated fat); 210mg cholesterol; 560mg sodium; 36g protein; 53g carbohydrates; 8g sugar; 8g fiber; 4mg iron; 160mg calcium.

PASTA

301 pappardelle with beef and mushroom ragù
PER SERVING: 605 calories; 16g fat (5g saturated fat); 53mg cholesterol; 914mg sodium; 46g protein; 69g carbohydrates; 6g sugar; 8g fiber; 7mg iron; 282mg calcium.

303 slow-cooker spinach and ricotta lasagna with romaine salad
PER SERVING: 472 calories; 24g fat (10g saturated fat); 53mg cholesterol; 1,321mg sodium; 27g protein; 40g carbohydrates; 15g sugar; 7g fiber; 5mg iron; 640mg calcium.

305 spaghetti with herbs, chilies, and fried eggs
PER SERVING: 558 calories; 23g fat (5g saturated fat); 217mg cholesterol; 201mg sodium; 22g protein; 66g carbohydrates; 2g sugar; 4g fiber; 4mg iron; 155mg calcium.

307 ravioli with Brussels sprouts and bacon
PER SERVING: 607 calories; 34g fat (10g saturated fat); 74mg cholesterol; 1,039mg sodium; 21g protein; 56g carbohydrates; 5g sugar; 7g fiber; 3mg iron; 197mg calcium.

VEGETARIAN

309 parsnip and fennel soup with dill
PER SERVING: 477 calories; 13g fat (4.5g saturated fat); 22mg cholesterol; 914mg sodium; 19g protein; 70g carbohydrates; 8g sugar; 8g fiber; 5mg iron; 249mg calcium.

311 cauliflower and chickpea stew with couscous
PER SERVING: 446 calories; 9g fat (1g saturated fat); 0mg cholesterol; 735mg sodium; 16g protein; 80g carbohydrates; 23g sugar; 13g fiber; 6mg iron; 119mg calcium.

313 black bean and sweet potato enchiladas
PER SERVING: 756 calories; 35g fat (14g saturated fat); 60mg cholesterol; 1,798mg sodium; 28g protein; 82g carbohydrates; 13g sugar; 10g fiber; 6mg iron; 554mg calcium.

315 flaky mushroom and Gruyère tarts
PER SERVING: 527 calories; 39g fat (11g saturated fat); 30mg cholesterol; 794mg sodium; 16g protein; 29g carbohydrates; 5g sugar; 4g fiber; 3mg iron; 280mg calcium.

SIDE DISHES

317 sautéed escarole and leeks
PER SERVING: 111 calories; 7g fat (1g saturated fat); 0mg cholesterol; 218mg sodium; 2g protein; 11g carbohydrates; 2g sugar; 5g fiber; 2mg iron; 96mg calcium.

319 baked potatoes with artichokes, olives, and lemon
PER SERVING: 347 calories; 19g fat (2g saturated fat); 0mg cholesterol; 262mg sodium; 6g protein; 41g carbohydrates; 2g sugar; 5g fiber; 2mg iron; 35mg calcium.

319 baked potatoes with ricotta and roasted tomatoes
PER SERVING: 278 calories; 9g fat (3g saturated fat); 16mg cholesterol; 535mg sodium; 9g protein; 41g carbohydrates; 3g sugar; 5g fiber; 3mg iron; 99mg calcium.

319 baked potatoes with arugula, sour cream, and bacon
PER SERVING: 308 calories; 12g fat (5g saturated fat); 34mg cholesterol; 330mg sodium; 10g protein; 39g carbohydrates; 3g sugar; 4g fiber; 2mg iron; 71mg calcium.

321 spinach and Gruyère gratin
PER SERVING: 407 calories; 30g fat (15g saturated fat); 239mg cholesterol; 678mg sodium; 24g protein; 14g carbohydrates; 3g sugar; 5g fiber; 4mg iron; 687mg calcium.

DRINKS

322 vodka cranberry cooler
PER SERVING: 355 calories; 0g fat (0g saturated fat); 0mg cholesterol; 13mg sodium; 0g protein; 65g carbohydrates; 58g sugar; 3g fiber; 0mg iron; 8mg calcium.

322 tequila grapefruit splash
PER SERVING: 214 calories; 0g fat (0g saturated fat); 0mg cholesterol; 12mg sodium; 0g protein; 22g carbohydrates; 10g sugar; 0g fiber; 0mg iron; 9mg calcium.

322 pineapple mint punch
PER SERVING: 210 calories; 0g fat (0g saturated fat); 0mg cholesterol; 4mg sodium; 0g protein; 25g carbohydrates; 24g sugar; 0g fiber; 0mg iron; 28mg calcium.

323 bourbon ginger snap
PER SERVING: 224 calories; 0g fat (0g saturated fat); 0mg cholesterol; 7mg sodium; 1g protein; 30g carbohydrates; 26g sugar; 0g fiber; 0mg iron; 25mg calcium.

323 spiked sparkling cider
PER SERVING: 165 calories; 0g fat (0g saturated fat); 0mg cholesterol; 0mg sodium; 0g protein; 14g carbohydrates; 11g sugar; 0g fiber; 0mg iron; 0mg calcium.

323 winter sangría
PER SERVING: 214 calories; 0g fat (0g saturated fat); 0mg cholesterol; 7mg sodium; 0g protein; 26g carbohydrates; 21g sugar; 1g fiber; 0mg iron; 11mg calcium.

DESSERTS

325 hazelnut ganache tart with sea salt
PER SERVING: 495 calories; 39g fat (20g saturated fat); 67mg cholesterol; 351mg sodium; 6g protein; 38g carbohydrates; 25g sugar; 2g fiber; 2mg iron; 42mg calcium.

327 chewy spice cookies
PER COOKIE: 84 calories; 4g fat (1g saturated fat); 5mg cholesterol; 72mg sodium; 1g protein; 12g carbohydrates; 7g sugar; 0g fiber; 13mg iron; 1mg calcium.

329 praline-topped blondies
PER BLONDIE: 219 calories; 10g fat (5g saturated fat); 45mg cholesterol; 171mg sodium; 2g protein; 30g carbohydrates; 23g sugar; 1g fiber; 1mg iron; 29mg calcium.

331 double-chocolate profiteroles
PER 3-PIECE SERVING (INCLUDES DARK CHOCOLATE SAUCE): 487 calories; 29g fat (16g saturated fat); 182mg cholesterol; 141mg sodium; 10g protein; 54g carbohydrates; 38g sugar; 2g fiber; 3mg iron; 102mg calcium.

331 dark chocolate sauce
PER 2-TABLESPOON SERVING: 129 calories; 7g fat (3g saturated fat); 0mg cholesterol; 0mg sodium; 2g protein; 23g carbohydrates; 21g sugar; 0.5g fiber; 1mg iron; 0mg calcium.

333 raspberry-almond Linzer cookies
PER COOKIE: 130 calories; 7g fat (3g saturated fat); 19mg cholesterol; 38mg sodium; 2g protein; 17g carbohydrates; 9g sugar; 1g fiber; 1mg iron; 14mg calcium.

baking-pan substitutions

When you don't have the pan a recipe calls for, others will often do just as well. The baking time will be shorter if the pan is bigger than the specified pan, since the batter will be shallower. (The metric figures given below are straight conversions of the U.S. figures. Metric pan sizes vary widely; look for the closest size.)

PAN SIZE	CAPACITY	SUBSTITUTIONS
8" x 2" round (20 x 5 cm)	6 cups (1.4 l)	9" x 2" round 8" x 8" x 2" square 11" x 7" x 2" rectangle 12-cupcake tin
9" x 2" round (23 x 5 cm)	8 cups (1.9 l)	8" x 2" round 8" x 8" x 2" square 11" x 7" x 2" rectangle Two 12-cupcake tins
8" x 8" x 2" square (20 x 20 x 5 cm)	8 cups (1.9 l)	9" x 2" round Two 12-cupcake tins
11" x 7" x 2" rectangle (28 x 18 x 5 cm)	8 cups (1.9 l)	9" x 2" round 8" x 8" x 2" square Two 12-cupcake tins
13" x 9" x 2" rectangle (33 x 23 x 5 cm)	12 cups (2.8 l)	Two 9" x 2" rounds Two 8" x 8" x 2" squares Two 12-cupcake tins
8½" x 4½" x 2½" loaf pan (22 x 11½ x 6 cm)	8 cups (1.9 l)	9" x 2" round 8" x 8" x 2" square 11" x 7" x 2" rectangle 12-cupcake tin
12-cupcake tin (½ cup per cupcake)	6 cups (1.4 l)	9" x 2" round 8" x 8" x 2" square 11" x 7" x 2" rectangle

cups to grams

Approximate equivalents for some common kitchen staples measured in cups in the United States but in grams elsewhere.

INGREDIENT	1 CUP
almonds: whole	140 g
sliced	105 g
barley, pearled	200 g
beans, dried	190 g
bread crumbs: dried	95 g
panko	110 g
bulgur	160 g
butter	225 g
cheese: hard, grated	85 g
soft or semisoft, grated	110 g
chocolate chips	165 g
cocoa powder	80 g
coconut, shredded	70 g
couscous	190 g
flour (spooned and leveled):	
all-purpose	110 g
whole wheat	130 g
honey	330 g
nuts, mixed: whole	140 g
oats, old-fashioned rolled	85 g
orzo	170 g
peanuts: whole	130 g
chopped	140 g
pecans: halves	105 g
chopped	120 g
quinoa	170 g
raisins	155 g
rice: brown or white	180 g
sugar: granulated	210 g
brown (packed)	210 g
confectioners'	120 g
walnuts: halves	105 g
chopped	125 g

measuring cheat sheet

pinch or dash	=	$^1/_{16}$ teaspoon					
1 teaspoon					=	5 ml	
$^1/_2$ tablespoon	=	$1^1/_2$ teaspoons	=	$^1/_4$ fl oz	=	7.5 ml	
1 tablespoon	=	3 teaspoons	=	$^1/_2$ fl oz	=	15 ml	
1 jigger	=	3 tablespoons	=	$1^1/_2$ fl oz	=	45 ml	
$^1/_4$ cup	=	4 tablespoons	=	2 fl oz	=	60 ml	
$^1/_3$ cup	=	5 tablespoons + 1 teaspoon	=	3 fl oz	=	80 ml	
$^1/_2$ cup	=	8 tablespoons	=	4 fl oz	=	120 ml	
$^2/_3$ cup	=	10 tablespoons + 2 teaspoons	=	$5^1/_2$ fl oz	=	160 ml	
$^3/_4$ cup	=	12 tablespoons	=	6 fl oz	=	180 ml	
1 cup	=	16 tablespoons or $^1/_2$ pint	=	8 fl oz	=	240 ml	
1 pint	=	2 cups	=	16 fl oz	=	475 ml	
1 quart	=	4 cups or 2 pints	=	32 fl oz	=	945 ml	
1 gallon	=	16 cups or 4 quarts	=	128 fl oz	=	3.8 l	
1 pound	=	16 ounces	=	0.45 kg			
1 ounce			=	28 g			

oven temperatures

°F	225°	250°	275°	300°	325°	350°	375°	400°	425°	450°	475°	500°
°C	110°	125°	135°	150°	160°	175°	190°	200°	220°	230°	245°	260°

meat cooking temperatures

The safest, most accurate way to tell when meats are done is to use an instant-read thermometer, inserted in the thickest part of the meat. The following are the Real Simple test kitchen's preferred cooking temperatures (which are considered safe by many experts) for meats cooked to juicy perfection.*

	FAHRENHEIT	CELSIUS
BEEF		
Rare	115°	40°
Medium-rare	130°	55°
Medium	140°	60°
Medium-well	150°	65°
Well-done	155°	70°
Ground beef	160°	70°
LAMB		
Medium-rare	130°	55°
Medium	140°	60°
Medium-well	150°	65°
Well-done	155°	70°
Ground lamb	160°	70°
POULTRY		
White meat	160°	70°
Dark meat	165°	75°
Ground poultry	165°	75°
PORK		
Medium	145°	65°
Well-done	160°	70°
Ground pork	160°	70°

*For maximum food safety, the U.S. Department of Agriculture recommends 165° F for all poultry; 160° F for ground beef, lamb, and pork; 145° F, with a 3-minute resting period, for all other types of beef, lamb, and pork.

helpful info / RECIPE INDEX

spring

summer

helpful info / RECIPE INDEX

fall

winter

helpful info / CREDITS

REAL SIMPLE

managing editor Kristin van Ogtrop
creative director Janet Froelich
executive editor Sarah Humphreys
deputy managing editor Jacklyn Monk
managing editor, RealSimple.com
Kathleen Murray Harris

STAFF FOR THIS BOOK

food director Allie Lewis Clapp
art director Eva Spring
senior editor Lygeia Grace
project editor Candy Gianetti
staff food editors Charlyne Mattox,
Dawn Perry
food assistant Lindsay Hunt
photo director Casey Tierney
photo editor Lauren Reichbach Epstein
associate photo editor Brian Madigan
copy chief Nancy Negovetich
copy editors Ben Ake, Jenny Brown,
Pamela Grossman, Janet Kim,
Terri Schlenger
research chief Westry Green
researchers Stephanie Abramson,
Kaitlyn Pirie, Rachel Shelasky
art assistant Jennica Johnstone
production director Albert Young
production manager Joan Weinstein
production associate Sara Reden
imaging director Richard Prue
imaging manager Claudio Muller

publisher Sally Preston
associate publisher Melissa Gasper
senior vice president, consumer marketing
Carrie Goldin
vice president, marketing Sarah Kate Ellis

TIME HOME ENTERTAINMENT

publisher Richard Fraiman
**vice president, business development &
strategy** Steven Sandonato
executive director, marketing services
Carol Pittard
executive director, retail & special sales
Tom Mifsud
**executive director, new product
development** Peter Harper

editorial director Stephen Koepp
**director, bookazine development &
marketing** Laura Adam
publishing director Joy Butts
finance director Glenn Buonocore
assistant general counsel Helen Wan
assistant director, special sales
Ilene Schreider
design & prepress manager
Anne-Michelle Gallero
book production manager
Susan Chodakiewicz
brand manager Nina Fleishman

SPECIAL THANKS

recipe developers and testers Abigail
Chipley, Kay Chun, Sarah Copeland,
Kristen Evans Dittami, Mary B. Freund,
Melissa Gaman, Sue Li, Charlyne Mattox,
Emily McKenna, Kate Merker, Gina Marie
Miraglia Eriquez, Dawn Perry, Sara Ques-
senberry, Colleen Riley, Melissa Roberts,
Vanessa Seder, Jessica Shapiro, Ivee
Stephens, Caroline Wright, Chelsea Zimmer.
food stylists Roscoe Betsill, Sara Jane
Crawford, Victoria Granof, Rebecca
Jurkevich, Brett Kurzweil, Jee Levine, Cyd
McDowell, Maggie Ruggiero, Susan Spungen,
Susan Sugarman, Christine Wolheim.
prop stylists Tiziana Agnello, Jocelyn
Beaudoin, Sarah Cave, Heather Chontos,
Helen Crowther, Linden Elstran, Julie Flynn,
Matthew Gleason, Carla Gonzalez-Hart,
Megan Hedgpeth, Linda Heiss, Lauren
Laborie, Christina Lane, Jeffrey W. Miller,
Christine Rudolph, Olivia Sammons,
Pamela Duncan Silver, Loren Simons,
Sara Wacksman, Deborah Williams,
Michelle Wong, Hiroshi Yoshida.
thanks also to Christine Austin, Jeremy
Biloon, Jim Childs, Rose Cirroncione,
Jacqueline Fitzgerald, Christine Font,
Lindsay Funston, Jenna Goldberg, Lauren
Hall, Carrie Hertan, Hillary Hirsch, Kelly
Holecheck, Noelle Howey, Suzanne Janso,
Mona Li, Amy Mangus, Robert Marasco,
Kimberly Marshall, Amy Migliaccio, Nina
Mistry, Megan Moore, Dave Rozzelle, Ellie
Sher, Adriana Tierno, Alex Voznesenskiy,
Vanessa Wu.

PHOTO CREDITS

COVER: Con Poulos, photographer;
Rebecca Jurkevich, food stylist; Sarah
Cave, prop stylist.
Christopher Baker: pages 5, 18, 24, 38, 44,
46, 48, 52, 66, 68, 70–71, 74–75, 78, 80, 82, 84,
100, 108, 120, 124, 134, 146, 150, 152, 154,
156, 178, 184, 196, 198, 200, 204, 206, 208,
222, 226, 272, 274, 306. **Grant Cornett:** 118,
236–237, 256–257. **Dwight Eschliman:** 254,
258, 322–323. **Mitchell Feinberg:** 324, 330.
Gentl & Hyers: 230, 232, 234, 238, 240, 316.
Hans Gissinger: 180, 194, 220, 262, 296, 298.
Brian Henn: 174. **Lisa Hubbard:** 22, 186,
224, 278, 284, 294, 310. **Ditte Isager:** 4, 36,
40, 50, 64, 192, 266. **Yunhee Kim:** 34, 128,
138, 144. **Charles Masters:** 92, 106, 132,
148, 210–211, 304. **Miha Matei:** 320.
Marcus Nilsson: 86. **Kana Okada:** 202–203,
242–243. **José Picayo:** 8, 32, 170, 172–173, 188,
244, 246, 248, 250, 260, 264, 282, 286, 302.
Con Poulos: 4, 6, 28, 30, 42, 54, 58, 60, 62,
94, 96, 112, 116, 130, 136, 142, 182, 214,
218, 228, 270, 292, 300. **David Prince:** 20.
Sang An: 5, 16, 88, 90–91, 98, 102, 114, 122,
126, 140, 160, 162–164, 168, 190, 212, 216,
252, 288, 308, 312, 314. **Tom Schierlitz:** 10–11,
56–57, 110–111, 176. **Victor Schrager:** 326,
328, 332. **Anna Williams:** 276, 280, 290.
James Wojcik: 12, 72, 158, 166, 318.
Romulo Yanes: 14, 26, 104, 268.

First printing 2012
ISBN 10: 1-60320-923-9
ISBN 13: 978-1-60320-923-6

Printed in the U.S.A.

We welcome your comments and suggestions
about Real Simple Books. Please e-mail us at
books@realsimple.com.